Inspiration
and
Interpretation

Evangelical Theological Society Publications

Emil Brunner's Concept of Revelation by Paul King Jewett

Israel and the Arameans of Damascus by Merrill F. Unger

Inspiration and Interpretation, edited by John F. Walvoord

Inspiration
and
Interpretation

Edited by

JOHN F. WALVOORD
President, Dallas Theological Seminary

AN EVANGELICAL THEOLOGICAL SOCIETY PUBLICATION

WM. B. EERDMANS PUBLISHING CO.
Grand Rapids, Michigan

EDITOR'S PREFACE

This contribution to contemporary Biblical literature is the third in a series of volumes by members of the Evangelical Theological Society. Unlike previous publications, this work is a symposium of ten outstanding scholars in their respective fields. Though published primarily for the benefit of the members of the Society, the papers contributed are offered in book form in the hope of casting new light on the basic problems of revelation and inspiration in relation to contemporary theology.

Grateful acknowledgment is made to publishers who have granted permission to the respective authors for quotations used. The editor also wishes to acknowledge the invaluable preliminary work of Dr. Burton L. Goddard, of Gordon Divinity School, who as former editor of the Society did much of the early work on this volume, and the careful work of Dr. John A. Witmer, of Dallas Theological Seminary, who prepared the index.

Though representing the theological conservatism which characterizes the Society, each author assumes responsibility as an individual for the views expressed in his paper. An attempt has been made to achieve uniformity in style, but it has seemed best to allow individual authors some liberty. The total contribution constitutes a timely word on a timeless subject, pivotal in contemporary theology.

JOHN F. WALVOORD, *Editor*
Evangelical Theological Society

Dallas, Texas

CONTENTS

LIST OF CONTRIBUTORS

EDWARD J. CARNELL, TH. D., PH. D
  President and Professor of Apologetics, *Fuller Theological Seminary*

R. LAIRD HARRIS, TH. M., PH. D.
  Professor, *Covenant College and Theological Seminary*

CARL F. H. HENRY, PH. D., TH. D.
  Editor, *Christian Today*

PAUL K. JEWETT, TH. M., PH. D.
  Associate Professor of Systematic and Historical Theology, *Fuller Theological Seminary*

KENNETH S. KANTZER, S. T. M., PH. D.
  Chairman, Department of Bible and Philosophy, *Wheaton College*

DAVID W. KERR, B. D., TH. M.
  Associate Professor of Old Testament, *Gordon Divinity School*

J. THEODORE MUELLER, PH. D., TH. D.
  Professor of Dogmatics and Exegesis, *Concordia Seminary*

J. BARTON PAYNE, TH. M., TH. D.
  Professor of Old Testament, *Trinity Theological Seminary*

GEORGE A. TURNER, S. T. M., PH. D.
  Professor of Biblical Literature, *Asbury Theological Seminary*

MERRILL F. UNGER, TH. D., PH. D.
  Professor of Semitics and Old Testament, *Dallas Theological Seminary*

Edited by John F. Walvoord, A. M., Th. D., President and Professor of Systematic Theology, *Dallas Theological Seminary*

ix

Chapter I

THE BIBLICAL INTERPRETATION OF IRENAEUS

By J. Barton Payne

Born in the early second century, and reared at Smyrna in Asia Minor, Irenaeus was intimate with those who had been the companions of the apostles. Years later he would say:

> For I have a more vivid recollection of what occurred at that time than of recent events . . . how the blessed Polycarp . . . would speak of his familiar intercourse with John, and with the rest of those who had seen the Lord; and how he would call their words to remembrance.[1]

In time official duties took him to southern France as a missionary, and he was appointed Bishop of Lyons upon the martyrdom of the aged incumbent, Pothinus, in A.D. 177. In the executive ministry to which he was called, Irenaeus served with distinction until his death some time after the year 190; but in his work as a theological writer, with ecumenical contacts and with a dominating influence against the rising heresies of his day, he was to leave his more lasting mark.[2] To combat the rationalistic speculations of the Gnostics, which were then threatening the Christian Church from within, Irenaeus produced his monumental *Against Heresies,* which has been characterized as at once "the polemic theological masterpiece of the ante-Nicene age,"[3] and "a work marked by ability, moderation, and purity in its representation of Christianity."[4] Books I and II are devoted to the description and refutation of the

---

1 *De Ogdoade,* in Eusebius, *Hist. Eccl.,* V:20; cf. *Adv. Haer.,* VI;3,4.
2 Richard Adelbert Lipsius, "Irenaeus," in William Smith and Henry Wace, *A Dictionary of Christian Biography* (London; John Murray, 1882). III:266. "It was . . . the conflict with Gnosticism which . . . inaugurated that revival of fundamental Christian and Pauline thought which distinguishes the theology of Irenaeus."
3 Philip Schaff, *History of the Christian Church* (New York: Scribner's, 1912), II:753.
4 L. Berkhof, *The History of Christian Doctrines* (Grand Rapids: Eerdmans, 1949), p. 66.

multiform Gnostic heresies; but in Books III, IV, and V appear his positive presentations of Christian faith. In the latter group of books, much space is devoted to the exegesis of Scripture, to principles of interpretation, and to the authority of the Bible. Although the original Greek text of *Against Heresies* is now found only in fragments, primarily in the writings of Hippolytus and Epiphanius, the work in its entirety has been preserved in an almost contemporary, though confessedly none too accurate, Latin translation.[5]

The importance of Irenaeus in the history of the interpretation of Scripture cannot be overestimated. Hitchcock has well remarked,

> Church historians of every age speak in a chorus of praise of his work and character. Jerome calls him 'the apostolic man'; Basil, 'the successor of the apostles'; Tertullian, 'a most careful investigator of every doctrine.'[6]

His significance may well be set forth in several categories and pertinent quotations as follows:

His personal merit.

> Zahn: Soundness of judgment, acuteness of perception, and clearness of exposition. In fact, he is the first writer of the post-apostolic period who deserved the title of a theologian.[7]

5 Reference will be made to the standard paragraphing of Massuet, Migne and the Edinburgh translation, followed in parenthesis by the paragraphing and volume and page number in Harvey's handy text; III:11,7 (11,10; ii:46) means Book III, Ch. 11, Paragraph 7, according to Massuet; Ch. 11, Paragraph 10 (of the same Book III), as found on page 46 in Vol. II of W. Wigan Harvey, *Sancti Irenaei Episcopi Lugdunensis Libros quinque adversus Haereses*, (Cambridge: Univ. Press, 1857), 2 vols. Quotations of text are taken from Harvey and most translations from Alexander Roberts and James Donaldson, editors, *The Ante-Nicene Fathers*, American reprint of the Edinburgh Edition, revised by Cleveland Coxe (Buffalo: Christian Literature Pub. Co., 1855), I:315-567. References to the fragments from lost writings, e. g., *Fr.* 16, likewise follow Coxe; while *Dem.* 6 indicates this paragraph from J. Armitage Robinson, *St. Irenaeus, The Demonstration of the Apostolic Preaching*, as translated from the Armenian, in Sparrow and Clark, *Translation of Christian Literature*, Series IV (London: S.P.C.K., 1920).

6 F. R. Montgomery Hitchcock, *Irenaeus of Lugdunum* (Cambridge: Univ. Press, 1914), p. 16.

7 T. Zahn, "Irenaeus," in Jackson Samuel Macauley, ed., *The New Schaff-Herzog Encyclopedia of Religious Knowledge* (New York: Funk and Wagnalls, c. 1910), VI:30.

Terry: The light of the Western Church.[8]

Briggs: The greatest of all the Christian writers and scholars of the second century.[9]

His position as representative of the earliest and purest form of Christianity.

Seeberg: The Antignostic Fathers . . . did not really present anything new, not even a distinctly enlarged understanding of Christianity. Their conception of Christian truth and life is that which prevailed already at the close of the first and the beginning of the second century. The only peculiarity is that the opposition encountered compelled them to a greater distinctness and lucidity, as well as to deliberate utterances with respect to the canon and doctrinal tradition.[10]

Dorner: No one in the second century represents as he does the purity and the fulness of the development within the church.[11]

His influence upon subsequent thought.

Schaff: The polemic literature against heresies . . . upon this was formed the dogmatic theology of the church. At the head of the old Catholic controversialists stands Irenaeus . . . the first among the fathers properly so called, and one of the chief architects of the Catholic system of doctrine.[12]

Zahn: His actual influence upon the development of the Church was greater than that of perhaps any other teacher of the first three centuries.[13]

Harnack: Tertullian and Hippolytus were to a great extent dependent on Irenaeus . . . the main problem therefore resolves itself into the question as to the position of Irenaeus in the history of the Church.[14]

8 Milton S. Terry, *Biblical Hermeneutics* (Grand Rapids: Zondervan, n.d.), p. 635.

9 Charles Augustus Briggs, *History of the Study of Theology* (New York: Scribners, 1916), I:78.

10 Reinhold Seeberg, *Text-Book of the History of Doctrines,* Charles E. Hay, trans. (Philadelphia: The United Lutheran Publication House, c. 1905), I:140.

11 Isaak August Dorner, *History of the Development of the Doctrine of the Person of Christ* (Edinburgh: 1861), 1:303.

12 Schaff, *op. cit.,* II:747-48.

13 Zahn, *op. cit.,* VI:31.

14 Adolph Harnack, *History of Dogma,* Neil Buchanan, trans. (Boston: Roberts Bros., 1899), II:16.

His repeated reference to Scripture as the ground of authority.

Hitchcock: His doctrine, founded upon the New Testament — the book he knew best — proved . . . decisive.[15]
Lawson: The most casual reader of S. Irenaeus cannot fail to observe . . . the extensive use made of Scripture. At times chapter after chapter is nothing other than a mosaic of Biblical quotations.[16]

Despite his inadequacies in specific theological areas, Irenaeus yet constitutes perhaps the most crucial figure in the historical establishment of Christianity as based upon the Bible, and in the present day his importance is accentuated by the special appeal which neo-supernaturalists have made to his writings. His thought may be approached by considering in order: his conception of Scripture, his principles for the interpretation of Scripture, and his methodology in the employment of Scripture.

I. IRENAEUS' CONCEPTION OF SCRIPTURE

It is an all too common assertion that the Church universal, Irenaeus not excepted, has refused to commit itself in regard to the nature of Scripture and of inspiration. The charge of a recent writer is quite representative of such allegations:

The Church has always honored the Bible as a book sacred and apart, of unique religious authority, and yet there has never been any dogma of inspiration. No definition of that in which this authority consists, and how it came to be, and how it acts, has ever been agreed upon by the whole Church. S. Irenaeus foreshadows this historic phenomenon. Though he is so eminently a Biblical theologian he has no definite doctrine of the inspiration of the Bible.[17]

But such claims, motivated by an ill-concealed desire to justify declination from Biblical authority, consistently misrepresent the testimony of the ancient Church. For while it is true that the mode of inspiration is left open — mechanical dictation as over against organic though infallible direction of the secondary

---

15 Hitchcock, *op. cit.*, p. 344.
16 Lawson, John, *The Biblical Theology of Saint Irenaeus* (London: Epworth Press, 1948), p. 23.
17 *Ibid.*, p. 25.

(human) authors — still the source of inspiration (the Holy Spirit), the nature of inspiration (the making of man's writings the equivalent of God's), and the extent of inspiration (plenary, or full), are so uniformly maintained as to have become axiomatic. Among the earliest apostolic fathers, Barnabas introduces Biblical quotations saying, "The Spirit of the Lord proclaims," [18] Clement of Rome speaks of "the Scriptures, which are the true utterances of the Holy Spirit,"[19] and Polycarp refers to Scripture simply as "the oracles of the Lord."[20] So too among the succeeding apologists. Justin Martyr affirmed, "We believe God's voice spoken by the apostles . . . and prophets."[21] Athenagoras unhesitatingly proclaimed,

> While deprived of their natural powers of reason [tōn en autois logismōn] by the influence of the divine Spirit, they uttered that which was wrought in them, the Spirit using them as His instruments, as a flute player might blow a flute.[22]

So Irenaeus could say of even the heretical Ebionites, Marcion, the Gnostics, and Valentinus, "Since . . . our opponents do bear testimony of us, and make use of these [documents], our proof derived from them is firm and true."[23] Though his writings called for no single treatment of Scripture, yet they so abound in presentations of his conception of the Bible that any attempt at exhaustive coverage becomes impossible. Whole sections[24] expound his principles; and, as Beaven notes, "Although here his example is more forcible than his precepts, it is satisfactory that he speaks very definitely, and to the purpose."[25] Specifically, his doctrine of Scripture may be resolved into the nature, the extent, and the mode of inspiration.

A. THE NATURE OF INSPIRATION

Irenaeus held to the inspiration of men, that is, that inspiration was a process commencing, at least, with human

---

18 *Epist.*, IX.
19 *Epist.*, I:45.
20 *Ea logia*, Epist. VII.
21 *Dial.*, CXIX.
22 *Leg. pro. Christ.*, IX.
23 *Firma et vera est nostra de illis ostensis*, III:11,7 (11,10; ii:46).
24 As IV:26 (40-41; ii:234-38).
25 James Beaven, *An Account of the Life and Writings of S. Irenaeus* (London: J.G.F. and J. Rivington, 1841), p. 135.

illumination. In reference to Paul he says, "Paul testifies";[26] "The apostle says to the Ephesians";[27] or, "Paul, when writing to the Romans, has explained this very point."[28] The same may apply to Moses, David, Isaiah,[29] or any other given writer of Scripture. Yet behind their messages lay divine authority: first, "God prepared for Himself those who should announce the Savior's advent";[30] and then came the impartation from God of those truths which they were destined to pronounce. Leaving aside, for the moment, the mode of this supernatural communication, one must observe that the revelation included factual content, that indeed it was primarily defined in terms of propositional truth; the prophets outstandingly "had foreknowledge of His future advent which they received from Him."[31] Because of this Irenaeus asserted with literalness, "The Spirit has spoken by Esaias,"[32] and applied to the apostles the words of Luke 10:16, "He that heareth you heareth Me."[33] For all practical purposes this equaled Justin Martyr's declaration, "We must not suppose that the language proceeds from the men who are inspired, but from the divine Word which moves them,"[34] though with the qualification that those who listened were, while hearing God, none the less hearing active, thinking men.

But Irenaeus also held to the inspiration of the Book, namely, that inspiration was a process resulting in the production of writings which were in fact the words of God. He therefore writes,

> Since the writings *(literae)* of Moses are the words of Christ, He does Himself declare to the Jews, as John has recorded in the Gospel: "If ye had believed Moses, ye would have believed Me: for he wrote of Me. But if ye believe not his writings, neither will ye believe My words." He thus indicated in the clearest manner that the writings of Moses are His words. If then to Moses so also, beyond a doubt, the words of the other prophets are His.[35]

26 IV;7,2 (13; ii:163).
27 V;13,2-3 *(ibid.;* ii:361-62).
28 III:16, (17,2; ii:84).
29 IV:36,1 (57,1; ii:147).
30 IV:36,1 (57,1; ii:273).
31 *Ab ipso praescentiam ante accepissent,* IV:11,1 (21,1; ii:175).
32 *Per Esaiam dixit Spiritus,* IV:2,4 (3,2; ii:148).
33 III:Pref. *(ibid.;* ii:1).
34 *Apol.,* I:36.
35 *Moysi literas suos esse sermones . . . et reliquorum sine dubio prophetarum sermones ipsius sunt,* IV:2,3 (3,1; ii:148). John 5:46-47.

Moreover, he makes statements such as

> God . . . bears witness unto Him by the Holy Spirit,
> saying in the Scripture, And Abraham believed, and it
> was counted unto him for righteousness.[36]

In so doing, he equates the words of the Bible, here Genesis,
with the words of God. That this identification holds for the
New Testament as well as the Old is seen when he quotes a
verse from Ephesians and links it, without distinction, to one
from Isaiah.[37] In another place he writes,

> The Spirit, through many men, and now by Paul bears
> witness, that "he believed God and it was imputed unto
> him for righteousness."[38]

Finally, for Irenaeus the inspiration of the Book transcends
that of the men. On occasion it is intimated that the human
writers did not comprehend the Spirit-inspired words, as when
he says that Christ's

> human nature could not be understood, prior to the
> consummation of those things which had been predicted,
> that is, the advent of Christ. And therefore it was said to
> Daniel the prophet: "Shut up the words, and seal the book
> even to the time of consummation."[39]

The Bible is described as "the Lord's Scriptures,"[40] and its
authority is brought forward with the simple phrase, "The
prophetic word declares."[41] In other words, though the human
element of Scripture is by Irenaeus everywhere maintained, it
may not be advanced either as a limiting factor upon the
possible content of Scripture or as a detracting factor from its
divine authority. From this appear two corollaries. First, the
Bible is absolute, though incomplete, truth, the absence of the
totality of truth in no way minimizing the perfection of what is
present. Non-Christians drift in relativism: "They always have
the excuse of searching [after truth], but never succeed in finding

36 *Dem.* 24.
37 III:21,6 (26,2; ii:117-17).
38 IV:8,1 (15; ii:165); cf. IV:32 (49,2; ii:259): *Quemadmodum et Moses
ait* (Gen. 1:3) . . . *et in evangelio* (John 1:3) *legimus . . . et apostolus
Paulus* (Eph. 4:5) *similiter;* II:22,2 (32,7; i:327); and IV:33,11 (55,1;
ii:265).
39 IV:26,1 (40,1; ii:234-35).
40 V:20,2 (*ibid.;* ii:379), and elsewhere; cf. Lawson, *op. cit.,* pp. 46-48.
41 *Propheticus sermo . . . ait,* II:34,4 (55,2; i:383).

it";[42] but as for Christians, "We follow for our teacher the one and only true God, and possess His words as the rule of truth."[43] Second, the Bible, rather than man, is and must be its own source of evaluation. Irenaeus states the matter thus:

> If we cannot discover explanations of all things in Scripture . . . we should leave things of that nature to God who created us, being most properly assured that the Scriptures are indeed perfect, since they were spoken by the Word of God and His Spirit, but we, inasmuch as we are inferior to, and later in existence than, the Word of God and His Spirit, are on that very account destitute of the knowledge of His mysteries.[44]

True criticism must have appreciation for the object criticized; it must deal with that object by methods congruous to its nature and characteristics. Thus all further developments within the doctrine of inspiration must have as their source the statements of Scripture, though synthesized by the yielded believer; as he says, "Proofs [of the things which are] contained in the Scriptures cannot be shown except from the Scriptures themselves" (III:12,9).

B. The Extent of Inspiration

All of the Scripture was, according to Irenaeus, given by God. Accordingly, Irenaeus had no patience with those who would limit the extent of inspiration either intensively, within any given passage, or extensively, in reference to the fixed Christian canon.[45] As regards the intensive aspect, the full and complete inspiration of all portions of Scripture insured the absence of error from the original writings. Of the writers of Scripture he laid down as a principle, "It is unlawful to assert that they

---

42 III:24,2 (38,2; ii:132).
43 *Et regulam veritatis habentes ejus sermones,* IV:35,4 (57,4; ii:276).
44 *Scripturae quidem perfectae sunt, quippe a Verbo Dei et Spiritus ejus dictae,* II:28,2 (41,1; i:349-50).
45 Hitchcock, *op. cit.,* p. 193. Hitchcock has well said, "In his exposure of the perversions the Gnostics made of the Scriptures, Irenaeus vindicated the unity and integrity of the Old and New Testaments. He also maintains their inspiration against those who would deny it in whole or in part. The critics and critical problems of his time were much the same as those of ours. His words are still a rebuke to those who, like the Marcionites, would remove the passages they dislike."

preached before they possessed perfect knowledge";[46] or, from the negative side, "Nor can they prove Luke guilty of falsehood, when he proclaims the truth to us with all diligence."[47] As Augustine later put it, "I firmly believe that no one of their authors has erred in anything in writing."[48] This conclusion was based upon the authority of Christ, as when Irenaeus says,

> Christ does Himself declare . . . in the clearest manner that the writings of Moses are His words . . . so also, beyond doubt, the words of the other prophets are His [words], as I have pointed out.[49]

The heretics indeed maintained

> that the apostles intermingled the things of the law with the words of the Savior; and that not the apostles alone, but even the Lord Himself, spoke as at one time from the Demiurge, at another time from the intermediate place, and yet again from the Pleroma . . . [but Irenaeus rejoined with passion] this is, indeed, to blaspheme their creator after a most impudent manner![50]

In other words, for a Christian the mind of Christ is determinative; and therefore when Christ and His apostles committed themselves to a view of inspiration equal to that of the most strict rabbis,[51] or, as Irenaeus put it, when Christ accepted the words of Scripture as His own, the question of any lower form of inspiration ceased to be one which could legitimately be entertained. The only alternative was that of the Gnostics, a kenotic theory that Jesus and His early disciples were Jews and as such shared to a greater or less extent the traditional opinions of their countrymen. Such a view, inconsistent with a true supernaturalism,[52] Irenaeus rejected, with these words:

46 *Perfectam haberent agnitionem,* III:1,1 (*ibid.;* ii:2); cf. III:12, 7 (12,8-9; ii:60-62).
47 *Neque Lucam mendacem esse possunt osterdere, veritatem nobis cum omni diligentia annuntiantem,* III:15,1 (*ibid.;* ii:79).
48 *Epist.* (*ad Hier.*), LXXXII:1,3.
49 IV:2,3 (3,1; ii:148); cf. *supra* p. 16.
50 III:2,2 (*ibid.;* ii:8).
51 L. Gaussen, *Theopneustia, The Plenary Inspiration of the Holy Scriptures,* David Scott, trans. (Chicago: The Bible Institute Colportage Assn., n.d.), pp. 80-105.
52 Cf. John Howard Raven, *Old Testament Introduction* (New York: Revell, c. 1910), p. 92: "If he was either essentially or temporarily merely a man, his dictum on religious matters has no greater authority than that of a man."

> Jesus Christ . . . and the apostles . . . are above all false-
> hood; for a lie has no fellowship with the truth, just as
> darkness has none with light, but the presence of one shuts
> out the other.[53]

Therefore, with Irenaeus, "degrees" of inspiration were an impossibility. If inspiration meant guaranteed truthfulness, then
a given writing either fell within the category or it did not;
there could be no half-way position. He argued at length that
the Scriptures must stand or fall together:

> We allege . . . against those who do not recognize Paul
> as an apostle that they should either reject the other words
> of the Gospel which we have come to know through Luke
> alone, and not make use of them; or else, if they do receive
> all these they must necessarily admit also that testimony
> concerning Paul when he [Luke] tells us the Lord spoke at
> first to him from heaven: "Saul, Saul, why persecutest thou
> Me? . . ." Those who do not accept him [as a teacher], who
> was chosen by God for this purpose . . . do separate
> themselves from the company of the apostles.[54]

Within the Lucan writings themselves he states even more
clearly:

> Now if any man set Luke aside, as one who did not know
> the truth, he will [by so acting], manifestly reject that
> Gospel of which he claims to be a disciple. . . . It follows
> then, as of course, that these men must either receive the
> rest of his narrative, or else reject these parts also. For no
> person of common sense can permit them to receive some
> things recounted by Luke as being true, and to set others
> aside, as if he had not known the truth.[55]

Of course, then as now, there were those who professed Christianity who did maintain with apparent success a view of partial
inspiration; yet Irenaeus' demand holds good for a decision
between plenary inspiration or none at all, even as in the statement of Christ quoted by Irenaeus, "If ye believe not his
[Moses'] writings, how shall ye believe My words?" A denial of
the divinely authenticated Scriptures bespeaks an underlying
distrust of Christ and the supernatural as a whole. Finally,

53 *Mendacium in eo non est . . . extra omne mendacium sunt,* III:5,1
   (*ibid.*, ii:18).
54 III:15,1 (*ibid.*, ii:78-9).
55 III:14,3-4 (*ibid.*, ii:76-8).

under the intensive extent of inspiration, there must be noted Irenaeus' assurance that the divine superintendence reached to the very words which were chosen. Following the example of his Master,[56] he was content to rest entire arguments upon single expressions or words, as "all things" in John 1:3,[57] or "Christ" in Matt. 1:18;[58] and in reference to a single letter in the text of the Greek New Testament he declared, "There shall be no light punishment on him who either adds or subtracts anything from the Scripture."[59] In summary, then, the view of Irenaeus was that of plenary, verbal inspiration, or, as described by Harnack, "The apostolic writings were inspired, that is in the full and only intelligible sense attached to the words by the ancients."[60]

As regards the extensive scope of inspiration, that is, the canon, the limits of the Old Testament were by the time of Irenaeus well known. The conviction of Irenaeus was that Ezra stipulated the limits of the canon,[61] a view which is probable but without Old Testament confirmation. Perhaps owing in part to his use of the Septuagint version, Irenaeus seems to have then departed from Apostolic precedent and to have accepted some of the Old Testament Apocrypha as well. A quotation from Wisdom may not be significant, 2:28,29, for no comment is made as to its source, but verses from Bel and the Dragon and from Susanna are quoted as true words of Daniel the prophet,[62] and passages from Baruch are imputed to Jeremiah.[63] His use of the Apocrypha, however, is limited to the passages cited. As concerns the New Testament, the works of Irenaeus, along with the Muratorian Fragment, constitute the most important historical witness to the recognition of the completed composition of Scripture. Schaff says that "Irenaeus is the first among patristic writers to make full use of the New Testament,"[64] and Lipsius testifies thus to his concept of the finished Bible:

> The prophets and the gospels together make up the totality of Scripture (*Universae Scripturae*, ii.27,2). The

56 Cf. Matt. 22:32, 44; John 10:34.
57 III:11,1 (11,7; ii:41).
58 III:16,2 (17,1; ii:82-83); III:18,2 (19,2; 88:95-96).
59 III:5,1 (*ibid.*; ii:18).
60 *Op. cit.*, II:54.
61 *Anataxasthai*, III:21,2 (23,2; ii:111), perhaps on the basis of 2 Esdras 12:44-45.
62 IV:5,3 and 26,3 (41,1; ii:237).
63 V:35,1 (*ibid.*; ii:424).
64 Schaff, *op. cit.*, II:751-52.

notion of the Bible as of one divinely inspired whole, consisting of both Old and New Testaments is now, in this way, clearly enunciated . . . the main divisions of the New Testament canon . . . constitute for Irenaeus a complete whole, like the Scriptures of the Old Testament.[65]

In his writings Irenaeus quotes from every book of the New Testament with the exception of the short epistles of Philemon and 3 John[66] and at the same time specifically rejects the non-inspired writings of his day.[67] He writes, "But those who are from Valentinus . . . while they put forth their own compositions, boast that they possess more Gospels than there really are."[68] As Hitchcock argues, there must have been a canon,

> if not formally made, at least generally recognized, in the days of Irenaeus. Otherwise his arguments against the falsification of the Scriptures by subtractions and additions would have had no point.[69]

There are, however, three major questions raised concerning Irenaeus' testimony on the canon. First, do his pronouncements depend upon a concept of apostolic authorship, or upon a concept of the character of the works produced? This question lies behind Lawson's assertion:

> One can rightly discuss what writings S. Irenaeus knew as Apostolic, but it slightly savors of anachronism to ask, "How many New Testament books did he regard as canonical?" . . . The determinative factor for faith is simply the preaching of the Apostles, whether written or unwritten, and . . . New Testament Scripture is essentially this witness as preserved in writing . . . the argument is essentially an historical one. It does not proceed from any theory that would separate this authority from its human origin, such as, that the apostles went into a trance and uttered oracles "straight from God," or that an angel brought a mysterious manuscript from heaven. . . . This does not raise the contents of the Gospels to a higher level

---

65 *Op. cit.*, III:270.
66 Cf. Coxe, *op. cit.*, I:599-602.
67 Uncertainty does exist about a single reference to the Shepherd of Hermas, IV:20,2 (34,2; ii:213-14) cf. Lawson, *op. cit.*, pp. 49-51.
68 II:11,8-9 (11,11-12; ii:50-52).
69 Hitchcock, *op. cit.*, p. 213.

of authority than any other authentic information about the Lord.[70]

Such a claim confuses the facts in at least three respects: (1) The "determinative factor for faith" is the truth of the gospel, irrespective of how presented. That God's inerrant truth of Scripture is no more "true" than any other authentic information proves nothing concerning the canon, for what constitutes canon, according to Irenaeus' definition, is whether or not any given information is on the level of authority of authentic words of God. (2) New Testament Scripture is therefore not "essentially the preaching of the apostles as preserved in writing," but rather those words of God which were mediated to man through apostolic writing. (3) That Irenaeus generally does not "separate this authority from its human origin" in the apostles cannot be adduced to disprove divine origin in the mind of God. To maintain such is to be guilty of the inexcusable though common error of failing to distinguish an assumed mode of inspiration, namely, mechanical dictation "straight from God," from an indicated extent of inspiration, namely, plenary-verbal, so that the end product is "as good as God's." Irenaeus would no more have accepted the first than he would have denied the second! The real question is not whether the canon is brought down to the level of apostolic authorship — this is sufficiently denied by his concept of inspiration — but whether apostolic authorship is brought up to the level of the canon. On the basis of the writings he knew, the New Testament canon was indeed the equivalent of "the writings of the evangelists and the apostles";[71] but if a fifth Gospel, of genuine apostolic origin, should have appeared, what would have been his verdict? His reverence for the apostles might well have led him to assume its inspiration and canonicity, yet he elsewhere wrote,

> It is not possible that the Gospels can be either more or fewer in number than they are . . . four. . . . Those who destroy the form of the Gospel are vain, unlearned, and also audacious, those who represent the aspects of the Gospel as being either more in number than as aforesaid, or, on the other hand, fewer. . . . Wretched men indeed![72]

70 *Op. cit.*, pp. 36, 87-88.
71 I:3,6 (6; i:31); cf. II:30,9 (47,2; i:367-68).
72 III:11,8-9 (11,11-2; ii:48-52).

For Irenaeus, then, the canon was the totality of those books which had God as primary author, the status of the human authors being, it would seem, ultimately secondary in importance.

A second question concerns the matter of degrees of inspiration within the canon. Lawson contends that, "We must be cautious in drawing from the statements of S. Irenaeus the consequence that he regarded the New Testament writings as inspired and canonical equally with the Old Testament."[73] Irenaeus did, it is true, recognize basic divisions within the sacred books, but it is not clear that these were concerned with the matter of inspiration, nor are the divisions hard and fast uniform ones. In one place he speaks of "the writings of the evangelists and the apostles . . . [and] the law and the prophets,"[74] but in another place of

> the preaching of the apostles, the authoritative teaching of the Lord, the announcements of the prophets, the dictated utterances of the apostles [letters], and the ministrations of the law — all of which praise one and the same Being, the God and Father of all.[75]

The divisions differ in number and follow no clear order of rank. There appears to be no difference in authority. If anything, a priority sometimes goes to the New Testament: "First apostles, secondarily [Old Testament] prophets."[76] In reference to the previously noted passages in which the Old Testament and the New Testament are linked as proofs without distinction,[77] Hitchcock observes,

> In these passages St. Paul is coordinated as an authority not only with the Old Testament and the Gospel but also

---

73 Lawson, *op. cit.*, p. 26. It should be noted that this author's sympathies lie with degrees of inspiration, even when represented by the Gnostic heretics: "It is natural to find the Gnostics denying the unity of the Old Testament, so as to separate it into elements of greater and of less authenticity and divine authority . . . This was the nearest approach of the ancient Church to the modern conception of progressive revelation. It is unfortunate that such exposition grew up as a part of systems of thought rightly condemned as heretical." *Ibid.*, pp. 26-27.

74 Cf. *supra*, note 71.

75 II:35,4 (58,2; i:387).

76 III:11,4 (11,8; ii:43).

77 Cf. *supra*, note 38.

with our Lord . . . Irenaeus . . . appealing to the very
words to establish a doctrine or confute a heresy.[78]

Even as he could permit no degrees intensively within plenary
inspiration, so likewise Irenaeus could allow no real distinction
in its external manifestation in the canon.

A third question is this: Granting the existence of the doctrine
of the completed canon in his writings, when was it that the
canon actually appeared? Harnack speaks of "the new canon of
Scriptures set up by Irenaeus and Tertullian,"[79] as if Irenaeus
were in some way its author, but here two matters must be
distinguished: namely, the origin of the canon and the original
recognition of the canon. In respect to the former, Irenaeus'
view, as stated for example about the Gospels, was that

> The Word, the Artificer of all, He that sitteth upon the
> cherubim, and contains all things, He who was manifested
> to men, has given us the Gospel under four aspects.[80]

Biblical books do not *become* canonical, that is, of divine
authority; they *are* canonical from the moment of composition
by virtue of their inspired nature. William Henry Green once
wrote, "The assumption that the books . . . were not written
with the design of being held sacred and divinely authoritative
is . . . a fundamental error."[81] The error is based upon an anti-
supernaturalistic bias foreign to the thought of Irenaeus. His
holding to the universal Christian recognition of the canon
required an extended period of prior consciousness, for

> The assignment of a rank and position to its [the
> church's] own writings equal if not superior to that of the
> Old Testament . . . must have been made some time
> previous to the composition of this great treatise [*Against
> Heresies*].[82]

And even Harnack concedes, "Refusal on the part of the heretics
to recognize this or that book is already made a severe reproach
against them."[83] Irenaeus' own view was that the

78 *Op. cit.*, pp. 223-24.
79 *Op. cit.*, II:55.
80 III:11,9 (11,12; ii:50).
81 William Henry Green, *General Introduction to the Old Testament,
the Canon* (New York: Scribner's, 1898), p. 26.
82 Hitchcock, *op. cit.*, p. 213.
83 *Op. cit.*, II:44.

reading [of the work of God] without falsification and
. . . without any forging of Scriptures . . .[had from the
first been characteristic of] the doctrine of the apostles and
the ancient constitutions of the church throughout the
world.[84]

As William Henry Green has stated it,

Each individual book . . . of anyone accredited as inspired by Him [God] to make known His will, was
accepted as the word of God immediately upon its appearance.[85]

It may well be, however, that the express denial by Irenaeus of
canonicity for the non-apostolic writings marked the final
realization by the Christian Church of the completion of
Scripture. As Seeberg puts it,

Christianity had adopted from Judaism the conception
of the canon; i.e., that certain books are holy and every
word in them is authoritative. To this was, however, now
added the Christian principle that this authority attaches
only to the original Christian documents.[86]

C. The Mode of Inspiration

When men have said of Irenaeus, "He had a glimpse of a
theory of inspiration which does justice to the human factor,"[87]
justice was hardly done to Irenaeus. In a day when the
mechanical mode of inspiration was widely held, Irenaeus maintained a consistently organic position of real human activity in
the production of Scripture. There might indeed be adduced
his statement about the writers of Scripture and their original
audiences that "they did not address them in accordance with
their [the hearers'] opinion at the time, but according to revealed truth."[88] This, however, while asserting the negative
restriction from error necessary for plenary inspiration by no
means teaches a positive dictation of words to be reproduced by
unthinking machines. Similarly, his statement that Christ
"availed Himself of the prophets who were under the law and

84 IV:33,8 (53,2; ii:263).
85 *Op. cit.*, p. 35.
86 *Op. cit.*, p. 137.
87 Schaff, *op. cit.*, II:754.
88 *Secundem veritatis manifestionem*, III:5,2 (*ibid.*, ii:19).

declared His own matters through their instrumentality,"[89] does not deny their active participation in these same declarations. Finally, a reference to Matthew is sometimes cited as a quotation in point:

> Matthew might certainly have said, "Now the birth of *Jesus* was on this wise"; but the Holy Ghost, foreseeing the corrupters [of the truth] and guarding by anticipation against their deceit, says by Matthew, "But the birth of *Christ* was on this wise."[90]

But this likewise is no proof that Matthew did not at the same time, and of his own volition, use the language required. God truly prepared the men. As Irenaeus says, "These are the voices of the disciples of the Lord, the truly perfect, who after the assumption of the Lord, were perfected by the Spirit,"[91] but this very perfection was that the voices might be their own.

Within the framework of the organic mode of inspiration it is further maintained that, "Regarding the exact way in which God acted upon those whom He inspired there are no more than a few hints"[92] — again, hardly a fair criticism. Irenaeus testifies that inspiration began with Jesus Christ:

> All who have known God from the beginning, and have foretold the advent of Christ, have received the revelation from the Son Himself, who also in the last times was made visible.[93]

The Son, in turn, for the immediate action upon the minds of the men employed "the Holy Spirit, through whom the prophets prophesied."[94] This was done through charism, in which, while the personality of the man was in no way minimized, "the gift" of divine truth was imparted: "Wherefore the prophets, receiving the prophetic gift from the same Word, announced His

---

89 IV:25,2 (57,2; ii:274); cf. III:15,1 (*ibid.*, ii:79).

90 III:16,2 (17,1; ii:83).

91 *Tōn alēthōs teleiōn meta tēn analēmpsin tou Kuriou dia pneumatos teleiōtentōn* III:12,5 (12,6 ii:58). There is some question here about what *dia pneumatos* modifies; cf. the Latin reading, *Qui post assumtionem Domine per Spiritum et perfecti exstiterunt*.

92 Lawson, *op. cit.*, p. 27.

93 IV:7,2 (13; ii:163).

94 *Dem.* 6.

advent."[95] The same was equally true for the apostolic writers of the New Testament, who "were invested with power from on high when the Holy Spirit came down, were filled from all His gifts, and had perfect knowledge."[96] Such statements are sufficient refutation of the claims that "he is content to establish the authority of the four Evangelists upon the natural ground of human knowledge,"[97] and that

> We have no certain evidence as to whether S. Irenaeus would have defined the inspiration of Moses and of the Prophets in more strictly supernatural, or, as some would say, more mechanical, terms.[98]

Irenaeus accepted neither of these alternatives. He held to the organic mode of inspiration, but not to mere human knowledge; and he held to the fully supernatural book, but not to a mechanical mode of inspiration. To be sure, the fallacy that the existence of a supernatural book necessarily implies a mechanical mode of inspiration and a renunciation of the human element is indeed widely entertained. For example, Lawson has said of Irenaeus,

> He plainly betrays an underlying assumption that S. Paul, when rightly understood, must display the fulness of divine truth in every word. This attitude hardly answers to an appreciation of the human element in the Epistles.[99]

But to Irenaeus, though plenary inspiration meant an undistorted communication from God, it was still the man acting at the fulness of his capacities who did the "foreseeing through the Holy Spirit."[100] At the same time, "We must not imagine that the truth was thus impaired by the human agent, or the significance of the words destroyed."[101] The divine charism forbade compromise, or any writing "for the dull according to their dullness; for those in error according to their error."[102]

95 *Ab eodem Verbo propheticum accipientes charism,* IV:20,4 (34,4; ii:215).
96 *De omnibus adimpleti sunt, et habuerunt perfectionem agnitionem.* III:1,1 (*ibid.,* ii:2).
97 Lawson, *op. cit.,* p. 30.
98 *Loc. cit.*
99 *Ibid.,* p. 31.
100 IV:11,1 (21,1; ii:174).
101 Brooke Foss Westcott, *An Introduction to the Study of the Gospels* (Cambridge: Macmillan, 1881), p. 427.
102 III:5,1 (*ibid.,* ii:19).

II. IRENAEUS' PRINCIPLES FOR THE INTERPRETATION OF SCRIPTURE

The science of hermeneutics was not the primary subject of *Against Heresies,* and the work contains no systematic presentation of Irenaeus' principles of interpretation. Indeed, theological systematization characterized no Christian writer at this period. But within the writings of Irenaeus is found an abundance of references to the theory of interpretation, and the following represent some of the more basic or more distinctive elements of his thought.

A. THE REDEMPTIVE MESSAGE OF SCRIPTURE

Irenaeus sums up the fundamental theme of the writers of Scripture as

> The plan of our salvation . . . which they did at one time proclaim in public, and, at a later period, by the will of God, handed down to us in the Scriptures, to be the ground and pillar of our faith . . . preaching the glad tidings of the good things from God to us, and proclaiming the peace of heaven to men.[103]

The origin of our salvation is in the will of God, graciously expressing the divine attributes: "The love of God, being rich and ungrudging, confers upon the suppliant more than he can ask from it."[104] In history, then, came the redemptive incarnation of Christ, who "bestowed salvation on the men included in the creation; thus commenced His teaching in the Gospel."[105] (John 1:1-5 is quoted following this remark.) Scripture mediates the blessing; the four Gospels in particular he describes as "breathing out immortality on every side and vivifying men afresh."[106] Therefore an appreciation of the redemptive nature of Scripture is the *sine qua non* of Biblical interpretation, and there can be no real comprehension of Scripture on the part of one blinded to the purpose of its primary author.[107]

---

103 *Fundamentum et columnam fidei,* III:1,1 (*ibid.*; ii:2).
104 III:Pref. (*ibid.*; ii:1).
105 III:11,1 (11,7; ii:41).
106 III:11,8 (11,11; ii:47).
107 "True knowledge, then, consists in the understanding of Christ, which Paul terms the wisdom of God hidden in a mystery, which the natural man receiveth not." *Fr.* 36 (Pfaff).

B. Progressive Revelation

The second principle, according to Irenaeus, follows from the first: "If anyone, therefore, reads the Scriptures with attention, he will find in them an account of Christ, and a foreshadowing of the new calling";[108] that is, salvation being the theme of Scriptures, the earlier revelations had of necessity to be limited to the shadowy, thus producing progressive clarification as redemption was historically revealed and enacted, as attested by the words:

> The one and the same Lord granted, by means of His advent, a greater gift of grace to those of a later period, than what He had granted to those under the Old Testament dispensation.[109]

Hitchcock observes in comment, "The progress of His revelation is uniform and orderly. The course of redemption was adapted to the spiritual life and development of man."[110] This is not to deny occasional lapses by Irenaeus from his own principle, for instance, his assignment to Abraham of the knowledge that "the Son of God would be a man among men."[111] In general, however, the theory of progressiveness remained and was applied by Irenaeus to related fields. He noted that prophecy was difficult to understand before its fulfillment,[112] and in reference to the Person of Christ he freely admitted that "His human nature could not be understood prior to the consummation of those things which had been predicted, that is, the advent of Christ."[113] In the field of ethics he concluded,

> Inasmuch, then, as all natural precepts are common to us and to them (the Jews), they had in them indeed the beginning and origin; but in us they received growth and completion.[114]

To this development he applied the Biblical figure,

> For the Lord is the good man of the house, who rules the entire house of His father; and who delivers a law

108 IV:26,1 (40,1; ii:234-35).
109 IV:11,3 (21,3; ii:175); cf. Hitchcock, op. cit., p. 200.
110 Ibid., p. 204.
111 IV:7,1 (12; ii:162).
112 IV:26,1 (40,1; ii:234-35).
113 Loc. cit.; cf. Coxe. op. cit., footnote, I:497.
114 IV:13,4 (24,3; ii:183).

suited both for slaves and those who are as yet undisci-
plined; and gives fitting precepts to those that are free, and
have been justified by faith.[115]

It is necessary, however, to subjoin qualifications against two
theories often associated with the matter of progressive revelation but which Irenaeus expressly denied. First, messages adapted
to the attainments of the hearers must never be interpreted, as
was done by the heretics, as permissive accommodations to their
failures:

> These most vain sophists affirm that the Apostles did
> with hypocrisy form their doctrines according to the
> capacity of their hearers, and gave answers after the opin-
> ions of their questioners.[116]

Second, simplicity or incompleteness in the earlier revelations
must never be interpreted as error to be overcome and replaced.
Degrees of illumination do not imply degrees of inspiration
and truth.[117] In reference to Christ's much misinterpreted words
of Matt. 5, "Ye have heard that it was said . . . but I say unto
you," Irenaeus remarked,

> For all these do not contain or imply an opposition to
> and an overturning of the [precepts] of the past . . . but a
> fulfilling and an extension of them. . . . This which He
> did command — namely, not only to abstain from things
> forbidden by the law, but even from longing after them —
> is not contrary to [the law], as I have remarked, neither is
> it the utterance of one destroying the law, but of one
> fulfilling, extending, and affording greater scope to it.[118]

Some have indeed maintained, as does Lawson, that
> the temporariness and imperfection of some of the com-
> mandments of the Mosaic Law was the provision of the
> true God in pursuit of an eternal and unchanging purpose,
> yet by methods temporarily adapted to the frailty of man-

---

115 IV:9,1 (18,2; ii:169).
116 III:5,1 (*ibid.*; ii:19). Against views of accommodation such as Briggs'
    dictum that "Jesus was not obliged to correct all the errors of His
    contemporaries [about Scriptural authorship]," Irenaeus aligned him-
    self with Raven's judgment, *op. cit.*, pp. 89-90, that "Truth in the
    lower sphere was essential to the 'faithful witness' in the higher
    sphere. . . . Doubting Christ on these so-called minor points is always
    preparatory to doubting Him on religious matters."
117 Vs. Lawson, *op. cit.*, pp. 26-27.
118 IV:13,1 (23,1; ii:181).

kind. S. Irenaeus had here [on divorce] grasped the essential principle of progressive revelation.[119]

But it should be observed that in this very matter of marriage and divorce Irenaeus taught a uniformity of grace, coupled with divine opposition to sin, not a replacement of an "imperfect" old morality by a correct and different new morality.[120] What Irenaeus had actually "grasped as the essential principle" is that

> the Lord Himself did speak in His own person to all alike the words of the Decalogue; and therefore, in like manner, do they remain permanently with us, receiving by means of His advent in the flesh extension and increase, but not abrogation.[121]

This leads directly into his next main interpretative principle.

C. THE UNITY OF SCRIPTURE

Even as salvation was unified, the death of One for the sins of men of all periods, so the record of that salvation possessed a unity, by virtue, moreover, of its origin through that very Person. He writes: "How do the Scriptures testify of Him, unless all things had ever been revealed and shown to believers by one and the same God through the Word?"[122] This principle Irenaeus had received from those who were before him, perhaps Polycarp, for he says,

> After this fashion also did a presbyter, a disciple of the apostles, reason with respect to the two testaments, proving that both were truly from one and the same God.[123]

From this then came two related standards, both occupying crucial positions in his system of Biblical interpretation: the harmony of Scripture, and the analogy of Scripture. In respect to the former, Irenaeus stated:

119 Lawson, *op. cit.,* p. 86.
120 IV:15,2 (26,2; ii:188); cf. the identity of teaching in Deut. 24:2 and Matt. 5:32. "If, therefore, even in the New Testament, the apostles are found granting certain precepts in consideration of human infirmity . . . it ought not to be wondered at, if also in the Old Testament, the same God permitted similar indulgences for the benefit of His people."
121 *Extensionem et augmentum, sed non dissolutionem, accipientia,* IV:16,4 (28,2; ii:192).
122 IV:11,1 (21,1; ii:174).
123 IV:32, 1 (49,1; ii:254).

> All Scripture, which has been given us by God, shall be
> found to be perfectly consistent . . . and through the many
> diversified utterances there shall be heard one harmonious
> melody in us, praising in hymns that God who created all
> things.[124]

This harmony was based on inerrancy and applied to both testaments.[125] Within the Old Testament he could assert in respect
to Moses,

> Expounding again the law to that generation which fol-
> lowed those who were slain in the wilderness, he published
> Deuteronomy; not as giving them a different law from that
> which had been appointed for their fathers, but as
> recapitulating this latter.[126]

Within the New Testament he insisted, as over against heretics
who would accept but part of the Gospels, that Christ "has
given us the Gospel under four aspects, but bound together by
one Spirit."[127] True, criticisms have been raised against his stand
for Biblical unity,[128] but then Irenaeus on his part felt that the
heretics did not do justice to the Lord's position when they
attempted to explain certain difficulties on the basis of differing
types of inspiration!

In respect to the analogy of Scripture, Irenaeus' view was that
of the Westminster divines:

> The infallible rule of interpretation of Scripture is the
> Scripture itself; and therefore, when there is a question
> about the true and full sense of any Scripture (which is

124 *Pasa graphē dedomenē hēmin apo Theou sumphōnos hemin
    heurethēsetai . . . kai dia tēs ton lexeōn poluphōnias hen sumphōnon
    melos en hēmin aisthēsetai.* II:28,3 (41,4; i:352).

125 IV: 35,2 (57,2: ii:274). "If, at His advent, He sent forth His own
    apostles in the spirit of truth and not in that of error, He did the
    same also in the case of the prophets [writers of the Old Testament].

126 *Fr.* 16.

127 III:11,8 (11,11; ii:274).

128 Lawson, *op. cit.*, p. 53. "We may feel that this position does not
    entirely do justice to our Lord's teaching. In the words of Jesus,
    ethics and piety rise to a level of purity, consistency, clarity and
    winning loveliness, which transcends all that has gone before."

not manifold, but one), it may be searched and known by other places that speak more clearly.[129]

For him the New Testament was not simply a permissible source; it was an essential source for determining the meaning of the Old. From John 8:56 he knew that Abraham rejoiced to see Christ's day;[130] and from Matt. 13:17, that the prophets prayed that they might see it.[131] When noting from Matt. 1:23 that Isaiah spoke of the virgin birth,[132] he explained that such New Testament clarifications were "the meaning of the [Old Testament] Scripture and the dispensation of God."[133] He further admonishes,

> All those other points which I have shown the prophets to have uttered by means of so long a series of Scriptures, he who is truly spiritual will interpret by pointing out . . . to what special point in the dispensation of the Lord is referred . . . knowing always the same God, and always acknowledging the same Word of God, although He has [but] now been manifested to us.[134]

D. Historicity

For Irenaeus the principle of the analogy of Scripture led directly into a consistently historical approach to Biblical literature. God's statements in the New Testament, far from imposing upon the former revelations content foreign to their original nature, served to guarantee their authenticity in matters both of fact and of interpretation. Irenaeus maintained, "Faith is produced by the truth; for faith rests on things that truly are. For in things that are, as they are, we believe."[135] Therefore, because "the prophetic word declares . . . ," he held to the origin of the human race as recorded in Genesis 1-2.[136] His statement, "Moses likewise [variant reading "himself"] says, 'God said, Let there be light: and there was light,' "[137] indicates his confidence,

129 *Conf. of Faith*, I:9.
130 IV:7,1-2 (11,5—ch. 13; ii:161-63).
131 IV:11,1 (21,1; ii:174).
132 III:21,3 (24,2—25,1; ii:114-15).
133 *Virtutem Scripturae et dispositionem Dei*, IV:11,3 (21,3; ii:176).
134 IV:33,15 (55,6; ii:269).
135 *Dem.* 3.
136 II:34,3 (56,2; i:383); cf. V:14,2 (*ibid.*; ii:361-6) and *Dem.* 13.
137 *Et* [var. *ipse*] *Moses ait*, IV:32,1 (49,2; ii:255).

not simply in fiat creation but also in the Mosaic authorship of its record. He had implicit faith in the authenticity of the words of God to Cain and to Noah,[138] and in the historicity of the tower of Babel[139] and of the call of Abraham.[140] The psalms which claimed Davidic authorship in their titles were for him genuine products of the shepherd-king.[141] He accepted the New Testament in the same way. The activity of Gabriel recorded in Luke 1 was factual,[142] and about the virgin birth there could be no question.[143] He acknowledged the apostolic authorship of Matthew and Revelation as well as of John.[144] The words of Christ during His public ministry were taken to be exactly as they had been preserved in the Gospels,[145] and 2 Timothy and Titus were recognized as authentic Pauline epistles, as claimed by the books themselves.[146] Irenaeus stated at length about the antediluvians and the prophets:

> It might seem to the men of the present day, who are ignorant of God's appointment, to be a thing incredible and impossible that any man could live for such a number of years, yet those who were before us did live [to such an age], and those who were translated do live as an earnest of the future length of days; and [as it might also appear impossible] that from the whale's belly and from the fiery furnace men issue forth unhurt, yet they nevertheless did so, led forth as it were by the hand of God, for the purpose of declaring His power; so also now, although some, not knowing the power and promise of God, may oppose their own salvation, deeming it impossible for God, who raises up the dead, to have power to confer upon them eternal duration, yet the skepticism of men of this stamp shall not render the faithfulness of God of none effect.[147]

This has indeed caused the comment, "One would be inclined to infer that 'saving faith' is here built upon the foundation of

138 V:14,1 (*ibid.*; ii:360-61).
139 *Dem.* 23.
140 IV:7,3 (13; ii:163-64).
141 Psa. 35 and 8, IV:11,3 (21,3; ii:175-76); though note too his Davidic assignment of Psa. 85, of the Korahites, III:5,1 (*ibid.*; ii:18).
142 III:11,4 (11,8; ii:43).
143 III:19 (20; ii:102-5).
144 III:1,1 (1,1-2; ii:2-6).
145 V:14,1 (*ibid.*; ii:360-61).
146 III:14,1 (*ibid.*; ii:73); I:16,3.
147 V:5,2 (5,2-3; ii:332-33).

acceptance of these stories";[148] and, although Irenaeus would not
have made knowledge of the ancient miracles a prerequisite to
salvation, still, that he did see a real connection between faith
in them and faith in Christ is not to be denied. Irenaeus'
Demonstration of the Apostolic Preaching is primarily a running
commentary on sacred history, chapters 11 to 23, for example,
being simply a paraphrase of Genesis 1-11. Of this work Robinson has said, "It is in no sense a manual for catechumens; it is a
handbook of Christian evidence . . . for an intelligent Christian,
explaining his faith";[149] and Irenaeus himself called it a
"manual of essentials."[150] In other words, Irenaeus' stand was for
a consistent supernaturalism. The God who took away sins
could, and did, take away Elijah; and, conversely, for the man
to whom the latter act was not historically real, neither could
the former be expected to be historically real. The determinative
demonstration of the necessity of historicity was the resurrection
of Christ. So it was that Irenaeus wrote,

> If He rose not from the dead, neither did He vanquish
> death and bring its reign to naught; and if death be not
> vanquished, how can we ascend to life, who from the
> beginning have fallen under death?[151]

E. TEXTUAL STUDY

The historical approach of Irenaeus to the Bible led him to a
recognition, however incomplete, of the need for grammatical
exegesis and textual criticism in interpreting Scripture. In
respect to the former he stated as a principle:

> If then one does not attend to the [proper] reading
> [of the passage], and [if he] does not exhibit the intervals
> of breathing as they occur, there shall be not only incon-
> gruities, but also when reading, he will utter blasphemy.[152]

On occasion he could base his arguments on the meaning and
use of a single word,[153] or even New Testament punctuation.[154]

148 Lawson, *op. cit.*, p. 78.
149 Robinson, *op. cit.*, p. 2.
150 *Dem.* 1.
151 *Dem.* 39.
152 III:7,2 (*ibid.*; ii:26).
153 III:11,1 (11,7; ii:40-41).
154 III:7,1 (*ibid.*; ii:25-26).

He was, of course, a child of his times in his ignorance of scientific grammar. Concerning this last reference, 2 Corinthians 4:4, with its Gnostic-like phrase, "The God of this world": "He is trying desperately to explain away the awkward phrase . . . by an utter wresting of the sense";[155] and his lack of familiarity with the Hebrew Old Testament is indicated by the following on Gideon's name:

> And when he did not choose to partake with them in their idol worship, they threw the blame upon him; for "Jerubbaal" signifies the judgment-seat of Baal.[156]

Still, the very discussion of such matters shows his awareness of the importance of such study.

Irenaeus was equally cognizant of the problem of Textual Criticism. His general conclusion was that the Biblical text had been transmitted "without falsification";[157] but in his *De Ogdoade* he felt it necessary to include, for the benefit of future scribes, a sharp warning lest they fail to take precautions against textual corruption.[158] At points in his Biblical exegesis could appear such a statement as:

> This occurred through the fault of copyists, as is wont to happen . . . others then received this reading without examination.[159]

The interpretation of Irenaeus himself of Genesis 1:1, "In the beginning, the Son," was based on a faulty text, *"Baresith bara, Elowin. . . ."*[160] The principle on which Irenaeus worked is explicit: to adopt those readings found "in all the more approved and ancient copies,"[161] but he nowhere describes his actual textual method — if indeed he had one. Further, he was aware of the differences within the Biblical versions of his day. He rejected as unworthy the readings of the Greek versions of

155 Lawson, *op. cit.,* p. 31.
156 *Fr.* 18.
157 IV:33,8 (53:2; ii:263).
158 Eusebius, *Hist. Eccl.,* V:20.
159 V:30,1 (*ibid.;* ii:406), though this very passage may not be genuine! Harvey styles it, "An evident interpolation," *op. cit.,* II:407.
160 *Dem.* 43. Even worse would appear to be a passage on God's preaching salvation to dead Israel, first mentioned by Irenaeus as from Isaiah, but later as from Jeremiah, III:20,4, cf. IV:22,1, but being in fact a verse otherwise totally unknown.
161 V:30,1 (*ibid.;* ii:406).

Aquila and Theodotion on Isaiah 7:14; he preferred the Septuagint reading, which taught the virgin birth.[162] Lawson says that in so doing he went too far, "even to the point of preferring it to the original,"[163] a claim based on the prejudiced assumption that the virgin birth is not taught in the Isaiah passage. Irenaeus seems to have anticipated Robert Dick Wilson[164] by branding such a denial as "setting aside the testimony of the prophets which proceeded from God."[165] It must be noted, however, that Irenaeus adopted Justin Martyr's addition to the *Letter of Aristeas,* for he held to an authority for the Septuagint equal to that of the Hebrew: "The Scriptures had been interpreted by the inspiration of God."[166]

F. Literary Interpretation

The heretical opponents of Irenaeus had no scruples against reading their own concepts into the Scriptures, but it has been questioned whether Irenaeus himself appreciated the need for interpreting Biblical literature in accordance with objective standards, assigning to given statements meanings in harmony with their contexts and true intent. Again Lawson has said,

> He saw the book [of Isaiah] as a mysterious oracle, to which one could turn to provide divine sanction for what one had to say. This attitude is not the scientific and historical, which approaches an ancient author with the question: "How can I understand what this writer has to say?"[167]

Of course, such criticism may be expected from those who fail to recognize the divine authorship behind the human, and hence the legitimacy of interpretation by the analogy of Scripture, but granting the divine unity of the Scriptures one discovers in Irenaeus' principles of literary interpretation a noteworthy contrast with the subjectivity of his day.

In the first place, Irenaeus recognized the problem:

162 III:21,1 (23; ii:110-11).
163 Lawson, *op. cit.,* p. 61.
164 "The Meaning of Alma (A.V. "Virgin") in Isaiah VII:14" *Princeton Theological Review* 24 (1926), 308-16.
165 III:21,1 (23; ii:110).
166 III:21,2 (24,1; ii:114).
167 Lawson, *op. cit.,* p. 61.

> They [the Valentinians] disregard the order and the connection of the Scripture. . . . By transferring passages, and dressing them up anew, and making one thing out of another, they succeed in deluding many through their wicked art of adapting the oracles of the Lord to their opinions.[168]

In the second place, and perhaps in reaction, Irenaeus advanced to a positive position of his own, maintaining the basic unity of Scripture and, at the same time, varying forms of expression appropriate to the differing human writers:

> It was requisite that certain facts should be announced beforehand by the fathers in a paternal manner, and others prefigured by the prophets in a legal one, but others, described after the form of Christ, by those who have received the adoption; while in one God are all things shown forth.[169]

In the third place, he attempted to assign to these forms of expression meanings contextually consistent, insofar as he was able. The remarks of Lipsius are in point:

> It must be allowed that Irenaeus himself in interpreting Scripture, especially when, like the Gnostics, he indulges in allegory, is not free from forced and arbitrary methods of exposition. But in opposition to the fantastic interpretations of the Valentinian school, he represents for the most part the historical sense of the written word.[170]

Of the presence in Scripture of symbolic or parabolic language and of the need for caution in its interpretation, Irenaeus was well aware, as when he wrote,

> The parables ought not to be adapted to ambiguous expressions. For if this be not done . . . the parables will receive a like interpretation from all, and the body of truth remains entire. . . . But to apply expressions which are not clear or evident to interpretations of parables, such as everyone discovers for himself [is absurd].[171]

He thus made a break in principle, both with the Gnostics and with those Christians of Alexandria who were characterized by

---

168 *Tēn men taxin kai ton heirmon tōn graphōn*, I:8,1 (1,14; i:67).
169 *Paternaliter a patribus . . . legaliter a prophetis . . . secundum formationem Christi ab his qui* . . . IV:25,3 (39; ii:234).
170 Lipsius, *op. cit.*, III:270.
171 From the section on "a sound mind," II:27,1 (40,1; i:347-48).

unrestricted figurative interpretation. Exception must be taken
to Farrar's conclusion that "his own exposition is based on the
same erroneous principles as that of his predecessors";[172] for
"there appear in his writings a greater justness of reasoning, and
a more unexceptional use of Scripture, than is found in the
writers of the Alexandrian school."[173] Specifically, Irenaeus' aim
was a "harmonious adaptation of its [the truth's] members, and
without any collision."[174] This harmony he sought, but not by
an imposition of questionable meanings.[175]

In particular, Irenaeus opposed the principle of Biblical
numerics, saying,

> They [the heretics] endeavor to bring forward proofs
> . . . sometimes through means of numbers and syllables of
> names, sometimes through those numbers which are, ac-
> cording to the practice followed by the Greeks, contained
> in [different] letters; — [this I say], demonstrates in the
> clearest manner their overthrow or confusion, as well as
> the untenable and perverse character of their knowledge.[176]

In the same discussion he demonstrated the absurdity of the
method by a Biblical list of things in fives, concluding,

> Any one, in fact, might collect many thousands of other
> things of the same kind, both with respect to this number
> and any other he chose to fix upon . . . that vain kind of
> labor; nor do we perversely force a creature well adapted
> by God to change itself into types of things which have no
> real existence.[177]

172 Frederic W. Farrar, *History of Interpretation* (London: Macmillan, 1886), p. 175.
173 Beaven, *op. cit.*, pp. 1-2.
174 *Simili aptatione membrorum, et sine concussione,* II:27,1 (40,1; i:347).
175 "To explain ambiguous passages of Scripture . . . no question can be solved by means of another which itself awaits solution . . . but things of such character receive their solution from those which are manifest, and consistent, and clear." *Ex manifestis et consonantibus et claris accipiunt absolutiones,* II:10,1 (11,1; i:273): cf. II:28,3 (41,4; i:352): The parables shall harmonize, *sumphōnēsousi* with those passages which are perfectly plain; and those statements the meaning of which is clear, shall serve to explain the parables.
176 II:24,1 (34,3; i:333); cf. II:24,2-6 (34,4—36,4; i:334-42).
177 II:24,4 (36,1-2; i:338-40); cf. II:25,1 (37,1; i:342-43): "Men ought not to connect these things with the number thirty, but to harmonize them with what actually exists, or with right reason . . . because every sort of hypothesis may at the present day be, in like manner, devised by anyone . . . they may be turned in many different directions."

Westcott, it is true, notes Irenaeus as "drawing arguments from isolated details of parables,"[178] but his reference appears to be to Irenaeus' use of verses such as Matt. 25:41 (cf. 3:12), which is found in a predictive rather than a parabolic context.[179] Furthermore, Westcott's argument is in itself a demonstration of the strict adherence of Irenaeus to the text, as Briggs summarizes it: "The literal method of exegesis."[180]

In regard to typology and allegory, Irenaeus has been subject to sharp criticism, as when Lawson wrote,

> The most casual reader of S. Irenaeus cannot fail to observe . . . that the interpretation of Scripture is most commonly allegorical. To modern eyes it is often strange to the point of the fanciful, or even the grotesque.[181]

Irenaeus did hold to the possibility of higher meaning in Biblical events, as in a reference to Hosea:

> It was not by means of visions alone which were seen, and words which were heard, but also in actual works, that He was beheld by the prophets, in order that through them He might prefigure and show forth future events beforehand. For this reason did Hosea the prophet take "a wife of whoredoms" prophesying by means of action "that in committing fornication, the earth should fornicate from the LORD," that is, the men who are upon the earth; and from men of this stamp it will be God's pleasure to take out a church which shall be sanctified by fellowship with His Son.[182]

Such a meaning was by no means foreign to the intent of Hosea, and the New Testament consistently validates Irenaeus' contention that Christ was in the Old Testament by "types and parables."[183] This typology, however, was not arbitrary but stemmed from the eternal plan of God working out in history

---

178 *Op. cit.*, p. 429.
179 A parallel might be his argument from the record of the rich man and Lazarus: "By these things, then, it is plainly declared that souls possess the form of a man so that they may be recognized, and retain the memory of things of this world," II:34,1 (55,1; i:381-82).
180 Charles Augustus Briggs, *General Introduction to the Study of Holy Scripture* (New York: Scribner's, 1899), p. 448.
181 Lawson, *op. cit.*, p. 23.
182 *Praefiguraret et praemonstraret futura*, IV:20,12 (34,12; ii:223).
183 *Per typos et parabolas*, IV:26,1 (40,1; ii:234).

one unified course of redemption.[184] Two qualifying principles, moreover, were advanced by Irenaeus as limiting factors on the use of typology. First, the typical nature must be inherent, designed by God from the start. He states his position positively:

> Observances had been given as a type of future things — the law typifying, as it were, certain things in a shadow, and delineating eternal things by temporal, celestial by terrestrial.[185]

Negatively, he says in respect to passages not so designed,

> If, however, any shall endeavor to allegorize [prophecies] of this kind, they shall not be found consistent with themselves in all points, and shall be confuted by the teachings of the very expressions [in question].[186]

Secondly, typical meaning must be revealed by God, in whose mind, and only in whose mind, was the true design to be found. Irenaeus equated "things spiritual and heavenly" with "such as require to be made known to us by revelation,"[187] and his condemnation of the methods of the Gnostics was that "their imaginations range beyond God, they in their hearts having surpassed the Master Himself."[188] Whether Irenaeus personally lived up to the principles he enunciated is, of course, another matter, but Terry has well summarized the general situation:

> These expositions [of Irenaeus] are sometimes manifestly erroneous, and occasionally farfetched and strange, but on the whole evince a thorough acquaintance with the sacred books, and avoid the most objectionable features of the typical and allegorical interpretations so prevalent at that time.[189]

As concerns prophecy, Irenaeus began with the fact that "our God, one and the same, is also their [the patriarchs'] God, who knows hidden things, who knoweth all things before they can come to pass."[190] Since the Bible consisted of the words of God,

---

184 IV:19,1 (32; ii:210). "The gifts, oblations and all the sacrifices, did the people receive in a figure as it was shown to Moses in the mount, from one and the same God, whose name is now glorified in the church among all nations."
185 IV:11,4 (21,4; ii:176).
186 V:35,1 (*ibid.*; ii:423).
187 II:28, (41,2; i:350).
188 IV:19,1 (32; ii:210).
189 *Op. cit.*, p. 636.
190 IV:21,2 (35,2; ii:226).

it followed that on its pages "the Spirit of God . . . announced
things future, revealed things present, and narrated things
past."[191] Moreover, behind the prophecies themselves lay a
definite philosophy of history, the key to the interpretation of
which lay, once again, in an appreciation of redemption. The
purpose of man is to glorify God. Irenaeus' analysis tended
toward supralapsarianism, for he said,

> God predestined that the first man should be of an
> animal nature, with the view that he might be saved by
> the spiritual One. For inasmuch as He had a pre-existence
> as a saving Being, it was necessary that what might be
> saved should also be called into existence, in order that
> the Being who saves should not exist in vain.[192]

After the fall, and the announcement found in Genesis 3:15,
though redemption was not actually accomplished until Calvary,
men were granted the opportunity to exercise saving faith in the
coming deliverance. Irenaeus put it thus:

> As in the beginning, by means of our first parents, we
> were all brought into bondage, by being made subject to
> death, so at last, by means of the New Man, all who from
> the beginning [were His] disciples, having been cleansed
> and washed from things pertaining to death, should come
> to the life of God.[193]

And even as all history was directed to the execution of the one
great plan of redemption, so all prophecy had salvation in
Christ as its central theme.[194] Predictive Messianic prophecy was

191 IV:33,1 (50; ii:256).
192 III:22,3 (33,1; ii:123).
193 IV:22,1 (36:1; ii:228). Cf. his famous statement on man's end being
redemption, "The business of the Christian is nothing else than to
be ever preparing for death," *Fr.* 11. Note also his uncompromising
attitude on the unity of salvation, particularly because of its denial
by Gnosticism: "Those who disallow his [Abraham's] salvation, and
frame the idea of another God besides Him who made the promise
to Abraham, are outside the kingdom of God, and are disinherited
from incorruption, setting at nought and blaspheming God, who
introduced, through Jesus Christ, Abraham to the kingdom of heaven,
and his seed, that is the church, upon which also is conferred the
adoption and the inheritance promised to Abraham," IV:8,1 (15;
ii:165).
194 IV:2,7 (4,1; ii:150). "For the law never hindered them [Israel] from
believing in the Son of God; nay, but it even exhorted them to do
so, saying that men can be saved in no other way from the old wound
of the serpent than by believing in Him who, in the likeness of
sinful flesh, is lifted up from the earth upon the tree of martyrdom,
and draws all things to Himself, and vivifies the dead."

not only possible but was required, both for the salvation of the pre-Incarnation saints and for the preparation of those that followed. So it was that Irenaeus wrote,

> The patriarchs and prophets . . . prefigured our faith and disseminated through the earth the advent of the Son of God, who and what He should be: so that posterity, possessing the fear of God, might easily accept the advent of Christ, having been instructed by the prophets.[195]

Finally, this unity in teaching extended to the future consummation as well, for

> John, there, did distinctly foresee the first "resurrection of the just" and the inheritance in the kingdom of the earth; and what the prophets have prophesied concerning it harmonize.[196]

Because of the unity of the divine prophetic plan Irenaeus believed in the final fulfillment of all that had been prophesied.[197] Furthermore, prophecy is to be fulfilled in precisely that historical and literal sense in which it was originally announced, as indicated in remarks pertaining to Isaiah:

> Says Isaiah . . . "And they shall build houses, and shall inhabit them themselves: and plant vineyards and eat of them themselves." For all these and other words were unquestionably spoken in reference to the resurrection of the just, which takes place after the coming of Antichrist, and the destruction of all nations under his rule; in which the righteous shall reign on the earth.[198]

Irenaeus admitted that there were cases, such as when Daniel was told to seal the book until accomplishment, which were "to men [full of] enigmas and ambiguities,"[199] but where he felt he had grasped the true and original sense, he was unwilling to allow its replacement by other concepts. An example is seen in his reference to Isa. 11:

195 IV:23,1 (37:1; ii:230).
196 V:36,3 (26; ii:429).
197 IV:21,1 (35,1; ii:225). "[Abraham] believed in things future, as if they were already accomplished, because of the promise of God; and in like manner do we also, because of the promise of God, behold through faith that inheritance [laid up for us] in the [future] kingdom."
198 V:35,1 (ibid.; ii:423).
199 *Aenigmata et ambiguitates sunt hominibus*, IV:26,1 (40,1; ii:234-36).

The lion shall eat straw as well as the ox. . . . I am quite aware that some persons endeavor to refer these words to the case of savage men, both of different nations and various habits, who come to believe, and when they have believed act in harmony with the righteous. But though this is true now . . . some other occasion, and not the present, is [to be sought] for showing that the lion shall [then] feed on straw.[200]

Lawson, it is true, claims that Irenaeus himself elsewhere spiritualized the passage,[201] but the reference in question hardly serves to deny his basic principle of literal fulfillment.[202] Concerning, however, a number of obscure points in prophetic interpretation Irenaeus could and did advise, "It is therefore more certain, and less hazardous, to await the fulfillment of the prophecy, than to be making surmises,"[203] and,

We will not . . . incur the risk of pronouncing positively as to the name of Antichrist; for if it were necessary that his name should be distinctly revealed in this present time, it would have been announced by him who beheld the apocalyptic vision.[204]

This leads then to a final principle.

G. Perspicuity

From the above it is evident that Irenaeus did not maintain that Scripture could be understood at all points, but even as

200 V:33,4 (*ibid.;* ii:418-19).
201 Lawson, *op. cit.,* p. 84.
202 "Now as to the union and concord and peace of the animals of different kinds, which by nature are opposed and hostile to each other, the Elders say that so it will be in truth at the coming of Christ, when He is to reign over all. For already in symbol He announces the gathering together in peace and concord, through the name of Christ, of men of unlike races and yet of like dispositions." *Dem.* 61. It should be noted, however, that a futuristic interpretation was not consistently maintained. He speaks of "the resurrection [of Christ] . . . as God promised by the prophet, saying: *And I will raise up the tabernacle of David that is fallen*; that is, the flesh that was from David. And this our Lord Jesus Christ truly fulfilled, when He gloriously achieved our redemption," *Dem.* 38. Cf. also IV:34,4 (56,3; ii:271) on Isa. 2:3-4, about which Lawson, *op. cit.* p. 59, comments, "This is certainly an applied meaning read into the text." For a list of passages both ways cf. *ibid.,* p. 60.
203 V:30,3 (30:2; ii:408).
204 *Loc. cit.* (30:3; ii:410).

his doctrine of the sacraments has caused Romanist apologists no little embarrassment,[205] so too his doctrine of the perspicuity of Scripture is that of the Reformation, namely, that insofar as essentials of faith are concerned, "the entire Scriptures . . . can be clearly, unambiguously, and harmoniously understood by all, although all do not believe them."[206] Again,

> Those things which God hath placed within the power of mankind . . . are such as fall [plainly] under our observation, and are clearly and unambiguously in express terms set forth in sacred Scriptures.[207]

He had, therefore, little patience with the contrary position of the heretics.[208]

Irenaeus did note two qualifications to his interpretative principle of general perspicuity. First, it was understood that the enlightening work of the Holy Spirit was necessary within the hearts of sinful men before the truth could assume its natural clarity. He therefore wrote,

> A spiritual disciple of this sort truly receiving the Spirit of God, who was from the beginning . . . does indeed "judge all men, but is himself judged of no man." For He judges . . . the Jews, who do not accept the word of liberty . . . nor are willing to understand that all the prophets announced His two advents.[209]

Secondly, it required serious human application to reap the full benefit of the Word. Characteristic of Irenaeus was the proviso, "If anyone read the Scripture with attention";[210] and this would appear to be the thought behind his much debated statement,

> Then shall every word also seem consistent to him, if he for his part diligently read the Scriptures in company with

---

205 Cf. *Fr.* 37, of Pfaff.
206 *In aperto, et sine ambiguitate, et similiter ab omnibus,* II:27,2 (40,2; i:348).
207 *Hosa phanerōs kai anamphibolōs autolexei en tais theiais graphais lelektai,* II:27,1 (40:1; i:347).
208 III:2,1 (*ibid.*; ii:7). "When, however, they are confuted from the Scriptures they turn around and accuse these same Scriptures as if they were not correct nor of authority, and assert that they are ambiguous, and that the truth cannot be extracted from them by those who are ignorant of tradition . . . depraving the system of truth."
209 IV:33,1 (50; ii:256).
210 *Intentus legat,* IV:26,1 (39; ii:234).

those who are presbyters in the Church, among whom is the apostolic doctrine.[211]
From this has been postulated a reliance upon authoritative, ecclesiastical interpretation, in opposition to his express statements of perspicuity, as when Lawson says,

> Historical ignorance forced the Catholic Christian into the same fast-and-loose game as the heretic, well aware though he was of the perils of religious subjectivity. . . . The Church roundly asserted that certain historical and certain allegorical interpretations, and they only, were legitimate. . . . Thus a commanding voice was raised to bear down the cavils of the heretics.[212]

Such an analysis, however, misrepresents the situation in two important respects: first, as previously noted, the spiritual interpretations advocated by Irenaeus had, in principle at least, their basis in the revelation itself and not in human subjectivity; and secondly, such spiritualizations as he did accept did not exclude the authority of their literal teachings. True, he spoke of the presbyters who "expound the Scripture to us without danger"; but this was not because of authority resident within the Church but because these men "neither blaspheme God, nor dishonor the patriarchs, nor despise the prophets."[213] Hitchcock summarizes his views thus:

> Irenaeus did not uphold the Church as the infallible interpreter of Scripture or commit himself to any such position, but he held that some standard such as the Church's "rule of truth" (regula veritatis, II.27.1, III.2.1) or "Preaching" (praeconium Ecclesiae, V.20.2) should be employed, as a sort of critical test by which "sound" views could be distinguished from the "unsound."[214]

Irenaeus had a high regard for the tradition of the apostles,[215] but the real value of the "succession of the bishops" lay in the fact that they handed down "a lawful and diligent exposition in harmony with the Scriptures."[216]

---

211 *Diligenter legerat*, IV:32,1 (49,2; ii:255).
212 Lawson, *op. cit.*, p. 95.
213 IV:26,5 (42,1; ii:238).
214 Hitchcock, *op. cit.*, p. 184.
215 Cf. *infra*, pp. 62 ff.
216 *Secundum Scripturas expositio legitima et diligens*, IV:33,8 (53,2; ii:263).

III. Irenaeus' Methodology in the Employment of Scripture

In Farrar's somewhat negative critique of Irenaeus appears the statement, "Whatever may be his other gifts he shows no special wisdom in the application of hermeneutic methods."[217] It is therefore well to observe certain outstanding aspects of the relationship of his actual practice of interpretation to his theory as outlined above.

A. The Consecrated Approach

Even as the most fundamental principle in Irenaeus' interpretation was the redemptive nature of Scripture, so his first requirement in its employment was consecration on the part of its user.[218] Scripture must be employed first of all as the means to one's own salvation, or all other study is meaningless:

> True knowledge, then, consists in the understanding of Christ which Paul terms the wisdom of God hidden in a mystery, which "the natural man receiveth not." . . . For the truth is unsophisticated . . . being easy of comprehension to those who are obedient. . . . For truly the first thing is to deny oneself and to follow Christ; and those who do this are borne onward to perfection, having fulfilled all their Teacher's will, becoming sons of God by spiritual regeneration, and heirs of the kingdom of heaven.[219]

There must then follow constant reliance for guidance upon the Holy Spirit, "the means of confirming our faith."[220] He repeatedly cautions:

> In regard to those things which we investigate in the Scriptures . . . as the apostle has said on this point, that, when other things have been done away, then these three, "faith, hope, and charity shall endure."[221]

For Irenaeus, then, this consecrated approach meant first an attitude of mind in using Scripture. His admonition was: "Place

---

217 *Op. cit.*, pp. 174-75.
218 II:26,1 (39,1; i:345). "It is better . . . that he should seek after no other knowledge except [the knowledge of] Jesus Christ the Son of God, who was crucified for us, than that by subtle questions and hair-splitting expressions he should fall into impiety."
219 *Fr.* 36.
220 *Confirmatio fidei nostrae*, III:24,1 (38,1; ii:131).
221 II:28,3 (41,3; i:351).

the fear of God supreme in the heart."[222] Specifically, one must yield assent to the inspired truth of Scripture, whether or not one could account rationally for all that appeared.[223] As Calvin later put it, "For our wisdom ought to consist in embracing with gentle docility, and without any exception, all that is delivered in the sacred Scriptures."[224] For those who opposed their minds to Scripture, Irenaeus could speak feelingly from 2 Corinthians 2:17 about the many who corrupted the Word of God,[225] stating that the apostles

> announced through the Holy Spirit that those who teach such doctrines were agents of Satan, sent forth for the purpose of overturning the faith of some, and drawing them away from life.[226]

Westcott observed, "Then only does he seem to forget his master's lessons of peace and love, when he contends against those who deny Christian truth."[227]

Indeed, Irenaeus' consecrated approach meant, secondly, an application of Scriptural standards to personal life. He sums it up in: "The pre-eminent gift of love, which is more precious than knowledge, more glorious than prophecy, and which excells all the other gifts."[228] Orthodoxy, though the goal of Irenaeus for the minds of his readers, was, if alone, not enough, because Christ "did throw blame upon those persons because they repeated indeed the words of the law, yet were without love."[229] As the basis for the true life Irenaeus says, "We should increase in the love of Him who has done, and still does, so great things

222 IV:26,3 (41,1; ii:236-37).
223 II:25,3 (37,3; i:344): "If, however, any one does not discover the cause of all those things which have become objects of investigation, let him reflect that man is infinitely inferior to God . . . that he cannot have experience or form a conception of all things like God." Cf. II:28,2 (41,1; i:349) and I:10,3 (4; i:94-97): It does not follow because men are endowed with greater or less degrees of intelligence, that they should therefore change the subject matter [of the faith] itself . . . for in reference to this . . . the apostle explains, "Oh! the depth of the riches both of the wisdom and knowledge of God; how unsearchable are His judgments, and His ways past finding out."
224 John Calvin, *Institutes of the Christian Religion*, John Allen trans. (Philadelphia: Presbyterian Board of Christian Education, n.d.) I:262.
225 IV:26,4 (41,1; ii:237-38).
226 III:16,1 (16; ii:82).
227 *Op. cit.*, p. 427.
228 IV:33,8 (52,2; ii:263).
229 IV:12,4 (24,1; ii:179).

for us."[230] The result will be then, not simply the response of love for the men Christ died to save, but also, and by this very response, the fulfilling of one of the prime prerequisites to a right use of Scripture. His recommendation for discerning the true Bible expositor included, "Adhere to those who . . . display sound speech and blameless conduct."[231] An important factor in the influence of Irenaeus himself was the extent to which he lived up to his name, Irenaeus, "the peaceful one."

B. SCRIPTURAL PROOF

A second basic method observable in the use of Scripture by Irenaeus is his employment of its words as his final authority. This followed from his belief in historicity and inerrancy. For him, proof-texts clinch an argument, as witness his formulas of citation: "I shall adduce proofs from the Scriptures";[232] "Let us revert to the Scriptural proof furnished by those apostles who did also write the Gospel";[233] "John, however, does himself put this matter beyond all controversy on our part when he says";[234] or simply, "As the Scripture says."[235] Yet while a firm believer in the "proof-text method" Irenaeus was aware that his arguments should have the support of total context as well; observe his dictum, "I judge it necessary to take into account the entire mind of the apostles regarding our Lord Jesus Christ."[236] He specifically rebukes the heretics for their violations in this respect, saying that, "Collecting a set of expressions and names scattered here and there [in Scripture], they twist them . . . from a natural to a non-natural sense."[237] He then goes on to show by a series of miscellaneous quotations from Homer how, when used out of context, they can prove almost anything. Furthermore, Irenaeus' use of the Scripture is not simply to illustrate his doctrines but to uncover their source. In his warning that God judges the man who "is not subject to His Word,"[238] is the demand for a total yielding to the mind of Christ; hence it is no

---

230 II:28,1 (41,1: i:349).
231 IV:26,4 (41,1; ii:237).
232 III:Pref. (ibid.; ii:1).
233 III:5,1 (ibid.; ii:18).
234 III:11,2 (11,7; ii:41).
235 IV:11,1 (21,1; ii:174).
236 III:16,1 (16; ii:82).
237 Ek tou kata phusin eis to para phusin. I:9,4 (1,20; i:85-6).
238 IV:11,2 (21,2; ii:175).

mere pious phrase when he asserts, "The Scriptures teach us."[239]
Lawson has indeed maintained,

> Religious authority as something fixed in historic and
> objective fact . . . is strongly asserted. In actual fact, how-
> ever, it always dissolves, and is bound to dissolve, into the
> tones of the *present* voice . . . the *"Living Voice,"* of the
> Church. . . . This *"Living Voice"* is the actual religious
> authority for S. Irenaeus.[240]

But Lawson is here reading his own liberal convictions back
into Irenaeus. He goes so far as to admit: "We may candidly
agree that he would probably not have recognized this as the
truth about himself."[241] It is true that at scattered points
Irenaeus may appear to be arguing his way around embarrassing
Scriptures; for example, after having stated that "we have been
saved through the flesh of our Lord, and through His blood,"
he adds,

> If, therefore, flesh and blood are the things which pro-
> cure for us life, it has not been declared of flesh and blood,
> in the literal meaning of the terms, that they cannot in-
> herit the kingdom of God; but [these words apply] to those
> carnal deeds already mentioned, which, perverting man to
> sin, deprive him of life.[242]

Again he says,

> "Judge not, that ye be not judged . . ." not certainly that
> we should not find fault with sinners, nor that we should
> consent to those who act wickedly; but that we should not
> pronounce an unfair judgment on the dispensations of
> God.[243]

But such attempts are either, at the best, careful exegesis, or, at
the worst, injudicious attempts to bring Scripture passages into
conformity with what he had already learned from Scripture.
As Seeberg puts it, "The decisive authority rests with the
Scriptures of the Old and New Testaments."[244]

Irenaeus' reliance on Scriptural proof did not prevent him,
however, from developing certain further conclusions on the

---

239 II:28,3 (41,4; i:353).
240 Lawson, *op. cit.*, p. 105.
241 *Loc. cit.*
242 V:14,3-4 (*ibid.*; ii:363).
243 IV:30,3 (46,3; ii:250).
244 Seeberg, *op. cit.*, p. 135.

basis of his own rational endeavor, sometimes with strange or even dangerous results. He inferred, for example, a growth for Adam and Eve, saying,

> [In Paradise] they were both naked, and were not ashamed, inasmuch as they, having been created a short time previously, had no understanding of the procreation of children: for it was necessary that they should first come to adult age, and then multiply from that time onward.[245]

> Again, Christ gave Himself as a redemption for those who had been led into captivity. And since the apostasy tyrannized over us unjustly and . . . alienated us contrary to nature, rendering us its own disciples, the Word of God did righteously turn against that apostasy, and redeemed from it His own property, not by violent means, so that neither should justice be infringed upon, nor the ancient handiwork of God go to destruction. . . . The Lord thus redeemed us giving His soul for our souls, and His flesh for our flesh.[246]

This is apparently one of the earliest expressions of atonement via a ransom to Satan. Yet at other times Irenaeus demonstrates a commendable restraint, as when he writes,

> If for instance one asks, "What was God doing before He made the world?" . . . no Scripture reveals to us what God was employed about before this event. The answer therefore to that question remains with God, and it is not proper for us to aim at bringing forward foolish, rash, and blasphemous suppositions.[247]

One recalls Calvin's somewhat less restrained quotation in answer to the same question: "What had God been doing before the creation of the world? He had been making hell for over-curious men!"[248]

C. Symbolism

Despite his emphasis on the historical meaning of Scripture, Irenaeus frequently demonstrated his previously noted consciousness of certain spiritual realities symbolically presented by Biblical facts and statement. For example, he concludes from Gen. 4:

245 III:22,4 (32,1; ii:123).
246 V:1,1 (*ibid.*; ii:314-15).
247 II:28,3 (41,4; i:352-53).
248 *Op. cit.,* I:178.

And so Abel died, slain by his brother; signifying thence-
forth that certain should be persecuted and oppressed
and slain, the unrighteous slaying and persecuting the
righteous.[249]

This would appear to be a reasonable interpretation. Those
who would divide the Church he compares with those who
divided the Israelitish kingdom, saying that they will "receive
the same punishment as Jeroboam did";[250] and against those
who cut themselves off from the Spirit and the Church he quotes
Jer. 2:13 about digging for themselves broken cisterns.[251]
Parables and apocalyptic literature, designedly figurative, were
treated by him as such. From Revelation, he associated the living
creatures with the divine attributes: "The first living creature
was like a lion, symbolizing His effectual working, His leader-
ship, and royal power,"[252] and so on; a legitimate methodology,
in spite of the possibility of disagreement in specific matters.

Two major criticisms, however, are to be leveled against
Irenaeus in his employment of symbolism. First, in matters truly
symbolic his assignment of interpretations may be open to
question. For example, he speaks of the meaning of the name
Jesus, saying

Jesus . . . contains . . . two letters and one half [the yodh]
and signifies that Lord who contains heaven and earth: for
Jesus in the ancient Hebrew language means "heaven"
while again "earth" is expressed by the words sura usser.[253]
Further, he states that the four faces of Ezekiel's cherubim and

249 Dem. 17.
250 IV:26,2 (40,2; ii:236).
251 III:24,1 (38,1; ii:131-32).
252 To emprakton auto kai hēgemonikon kai basilikan charaktērizon.
    III:11,8 (11,11; ii:47).
253 II:24,2 (34,4; i:334); his point is uncertain but he seems to equate
    ysw (Hebrew) with yhwh smym wrs. Cf. his reference to the number of
    the beast, 666, in Rev. 13:18, "That number which [expressed] the
    digit six, being adhered to throughout, indicates the recapitulations
    of that apostasy, taken in its full extent, which occurred at the be-
    ginning, during the intermediate periods, and which shall take place
    at the end." He concludes that lateinos "is a very probable
    [solution]" but teitan "among all the names which are found
    among us, is rather worthy of credit," one of his reasons being, "For
    it has in itself the predicted number, and is composed of six letters,
    each syllable containing three letters." But even here he shows a
    commendable open-mindedness in his observation that "many names
    can be found possessing the number mentioned." V:30,1 and 3 (ibid.;
    ii:406-9).

of the living creatures of Revelation refer to the Son of God.
He then adds, "The Gospels are in accord with these things,
among which Jesus is seated,"[254] and proceeds to equate John
with the lion, Luke with the calf, Matthew with the man, and
Mark with the flying eagle. Note that he claims no dogmatic
identification; it is simply an analogy "in accord with" these
things. Though others have employed a different order in making this association, many would agree with the thought he
expresses:

> Such, then, as was the course followed by the Son of
> God, so was the form of the living creatures; and such as
> was the form of the living creatures, so was the character
> of the Gospel.

But when he adds, "For this reason were four principle covenants given to the human race,"[255] he is, to say the least,
violating his own principle of the interpretation of the obscure
by the manifest. The second major criticism is that in passages
not truly symbolic he may assign spiritual meanings in disregard
of context. He thus describes Rahab's token: "The sign of the
scarlet thread, which meant the passover, and the redemption
and exodus of the people from Egypt";[256] and in the parable
of the prodigal son he goes beyond the one truth symbolically
presented and interprets the sacrifice of the fatted calf as the
atoning death of Christ.[257] Irenaeus was not always innocent of
"making one thing out of another," his accusation against the
Valentinians.[258]

D. Typology

It has been maintained that "Irenaeus anticipates the thoughts
and language of Origen,"[259] that is to say, by employing extreme
forms of typical and allegorical interpretation. In a sense, such
a judgment might seem misleading, both because an un-
restrained typology, inherited from Philo's type of Judaism, had
characterized the writings of Barnabas, Clement of Rome, and
others, long before the days of Irenaeus, and also because in his

254 III:11,8 (11,11; ii:48).
255 *Loc. cit.* Cf. for the same reason, his argument that it was impossible
    for there to be more or fewer Gospels than four.
256 IV:20,12 (34,12; ii:224).
257 III:11,8 (11,11; ii:48).
258 Cf. *supra*, p. 39.
259 Westcott, *op. cit.*, p. 428.

previously noted theoretical principles he had taken a markedly cautious stand in the matter. But in his actual employment of typology there does appear, at least at times, a patent disregard for his own limiting standards. He had restricted the meanings within true types to those revealed by God; but that the seven-branched candlestick of the tabernacle was on the pattern of seven heavens[260] is hardly the clear statement of Heb. 8:5, nor does he appear justified in concluding from verses such as 1 Cor. 10:1-4 that "the whole exodus of the people out of Egypt, which took place under divine guidance was a type and image of the exodus of the church which should take place from among the gentiles."[261] More serious, however, appears the violation of his other limiting standard, namely, that typical nature itself must be inherent, from the first so designed by God, and not at a time long afterward so designated by men. To him, Gideon's fleece was a type of Israel, first with the dew of the Holy Spirit, and then dry;[262] the three (!) spies who came to Rahab signified "doubtless the Father and the Son together with the Holy Spirit";[263] and when it says that Balaam mounted upon his ass, "the ass was a type of the body of Christ, upon whom all men, resting from their labors, are borne as in a chariot. For the Saviour has taken up the burden of our sins."[264] Nor was the New Testament, despite its lesser natural adaptability, exempt: the Last Supper and Gethsemane were types of the descent into hell,[265] and the Good Samaritan was a type of the work of the Holy Spirit.[266] Other similar examples could be cited as well. On occasion Irenaeus even threw open to a second allegorical meaning almost every statement in an account. Thus, in referring to the patriarch Jacob, he wrote,

> If anyone . . . will look into Jacob's actions, he shall find them not destitute of meaning, but full of import with regard to the dispensations . . . for with God there is nothing without purpose or signification.[267]

260 *Dem.* 10.
261 IV:30,4 (47; ii:251).
262 III:17,3 (18,2; ii:251).
263 IV:20,12 (34,12; ii:224).
264 *Fr.* 23; cf. the two sons of Tamar, IV:25,2 (39; ii:233); Samson's jaw bone, *Frs.* 27 and 41; and Elisha's axe-head, *Fr.* 28.
265 IV:22,1 (36,1; ii:228-29).
266 III:17,3 (18,2; ii:93).
267 IV:21,3 (35,3; ii:226-28).

Following this, he proceeded to equate the grasped heel with Christ's victory, the right of the first-born with Christ the first-begotten, Esau's contempt with the persecution of Christians by Jews, the twelve sons born in a foreign country with the twelve-pillared church founded in the world, Jacob's wages of marked sheep with Christ's winning men of all nations, the begetting via the two daughters with Christ's regenerating via the two laws, the preference for Rachel with the superiority of the Church age, and the handmaids with the conversion of slaves and free men.

An attempted explanation for this sort of thing has been that it was the failure of the Scripture to teach in itself the desired facts, which led to the spiritual supplementing; for example, Lawson took Irenaeus' words, "When at this present time the law is read to the Jews, it is like a fable; for they do not possess the explanation of all things pertaining to the advent of the Son of God," and from them concluded, "Irenaeus himself unconsciously confesses to the difficulty which was the mainspring of such [allegorical] exposition."[268] But Lawson confuses the unregenerate man's misunderstanding of what Scripture truly teaches, the phenomenon with which Irenaeus is here dealing, and the Christian's subsequent supplementing, the phenomenon under examination. Irenaeus, and indeed all believing Christians, have agreed that the Old Testament ceremonies not only were promulgated in anticipation of Christ but also are in fact otherwise incomprehensible. It is true that Irenaeus, like Augustine after him,[269] did occasionally use allegory in connection with a difficulty in Scripture. The exodus, for example, furnished a moral problem: "The people did, by God's command, upon the eve of their departure take vessels of all kinds and raiment from the Egyptians and so went away." Irenaeus then explained:

> For if God had not accorded this in the typical exodus, no one could now be saved in our true exodus . . . for from what source do we derive the houses in which we dwell . . . and everything else of our everyday life, unless it be from those things which, when we were Gentiles, we acquired by avarice, or received them from heathen par-

268 *Op. cit.*, p. 85.
269 J. Barton Payne, "Biblical Problems and Augustine's Allegorizing," *The Westminster Theological Journal*, 14:1 (Nov. 1951), 46-53.

ents, relations, or friends who unrighteously obtained them.[270]

Again in respect to the incest of Lot with his daughters, the reprehensibleness of which Irenaeus did not apparently appreciate, he says,

> With respect to those actions . . . on which the Scriptures pass no censure . . . we ought not to become the accusers . . . but we should search for a type. For not one of those things which have been set down in Scripture without being condemned is without significance.[271]

But that the true basis for Irenaeus' allegorizing is not to be found in this direction is indicated by three facts: (1) The above two instances are almost unique and do not find parallels in his other numerous types. (2) Both are examples of exegesis not originating with Irenaeus but are introduced "as also the presbyter remarked." (3) In both cases he maintains the original historical truth of the incidents and goes out of his way to explain, with varying success, the moral difficulties on other grounds, as in the former case:

> The Egyptians were debtors to the people, not alone as to property, but as to their very lives, because of the kindness of the patriarch Joseph in former times.[272]

and in the latter case:

> For there was no other person who could impart to them quickening seed. . . . Thus, after their simplicity and innocence did these daughters so speak, imagining that all mankind had perished, even as the Sodomites had done, and that the anger of God had come down upon the whole earth.[273]

The reason for Irenaeus' excessive typology lies rather in his over-application of, and over-enthusiasm for, a method of interpretation not simply validated by New Testament example but implicit in the unity of Scripture, of history, and of salvation. "The ancients may have carried this principle too far, but as a principle it receives countenance from our Lord Himself and His apostles."[274] Hitchcock concludes,

270 IV:30,1 (46,1; ii:248).
271 IV:31,1 (47; ii:251).
272 Cf. *supra,* note 270.
273 Cf. *supra,* note 271.
274 Coxe, *op. cit.,* I:504.

With regard to the mystical method of Scriptural interpretation which we found in Irenaeus . . . it is but a
cheap wit that would regard the underlying principle with
contempt because of the extravagance of its application.
Rationalism and common sense revolt against searching
the Old Testament for symbols of another set of symbols
in the New. . . . But the mystical interpretation . . . is
undoubtedly the true one. . . . As we go to school with the
Fathers who were in closer touch with the great realities,
we may come to see something in the Scriptures which this
enlightened age cannot discern so long as it solely employs
the rational method.[275]

E. Prophecy

Whatever may have been the disparity between theory and
practice in the matter of typology, Irenaeus was consistent in
the application of his principles of prophetic interpretation.
Because of his conviction regarding the unity throughout all
ages both of the plan of salvation and of the expression of that
plan in Scripture, he was able to, and did, fill his writings with
such statements as, "What has been declared by David concerning the Son of God was accomplished in His own person."[276]
Because of its association with the Messianic age, Daniel's fourth
kingdom is identified as "Latin."[277] In one section Irenaeus lists
almost fifty distinct Messianic prophecies, each authenticated
from the New Testament, although doubt might well be expressed as to the legitimacy of referring "I have spread out my
hands all the day" to the crucifixion, either in Isa. 65:2 or in
Rom. 10:21.[278] By some, Irenaeus' methods are criticized as
subjective: "As was but natural the fourth 'Servant Song' was
also given a most extended allegorical exegesis";[279] but such
negative criticisms appear only if one has rejected his basic
principles. Taking for example this Servant Song, Isa. 52:13-
53:12, one discovers that Irenaeus' use of these verses is logically

275 *Op. cit.,* p. 191.
276 IV:11,3 (21,3; ii:176); cf. III:16,2 (17,1; ii:82-83).
277 V:30,3 (*ibid.;* ii:410).
278 IV:33,11-14 (55,1-6; ii:265-69). Occasionally too he may make a statement such as, "David says, prophesying His birth from a virgin, and
the resurrection from the dead, 'Truth has sprung out of the earth,'"
Psa. 85:11, III:5,1 (*ibid.;* ii:18-19); cf. also his seeing the virgin birth
in Isa. 66:7, *Dem.* 54.
279 Lawson, *op. cit.,* p. 63.

consistent in the light of the analogy of Scripture and identical
with their employment in the New Testament. Irenaeus states,

> The divine Scriptures do . . . testify of Him . . . that He
> was a man without comeliness and liable to suffering.[280]
> That He Himself 'shall take our weaknesses and bear
> our sorrows' proclaimed those works of healing which were
> accomplished by Him.[281]
> Now what follows in Isaiah is this: By His stripes we are
> healed. All we like sheep went astray: a man in his own
> way went astray: and the Lord delivered Him up to our
> sins. It is manifest therefore that by the will of the Father
> these things occurred to Him for our salvation.[282]

Only in the case of Isa. 53:8, "His generation,"[283] which he took
as speaking of Christ's eternal generation,[284] did Irenaeus mis-
understand the Word.

Dispensational distinctions, although subordinate to the basic
unity in salvation, were recognized within the prophetic plan by
Irenaeus. First there was the main division between the Old
Testament and the New Testament, "our covenant," and "the
Jews' covenant,"[285] a primary matter with Irenaeus and not to
be confused. He declares that

> if anyone do maintain that this new covenant consisted
> in the rearing of that temple which was built under
> Zerubbabel . . . let him know that that temple was indeed
> rebuilt . . . yet no new covenant was given . . . but from

280 III:19,2 (20,2; ii:104).
281 IV:33,11 (55,2; ii:266-67).
282 *Dem*. 69; cf. IV:33,12 (55,3; ii:267): "Some of them [the prophets]
   moreover — as a weak and inglorious man, and as one who knew
   what it was to bear infirmity . . . and that he should be led as a
   sheep to the slaughter — prophesied His coming in the character of
   a man as He entered Jerusalem, in which by His passion and crucifixion He endured all the things which have been mentioned" IV:33,2
   (37,2; ii:231). "Philip, when he had discovered the eunuch of the
   Ethiopians' queen reading these words which had been written . . .
   which the prophet proceeded to relate in regard to His passion and
   His coming in the flesh, and how He was dishonored by those who
   did not believe Him; easily persuaded him to believe on Him, that
   He was Christ Jesus, who was crucified under Pontius Pilate, and
   suffered whatsoever the prophet had predicted, and that He was the
   Son of God, who gives eternal life to men," III:12,8 (12,10; ii:62);
   and *Dem*. 68.
283 tēn genean aut ou.
284 II:28,5 (42,3; i:355) and III:19,2 (20,2; ii:103-4).
285 IV:13,4 (25; ii:183); cf. *Fr*. 27, "Two covenants," and IV:9,3 (19,2;
   ii:170).

the Lord's advent, the new covenant which brings back
peace, and the law which gives life, has gone forth over
the whole earth.[286]

Then within these two appeared the various lesser covenants:
Christ was

revealed to men as God pleased; that they might always
make progress through believing in Him, and by means of
the [successive] covenants, should gradually attain to perfect salvation. For there is one salvation and one God; but
the precepts which form the man are numerous, and the
steps which lead to God are not a few.[287]

Irenaeus speaks of four chief covenants or the fourfold course
of the Lord, though the stages differ: Noah, Abraham, Moses,
and the Gospels; Adam, Noah, Moses, and the gospel; or the
patriarchs, Moses, the incarnation, and the Spirit.[288] As Beaven
notes:

The whole history of mankind has been a series of dis-
pensations . . . planned from the beginning; and he states
them to have been carried into execution by God the Son
exhibiting Himself to mankind under four different
aspects. . . . Thus in various ways God prepared mankind
for salvation, providing them laws suited to their various
states of preparation.[289]

This meant distinctions: "The laws of bondage . . . given for a
sign to them, He cancelled by the new covenant of liberty."[290]
But that there was no complete separation, Abraham, Moses,
and Paul having basically much in common, is apparent from
certain observations which he makes:

The Lord did not abrogate the natural [precepts] of the
law . . . which also those who were justified by faith, and
who pleased God, did observe previous to the giving of
the law.[291]

But He has increased and widened those laws which are
natural and noble, and common to all, granting to men
largely and without grudging, by means of adoption, to

286 IV:36,4 (56,3; ii:271).
287 IV:9,3 (19,2; ii:171).
288 III:11,8 (11,11; ii:50).
289 *Op. cit.,* pp. 115, 117.
290 IV:16,5 (28; ii:192).
291 IV:13,1 (24,1; ii:180-81).

know God the Father and to love Him with the whole heart.[292]

Since therefore the gospel age was not simply related to that which preceded, but was indeed a climax and goal, he placed the fulfillment of much Old Testament prophecy within the Church, as that Japheth's dwelling in the tents of Shem was fulfilled by the universal preaching of the Church;[293] and he says that

> In it [Deuteronomy] were written many prophecies concerning our Lord Jesus Christ and concerning the people, and also concerning the calling of the Gentiles, and concerning the kingdom.[294]

It is to be noted also that Hos. 2:23 is applied to the Church, as per Rom. 9:25;[295] the "inheritance of the holy Jerusalem" is for Christians;[296] and in fact the first full half of Book IV of *Against Heresies* is devoted to the elucidation of the preparatory nature of the pre-gospel periods.

But for Irenaeus the fulfillment of much prophecy lay still in the future, for he contends that "all the prophets announced His two advents: the one indeed in which He became a man subject to stripes . . . but the second in which He will come on the clouds, bringing on the day which burns as a furnace."[297] Furthermore, because of his principle of historical and literal fulfillment, the rule of Christ was for him visible, material, and temporal. As Schaff has remarked, though with a definition of orthodoxy to which many might take exception,

> Irenaeus is . . . on the whole, the most orthodox of the ante-Nicene fathers. We must, however, except his eschatology. Here, with Papias and most of his contemporaries, he maintains the pre-millennarian views which were subsequently abandoned by the Catholic Church.[298]

Specifically, Irenaeus held that the contemporary Roman Empire would be overthrown by ten kings, the toes of Daniel's image, and then would follow the appearance of the Antichrist,

292 Cf. *supra*, note 290.
293 III:5,3 (*ibid.*; ii:20).
294 *Dem.* 28.
295 III:9,1 (*ibid.*; ii:30-31).
296 IV:26,1 (40,1; ii:235).
297 IV:33,1 (50,1; ii:256).
298 *Op. cit.*, II:751.

who is the abomination of desolation, and whose name contains the number 666.[299] Concerning the date, he suggested:

> For the day of the Lord is as a thousand years; and in six days created things were completed; it is evident, therefore, that they will come to an end at the six thousandth year.[300]
>
> But when this Antichrist shall have devastated all things in this world . . . then the Lord will come from heaven in the clouds, in the glory of the Father, sending this man and those who follow him into the lake of fire; but bringing in for the righteous the times of the kingdom, that is, the rest, the hallowed seventh day; and restoring to Abraham the promised inheritance, in which kingdom the Lord declared, that many coming from the east and from the west should sit down with Abraham, Isaac, and Jacob. . . . This creation, which is renovated . . . Abraham . . . together with his seed, that is, those who fear God and believe in Him, shall receive at the resurrection of the just. For his seed is the Church.[301]

The purpose of the earthly rule is preparatory, "by means of which kingdom those who shall be worthy are accustomed gradually to partake of the divine nature."[302] Two concluding points are particularly to be noted: (1) The kingdom is located in Jerusalem and has Israelitish qualities,[303] but it is the Church that constitutes Israel. (2) The two resurrections are separated by the millennium, but that of the just is one unified event at the Lord's return to rule, premillennial but posttribulationist.

F. Tradition

Corresponding to Irenaeus' interpretative principle of the perspicuity of Scripture, there remains the question of his practical employment of Scripture in relation to church tradition. On the danger of tradition, Irenaeus knew the truth of Isa. 29:13:

> "In vain do they worship Me, teaching the doctrines and commandments of men." He does not call the law

299 V:26,1 (*ibid.*; ii:394-95).
300 V:28,3 (*ibid.*; ii:403).
301 V:30,4 and 32,2 (*ibid.*; ii:410,15).
302 V:32,1 (*ibid.*; ii:414).
303 V:35,1 (*ibid.*; ii:426-28).

given by Moses commandments of men, but the traditions of the elders themselves which they had invented.[304]

But at the same time he had grown up in the atmosphere of the oral traditions of Polycarp and others, in the integrity of whom he had perfect confidence, who had been pupils of the apostles. Through the apostles, moreover, Christ had Himself spoken and the New Testament had been transmitted. It is not surprising, therefore, that for them, for the church they had built up, and for the tradition they had left, Irenaeus had a high regard. He therefore writes,

> The apostles . . . lodged in her [the Church's] hands most copiously all things pertaining to the truth. . . . Make choice of the things pertaining to the church with utmost diligence and lay hold of the tradition of the truth. . . . For how should it be if the apostles had not left us writing? Would it not be necessary [in that case] to follow the course of the tradition which they handed down to those to whom they did commit the churches?[305]

Or again,

> To which course [that of apostolic tradition] many nations of the barbarians who believe in Christ do assent, having salvation written in their hearts by the Spirit, without paper or ink . . . who in the absence of written documents have believed this faith.[306]

As a result, some have concluded that for Irenaeus, "traditional authority is determinative for Scripture,"[307] but "ecclesiastical tradition is certainly represented as a self-sufficient authority."[308]

Such a conclusion, however, represents a misunderstanding of the problems at issue. First of all, the above statements by Irenaeus are theoretical: it was not necessary to follow the course of traditions, because the apostles *had* left writings; barbarians might be without paper and ink, but Irenaeus was not reduced to such straits. On the contrary,

> he goes to the Scripture as the only authentic record of revelation; and it is evident that, on his own account, he would never have appealed to any other authority in sup-

304 *Traditiones presbyterorum,* IV:12,4 (33:1; ii:179).
305 *Veritatis traditionem,* III:4,1 (*ibid.*; ii:15).
306 III:4,2 (4,1; ii:16).
307 Lawson, *op. cit.,* p. 102; cf. p. 140f.
308 *Ibid.,* p. 103.

port of the great and leading doctrines he had to deal with.[309]

Secondly, the above statements have as their subject the facts which one must accept to be saved, and not the degree of authority which lies behind any given medium. In this latter regard it appears from the practice of Irenaeus that

> he is careful to put the gospel before tradition. . . . In his letter to Florinus he says that "everything that Polycarp related was in agreement with the Scriptures." The Scriptures were then his chief authority and test of truth.[310]

Thirdly, the above statements assume that the truths of the tradition are in fact those recorded in the Scriptures. In the second quotation the list of doctrines which Irenaeus proceeds to name as believed by the barbarians is eminently Biblical, nothing new. He himself explains elsewhere,

> The preaching of the church is everywhere consistent, and continues an even course, and receives testimony from the prophets, the apostles, and all the disciples — as I have proved — through those in the beginning, the middle, and the end.[311]

Similarly, his much misquoted assignment of priority to the church at Rome is based simply on its greater knowledge of the truth:

> For it is necessary that the whole church, *i.e.* those from all places who are believers, should come, on account of its more potent leadership to that church in which has been preserved by believers from all places those things which are a tradition of the apostles.[312]

At another point it is the Scripture that Irenaeus calls the "ground and pillar of faith,"[313] about which it has been said,

> It is very remarkable that he should use this very phrase in speaking of the Gospel, which St. Paul had used in speaking of the Church itself; showing apparently that it

---

309 Beaven, *op. cit.*, p. 137.
310 Hitchcock, *op. cit.*, p. 197.
311 III:24,1 (38,1; ii:131).
312 *Potentiorem principalitatem*, III:3,2 (3,1; ii:9), from Seeberg's translation, *op. cit.*, p. 415.
313 III:1,1 (*ibid.*; ii:8-9).

was by the custody of the Scriptures that the Church was to sustain its office.[314]

Even in respect to what are probably Irenaeus' two most questionable references to church tradition, the reaching by Jesus of an age of fifty years (II,22,5), and the millennial vine with the ten thousand branches (V,33,1), Lawson characterizes the former as " a stupid misunderstanding of John 8:57,"[315] and the latter, though attributed to Christ, was derived from prophetic statements of the Bible. This serves to explain Irenaeus' limitation of tradition to the well known, as when he says,

> It is within the power of all, therefore, in every church, who may wish to see the truth, to contemplate clearly the tradition of the apostles manifested throughout the whole world . . . for if the apostles had known hidden mysteries . . . they would have delivered them especially to those to whom they were also committing the churches themselves.[316]

As Hitchcock concludes,

> It is to be remembered that there is no doctrine put forward by Irenaeus which was, if not literally, at least in spirit and in truth professed by the apostles and expressed or implied in the New Testament.[317]

But the fact remains that Irenaeus made regular use of the traditional argument. Lipsius' analysis is that,

> In the controversy with the Gnostics refutation out of Scripture was not sufficient. Both parties appealed to Scripture in support of their opinions; the victory was doubtful, at least it was disputed. Tertullian's advice was therefore in such cases to forego the Scripture argument.[318]

But Irenaeus was not one to substitute tradition for the Bible; his argument is always basically Scriptural. The most adequate evaluation in this matter would therefore appear to be as follows:

> In what way then does he appeal to tradition? . . . He calls it in as establishing the same *general* views, which he confirms at length from Scripture; as preparing the mind

314 Beaven, *op. cit.*, p. 136.
315 *Op. cit.*, p. 91.
316 III:3,1 (*ibid.*; ii:2).
317 *Op. cit.*, p. 57.
318 *Op. cit.*, III:271.

to believe that the view he takes of Scripture is the true one.[319]

It was a historically comprehensible and necessary, but an abnormal path, into which these ideas conducted.[320]

In conclusion one can well quote the words of Seeberg and of Lawson that "Irenaeus is a Biblicist and the first great representative of Biblicism."[321]

Moreover, his masterpiece is entitled *Against Heresies;* and it is true that

> these heresies . . . are by no means defunct, and the arguments of Irenaeus are by no means obsolete. For the same ideas which he assailed are still germinating in human minds, and are constantly reappearing in new forms . . . Marcion, like a modern advanced critic, openly employed a sword rather than a pen, making selections . . . to suit his own ideas.[322]

The modern evangelical, therefore, does well to follow Job 8:8 and "apply himself to that which this father hath searched out."

319 Beaven, *op. cit.,* pp. 146-47.
320 Seeberg, *op. cit.,* p. 137.
321 Lawson, *op. cit.,* p. 24.
322 Hitchcock, *op. cit.,* pp. 333,331.

Chapter II

AUGUSTINE OF HIPPO

By David W. Kerr

Aurelius Augustine, bishop of Hippo, is so well known in the Christian Church as to need no introduction. Such is his stature among Christian theologians that he serves as a dividing point between the ancient and the medieval periods of the Church.

Augustine wrote his work, *De Doctrina Christiana,* to set forth his principles of Biblical interpretation. It might be supposed, therefore, that by simply condensing this work we should have an accurate presentation, as if from the author's own hand, of the way he handled the Scriptures. Unfortunately that is not altogether the case. Augustine had been interpreting the Scriptures for many years before he wrote *De Doctrina Christiana.* That work, moreover, is not so much a summary of his own methods as of the methods he would prescribe for other Christian teachers. His famous statement about the fourfold interpretation of Scripture is found in another work altogether, *De Utilitate Credendi.* Augustine was a man of the Word. His controversial writings, his letters, his sermons and his commentaries all provide examples of his own way of interpreting the Bible.

In setting forth his rules for interpreting Holy Scripture, Augustine develops at some length a philosophy of "things" and "signs." A "thing" is an object which is never used as a sign of anything else. A "sign" is an object, such as a word, which is used to designate something else. Indeed, words are always signs. Since the Bible is a book and consists entirely of words, or signs, the task is to determine precisely what these signs mean.[1] One feels, however, that Augustine in this line of argument is not getting at his own presuppositions but is rather laying a foundation for his own use of allegorical interpretation.

---

1 *De Doctrina Christiana,* I, ii, 2. English translation, *The Works of Aurelius Augustine,* ed. by Marcus Dods (Edinburgh: Clark, 1873), vol. IX.

The master-key which opens the Scriptures to our understanding is the love of God and of our neighbor. "We should clearly understand that the fulfillment and end of the Law and of all Holy Scripture is the love of an object which is to be enjoyed, and the love of an object which can enjoy that other in fellowship with ourselves . . . Whoever, then, thinks that he understands the Holy Scriptures, or any part of them, but puts such an interpretation upon them as does not tend to build up the twofold love of God and our neighbor, does not yet understand them as he ought."[2] This same rule may, as a matter of fact, be used to decide whether a given passage should be taken literally or figuratively. "Whatever there is in the Word of God that cannot, when taken literally, be referred either to purity of life or soundness of doctrine, you may set down as figurative. Purity of life has reference to the love of God and one's neighbor; soundness of doctrine to the knowledge of God and one's neighbor."[3] There is something of a parallel, therefore, between the place which the first and great commandment is given in Augustine's handling of the sacred work and that which the sovereignty of God receives at Calvin's hand.

A number of the rules of interpretation which Augustine suggests are common to most Biblical expositors. His reasons for suggesting such rules, however, derive in most instances from the times in which he lived. For example, in order to have a right understanding of God's Word the student should know the original languages of Scripture. One value of such knowledge is to remove any possible confusion where the words used in a given translation might have variant shades of meaning. In some languages, too, there are words which cannot be translated into the idiom of another language. Besides these reasons, Augustine felt that it was imperative to have a knowledge of Greek and Hebrew because of the great variety of Latin versions. He complains that in the early days of the faith every man who happened to get his hands on a Greek manuscript, and who thought he had a little knowledge of the two languages, ventured upon a translation.[4]

2 *Op. cit.*, I, xxxv, 39 — xxxvi, 40.
3 *Op. cit.*, III, x, 14.
4 *Op. cit.*, II, xi, 16.

The student must carefully inquire, also, in regard to any given expression, Is it literal or is it figurative?[5] What is the author trying to say? Augustine would not have agreed, it would seem, with those who approach the Bible determined to interpret it literally wherever possible. We must, indeed, disagree with the tests he applied to determine whether an expression is literal or figurative, yet the principle he enunciated is sound.

It is important to remember that the same word does not always signify the same thing. "We are not to suppose that there is any rule that what a thing signifies by likeness in one place it is to be taken to signify in all other places. For our Lord used 'leaven' both in a bad sense, as when He said, 'Beware of the leaven of the Pharisees,' and in a good sense, as when He said, 'The kingdom of heaven is like unto leaven.' "[6]

Obscure passages of Scripture are to be explained by those which are clearer. It may be necessary, if no undoubted evidence from Scripture may be found, to decide upon the meaning by the use of reason, but this is a dangerous practice. It is far safer to walk by the light of Holy Writ.[7] This amounts to saying with the later Reformed confessions that the infallible rule of interpretation of Scripture is the Scripture itself. It is evidence also that in Augustine there was a strain of thought which was entirely contrary to the idea that the Church is the infallible interpreter of Holy Scripture.

An example of the way he applies this rule is found in connection with Paul's statement that God "will have all men to be saved."[8] The problem here, of course, is not that the meaning of the words in themselves is obscure, but that the statement seems to conflict with other parts of Scripture and with experience. If, as the Psalmist says, God hath done whatsoever He pleased, and if this verse means that God wills to save all men everywhere, then why are they not all saved? Or how explain, for that matter, that the Lord was unwilling to work miracles among those who, He Himself said, would have repented if He had done them? Augustine's answer is that the apostle is speaking in the verse quoted about prayer for the human race in all its varieties of rank and circumstances. Out of every class God

5 *Op. cit.*, III, xxiv, 34.
6 *Op. cit.*, III, xxv, 35.
7 *Op. cit.*, III, xxviii, 39.
8 1 Tim. 2:4.

wills that men should be saved in all nations through our Lord. In support of this view Augustine says that Jesus used the same mode of speech when He said to the Pharisees, "Ye tithe mint and rue and every herb." The Pharisees did not tithe every herb from every land, but every herb used by themselves. "As then, in this place we must understand by 'every herb' every kind of herbs, so in the former passage we must understand by 'all men' every sort of men."[9] Generously enough, Augustine grants that one may interpret the passage in any other way he pleases so long as we are not compelled to believe that the omnipotent God has willed anything to be done which was not done. The Scripture must agree with itself and God must be true to His own nature.

Augustine recommends to the serious student that he have some acquaintance with various profane fields of knowledge such as logic, dialectic, rhetoric and even of such arts as medicine, agriculture and navigation. Of the sciences known to his day he takes exception only to astronomy which was, of course, hardly distinguishable from astrology. He feared that this study might lead to the practice of divination, which was forbidden by God. The secular training which Augustine felt to be desirable was perhaps the ancient equivalent of a liberal arts course. He says, however, "Now of these arts a very superficial and cursory knowledge is to be acquired, not with a view of practicing them, but with a view to forming a judgment about them so that we may not be wholly ignorant of what Scripture means to convey when it employs figures of speech derived from these arts."[10]

In this connection Augustine refers us to his philosophy of "things." "Ignorance of things renders figurative expressions obscure, as when we do not know the nature of animals or minerals or plants which are frequently referred to in Scripture by way of comparison."[11] For example, the injunction of our Lord to be wise as serpents takes on new meaning if we know that the serpent gets rid of its old skin by squeezing itself through a narrow hole and thus acquires new strength, for how appropriately it fits in with the apostle's saying that we must put off the old man with his deeds. And we must put it off, too,

---

9 *Enchiridion,* Chap. CIII, Eng. trans. ed. by Marcus Dods cited in I, above.
10 *De Doctrina Christiana,* II, xxx, 47.
11 *Op. cit.,* II, xvi, 24.

by coming through a narrow place according to the saying of the Lord, "Enter ye in at the narrow gate!"

The keen student must also be acquainted with numerology if he would delve into the mysteries of the Bible. That there is a definite numerology of Scripture will be readily granted by most orthodox interpreters, although most of these would confine the mysteries of numbers chiefly to apocalyptic literature. Augustine, however, takes flight into fanciful realms as many other numerologists have done. In the Christian religion, he says by way of illustration, the number fifty has no ordinary sacredness attached to it on account of Pentecost. This number taken thrice, "on account of the name of the Father, Son and Holy Spirit, and the Trinity itself being added over and above, has reference to the mystery of the Holy Church and reaches to the number of the one hundred and fifty-three fishes which were taken after the resurrection of our Lord. And in the same way many other numbers and combinations of numbers are used in the sacred writings to convey instruction under a figurative guise, and ignorance of numbers often shuts the reader out from this instruction."[12]

It is only fair to say that Augustine was not always as extravagant in his interpretation of numbers as this. As an example of a more moderate view, he understood the number seven to represent completeness or universality, a widely accepted canon of numerology. The monastics in the Church took literally the statement of Psalm 119:164, "Seven times in the day do I praise thee." They arranged their day to allow for seven periods of devotion. Augustine, however, says that the Psalmist's words mean just the same as "His praise shall continually be in my mouth," since the number seven here represents time universal.

At the conclusion of his rules of interpretation, Augustine mentions a work on the subject by a Donatist named Tychonius, which he says is worthy of some attention. Augustine disapproves of Tychonius' evident conceit and of the manner in which he expresses himself, yet he subscribes to certain of the principles of Tychonius and one of these is the principle of *recapitulation*. "Certain occurrences are so related that the narrative appears to be following the order of time or the continuity of events, when it really goes back without mentioning it to previous occurrences

---

12 *Op. cit.,* II, xvi, 25.

which had been passed over in their proper place."[13] Several passages from Genesis are adduced by way of illustration, including Gen. 2:8-9. Literary critics, in separating Genesis into its supposed documents, have usually contended that Gen. 2:8-9 contradicts Gen. 1 and represents a diverse Creation narrative. The conservative answer continues to be that of Augustine,[14] who at many points seems to anticipate the skepticism of our modern age. The recapitulation theory has been applied in a thorough way to the Revelation in some recent commentaries, some of which trace the principle back to Augustine.[15] Augustine himself credits the principle to Tychonius and does not claim originality for it.

Though he himself possessed great powers of logic, it has been observed already that Augustine felt it was wrong to put human reasoning above the Scripture. So great was his respect for the written Word of God that he recommended secular education chiefly for the ability it would give the Christian student to understand the Scriptures better. No other Christian writer, whether in the Bible or out of it, has expressed greater reverence for the Word or greater confidence in its divine inspiration and authority.

With respect to the inspiration of the Bible, Augustine declares that the canonical Scriptures are "the revered pen of thy (i.e., God's) Spirit."[16] In reading the Holy Scripture "men seek nothing more than to find out the thought and will of those by whom it was written, and through these to find out the will of God, in accordance with which they believe these men to have spoken."[17] Like the writer of the Epistle to the Hebrews, Augustine says not that a certain human writer spoke or wrote, but "the Holy Spirit . . . with admirable wisdom and care for our welfare arranged the Holy Scriptures."[18] That his doctrine is

---

13 *Op. cit.*, III, xxxvi, 52.
14 Cf. e.g., E. J. Young, *Introduction to the Old Testament* (Grand Rapids: Eerdmans, 1949); pp. 55-56.
15 B. B. Warfield, in *Biblical Doctrines* (Oxford, New York, 1929), article on the Millennium and the Apocalypse, p. 645, states that this principle of *recapitulatio* was announced by Augustine in his *De Civitate Dei*, XX, 7ff. Although he interprets the millennium in a spiritual way and thus agrees with recapitulationists in their results, it is not clear that he consciously applied the principle to the whole of the Book of the Revelation.
16 *Confessiones*, VII, 21, 27.
17 *De Doctrina Christiana*, II, v, 6.
18 *Op. cit.*, II, vi, 8.

that of verbal inspiration is virtually beyond all doubt and it is needless to quote from the numerous passages in which he stresses the importance of individual words as expressing the divine revelation.

One corollary of inspiration is inerrancy. To this Augustine subscribes in the boldest fashion. In a letter to Jerome he says, "For I confess to your charity that I have learned to defer this respect and honor to those Scriptural books only which are now called canonical, that I believe most firmly that no one of those authors has erred in any respect in writing."[19] This did not mean that all the customs or even the commandments of the Old Testament were to be approved by Christians. Some of the things permitted by the Old Testament, such as polygamy and divorce, were repugnant to the Christian Church. The moral standards of the patriarchs needed to be improved by later revelation. It is necessary to consider what is suitable to times and places and persons. It is impossible to say what Augustine's answer would have been had he been confronted with the Copernican or more recent theories of the universe, but it is safe to assume that he would have found it possible to reconcile them with his conviction of the infallibility of Scripture.

It may be seen from the statement that the moral standards of the patriarchs needed to be improved by later revelation, that Augustine adhered to the idea of progressive revelation. For anyone who believes, as he did, that the Old Testament fore-shadows or prepares for the New, revelation must be progressive. The progression does not mean, however, that the Old Testament is either abrogated or contradicted by the New. "The New is in the Old concealed; the Old is in the New revealed."[20]

A second corollary of inspiration is authority. On this subject Augustine could hardly have used more decided language. Holy Scripture has been established upon the highest and heavenly pinacle of authority,[21] and every pious mind submits to it. Such is the eminence of Scripture that "though it be but a single prophet or apostle or evangelist that is shown to have placed anything in his Scriptures, . . . we are not permitted to doubt that it is true."[22] So far did he go in this direction that he would

19 *Epistolae*, 82, i, 3.
20 *Quaestiones in Exodum*, LXXIII, Comment on Ex. 20:19.
21 *Epistolae*, 82, ii, 5.
22 *Contra Faustum Manichaeam*, xi, 5.

not for an instant have allowed the propriety of handling the
Scriptures in the subjective fashion of the several schools of
modern literary criticism. "This [i.e., subjecting the Scripture
to the rationalistic criticism of his day] is not to be subject for
faith to the authority of Scripture, but to subject Scripture to
ourselves; instead of approving a thing because it is read and
written in the sublime authority of Scripture, it seems to us
rightly written because we approve of it."[23] To the argument
that such an attitude is unscientific, Augustine would very likely
have replied that it is not scientific to try to subject the divine
mind to the human mind.

Any volume which comes from God's Spirit in such a way
that it may be called the very pen of God will be a veritable
mine of wisdom, and inexhaustible source of truth. It seems as
though for Augustine the Scriptures are almost as incomprehensible as God Himself. "Such is the profundity of the
Christian Scriptures," he says, "that even if I were to attempt to
study them and nothing else from early boyhood to decrepit
old age, with the utmost leisure, the most unwearying zeal and
greater talents than I have, I should still daily find something
new in them. Not that there is any great difficulty in arriving at
the things necessary to salvation from them, but when anyone
has accepted these truths with the faith indispensable to a life
of piety and uprightness, so many things remain to be apprehended by those who are progressing in this study, and so great
is the depth of wisdom not only in the words in which these
have been expressed but also in the things themselves which
are to be understood, that the experience of the oldest, the
ablest and the most eager students of Scripture illustrates what
the Scripture itself hath said, namely, 'When a man hath done,
then shall he begin.' "[24]

If we add together the three factors which are bound up with
Augustine's high view of inspiration, that is, inerrancy, authority
and incomprehensibility, we shall quite readily see why he
insists that one must approach the Bible with faith if he is to
understand it at all. If he who comes to God must believe that
He is, then he who comes to God's Word must believe what it
says. Understanding cannot, therefore, precede faith. It must
follow. Thus Augustine declares, "Understanding is the reward

23 *Op. cit.,* xxxii, 19.
24 *Epistolae,* 137, i, 3. The quotation is from Ecclus. 18:6.

of faith. Therefore seek not to understand that thou mayest believe, but believe that thou mayest understand."[25] His advice to a congregation is, Understand in order that thou mayest believe my words; believe in order that thou mayest understand the word of God."[26]

Faith, however, is never blind credulity. It may go beyond rational knowledge, but it is a belief growing out of a conviction of the truth of the thing believed. A man must be convinced of the authority of Scripture if he is to acknowledge that authority. Destroy his confidence in the written Word and you destroy his confidence in what it teaches. "Faith will totter if the authority of Scripture begins to shake."[27] Once again it would seem as if Augustine were anticipating the problems of a later age. It has been argued frequently by the older liberal critics that Christian faith does not depend upon the veracity of every part of Scripture. It was contended that while many of the sacred writings were pious frauds we might recognize and believe the essential truths contained in them. The neo-orthodox view is that the Scripture is, as a matter of fact, a quite fallible witness to the truth. It is an authority only in the sense that nowhere else is there such a witness through which the Spirit of God speaks to men. To Augustine such arguments would probably have seemed to be devoid of common sense. His own reasoning follows some such pattern as this: The Bible is to be believed because it is authoritative; it is authoritative because it is inerrant; it is inerrant because it is inspired; it is inspired because holy men of old spake as they were moved by the Holy Ghost.

Such reasoning moves in a circular direction, of course. It needs only one more step to complete the circle and that is to say that the same Holy Ghost who inspired the writers of Scripture also moves the believer to recognize the authority or truth of Scripture. This step Augustine never clearly took. He stated over and again that faith is a gift of God wrought in man by the Holy Spirit, but this is the faith which lays hold of Christ, not the faith which is necessary for understanding the Bible.

25 *In Joannis Evangelium tractatis*, XXIX, 6.
26 *Sermones*, XLIII, vii, 9. The quotations here and in a number of other instances are from Erich Przywara, *An Augustine Synthesis* (London; Sheed & Ward, 1945).
27 *De Doctrina Christiana*, I, xxxvii, 4.

He concludes his dissertation on the interpretation of the Scriptures by saying that it is "especially and before all things necessary" for students "to pray that they may understand them. For in these very books on the study of which they are intent they read, 'The Lord giveth wisdom: out of his mouth cometh knowledge and understanding' and it is from him they have received the very desire for knowledge, if it is wedded to piety."[28] Nevertheless, the desire for knowledge is not the inward illumination of the Spirit of God which is necessary for the saving understanding of such things as are revealed in the Word.

Since it would be unnatural for a man of Augustine's ability to leave such a gap in his reasoning, it is no surprise that in the place of the illumination of the Holy Spirit he puts another factor, that is, the influence of the Catholic Church. It is this link, indeed, which serves to join together two apparently inconsistent strains of thought in Augustine, the reverence he had for Scripture as the only infallible rule of faith and manners, and the reverence he had for the Church and its traditions.

It has been well pointed out that Augustine, having tested everything that the old world had to offer and found it wanting, had given himself at last to Catholic Christianity with no reserves.[29] Catholicism frankly became his passion and into its maintenance he threw all his force. It was primarily as a Catholic Christian, therefore, that he thought and worked and lived. He loved to say, "This is the Catholic faith and it is therefore also my faith." He urged his admirers not to love him more than the Catholic faith and warned those who disagreed with him not to love themselves more than the Catholic truth.[30]

The place which the influence of the Church assumed in Augustine's thinking may hardly be regarded as an intrusion. Indeed, as far as his view of Scripture is concerned, the place which he gave to the Church is exactly that which it had filled in his experience. That he did not see that the Church was the secondary and the Spirit of God the prime mover is regrettable but understandable.

At the same time, let it be kept in mind that Augustine did not suspend the *authority* of Holy Scripture upon the judgment

28 *De Doctrina Christiana*, III, xxxvii, 56.
29 Cf. B. B. Warfield, *Studies in Tertullian and Augustine* (New York; Oxford University Press, 1930), p. 119.
30 *De Trinitate*, I, iv, 7; III, pref. 2.

of the Church. He would not have said, as some Roman Catholic theologians have tried to make him say, that above the Scripture is the authority of the living Church. Instead, in his controversy with the Donatists he explicitly declared that bishops and councils may err,[31] and in another writing he stated that he felt free to use his own judgment upon the writings of Catholic authors, since he owed unhesitating consent to nothing but the canonical Scriptures.[32] When, then, Augustine said as he did, "I would not have believed the gospel if the authority of the Church had not moved me"[33] he undoubtedly spoke of the authority of the Church as a witness. It is this witness of the Church which holds in his theology the same place as the illuminating work of the Holy Spirit in Reformed theology.

To mention the authority of the Church is to introduce the second important presupposition of Augustine's approach to the Bible. The first, which has already been discussed, was his high view of inspiration. For Augustine, the Catholic Church was much more than a witness to the truth of Scripture. It was the true Body of Christ outside of which no one might be saved.[34] Moreover, to hold fast to the Christian religion is to hold fast to the communion with that Church which is Catholic and is called Catholic.[35] The key to the Scriptures is love for God and man, but these are found in their true form only in that Church whose members are linked together in the body and by love made one in their Head.[36]

The Catholic Church which Augustine revered so greatly is not one whose papal head alone speaks infallibly. Neither is it the church in its hierarchial organization, nor yet the church meeting in council. It is just this point which is missed by so many of the Roman Catholic writers, but not because Augustine failed to speak plainly enough on the matter. For him the Catholic Church is the congregation of believers extended through space and time. "We are Holy Church. But I did not

31 *De Baptismo contra Donatistes*, ii, 12.
32 *De natura et gratia*, lxi, 71.
33 *Contra Epistolam Manichaei Fundamenti*, v, 6.
34 *Epistola ad Catholicos contra Donatistes*, xix, 49: "No one, indeed, attains to salvation and eternal life except he who has Christ as his head. But no one can have Christ as his Head, except he who is in His Body which is the Church."
35 *De vera religione*, vii, 12.
36 *De unitate ecclesiae*, ii, 2.

say 'we' as if I meant we who are here present, you who are now listening to me. I do mean the many faithful Christians as are by God's favor here in this church, in this city; as many as are in this province, as many as are across the sea, as many as are in the whole wide world; for from the rising of the sun to the going down of the same, the name of the Lord is praised. Thus is constituted the Catholic Church, our true mother, the true Spouse of that Bridegroom."[37]

Nevertheless, the Church does speak through its councils, whose decrees have been formulated into creeds. It speaks through its bishops, its theologians, its writers. The creeds of the Church and the traditions of the fathers bore tremendous weight with Augustine. Accordingly, when he wrote his treatise on the Literal Interpretation of Genesis, *De Genesi ad Litteram,* and on the Holy Trinity, *De Trinitate,* he prefaced them with a summary of the Catholic faith on these matters declaring, as it has been remarked, with complete simplicity, "This is my faith, too, since it is the Catholic faith."[38]

It is evident, then, that in Augustine's thought the Church was practically a mediatrix of true knowledge, in somewhat the same way that it was the sole mediatrix of grace, yet he did not consider that the authority of the mediatrix was higher than that of the Scriptures. If, however, one must believe in order to understand, and if one believes truly only when he believes what the Catholic Church teaches, then the Church becomes the intermediary between man and God's Word. Yet it must be kept in mind at the same time that according to Augustine only that is Catholic which is declared by Catholic expositors who teach according to the Scriptures.[39]

To Augustine the suggestion that all believers have the right of private interpretation would have seemed preposterous. To be sure, there can be no more profitable exercise for anyone who can read than to read the Bible. To be sure, again, the Scriptures speak plainly enough on matters requisite to salvation. But the end of man's salvation is that he may, through all eternity, know and love God perfectly. In the earthly phase of man's existence his knowledge at best is imperfect. The intellectual faculties are darkened by sin. In this life, only those who

37 *Sermones,* CCXIII, vii, 7.
38 Cf. Warfield, *Studies in Tertullian and Augustine,* p. 217.
39 *De Trinitate,* I iv, 7.

are regenerated by the Holy Spirit working in and through the means of grace can have any saving knowledge of God at all. Of those who have such knowledge only a few spiritual men are able to explore with any degree of certainty the depths of divine truth.[40] These spiritual men, in their speaking and writing, are the voice of the Catholic Church. In his day, of course, the masses were uneducated and were dependent upon their teachers to a greater extent than people of later ages. Yet it was not the inability of the masses or their ignorance which deprived them of the right of private interpretation. Even the instructed members of the Church, of whom Augustine surely considered himself to be one, must hesitate to advance any teaching which might be contrary to the faith of the Catholic Church.

The reasoning which underlies this conception of the authority of the Church in matters of Scripture interpretation is perfectly consistent with other aspects of Augustine's theology. As over against the Pelagians he had taken a serious and Biblical view of human sin. The remedy for the disabilities caused by sin is to be found in divine revelation and divine grace. The revelation serves to set the truth before erring minds. The grace serves to repair the damage done to the mind and so to render it capable of grasping the truth. It is in the Church that both revelation and grace are mediated, and through the Church, therefore, that sinful human beings may attain to that knowledge of the truth which brings eternal life.[41]

The influence of the Catholic Church is predominant in Augustine's attitude toward the canon of Scripture. It is altogether likely that he included among the canonical books of the Old Testament six apocryphal books, Tobias, Judith, 1 and 2 Maccabees, Sirach and Ecclesiasticus. His language, however, is by no means unambiguous. "The most skillful interpreter of the sacred writing," he says, "will be he who has read them all and retained them in his knowledge, if not yet with full understanding, still with such knowledge as reading gives — those of them at least that are called canonical."[42] He then speaks of other writings, apparently among the sacred writings he has mentioned, which may be read with greater safety, since if the

40 *Contra Epistolam Manichaei Fundamenti,* i, 4, 5.
41 Cf. Warfield, *Studies in Tertullian and Augustine,* p. 221.
42 Cf. *De Doctrina Christiana,* II, viii, 12, 13 for Augustine's discussion of canonicity.

reader were not first reinforced by the truth of the canonical books he might be deceived by dangerous falsehoods and delusions.

With regard even to the canonical Scriptures the student must exercise a certain judgment. He will prefer those which are received by all the Catholic churches to those which some do not receive. Among those which are not received by all, he will prefer those which have the sanction of the greater number of churches and those of greater authority. If he should find that some books were held by the greater number of churches and others by churches of greater authority, Augustine felt that the weight on both sides was likely to be about equal and, presumably, all the books concerned should be accepted.

The situation may seem to be made perfectly plain when Augustine states, "Now the whole canon of Scripture on which we say this judgment is to be exercised is contained in the following," . . . after which he proceeds to name the books. At the conclusion of the list again he says, "The authority of the Old Testament is contained within the limits of these 44 books."[43] Yet other statements betray the fact that the whole matter of canonicity was as yet unsettled by him.

When he speaks of sacred writings, Augustine must mean not only the writings which he believed to be unquestionably canonical, but other writings also which were hallowed by tradition and antiquity, such as the Similitudes of Enoch or the Shepherd of Hermas. These latter might prove to be profitable reading though they did not have the authority of the canonical books.

As far as the student's exercising of judgment over the canonical books is concerned, there is evidence that there was still some uncertainty in Augustine's mind about the final authority of the apocryphal books, which were the only ones seriously questioned by any part of the Church in his day. In his own writings he quotes freely from Wisdom and Ecclesiasticus and only rarely from the other apocryphal books. Perhaps he attached to these latter books a lower estimate in much the same way that the Jews did when they claimed that Moses' inspiration was of a higher type than that of any other writer of Scripture.

43 *De Doctrina Christiana*, II, viii, 13.

On occasion Augustine even seems to reject outright the real canonicity of some apocryphal books. He concedes that things which are not written in the canon accepted by the Jews cannot be adduced with confidence against opponents.[44] The suggestion had been made by certain Donatists that suicide is permissible under certain circumstances. Augustine denied the argument vigorously and in so doing denies the final authority of 2 Maccabees, the book in which an act of suicide is approved. The book, he says, "is received by the Church not without advantage, *if it be read and heard soberly.*"[45]

It is evident that Augustine was involved in the state of confusion which existed in the Church at that time concerning the precise limits of the canon. Jerome, the contemporary of Augustine, and an authority on Hebrew, rejected the apocryphal books. The Jews did not consider them as canonical and it appeared certain that Jesus and His apostles accepted the canon of the synagogue. No concrete decision on the matter was reached in the Church until the turbulent days of the Reformation, when the Reformers accepted the judgment of Jerome, while the Romanists followed, for the most part, the conclusions of Augustine. It is surprising that Augustine, who based his conviction of the inspiration of the New Testament Scriptures largely upon their apostolicity, did not agree with Jerome's viewpoint, but he did not, apparently because of his adherence to the principle of Catholicity. It was the authority of the Catholic Church rather than any other consideration which gave rise to the confusion or inconsistency which marks Augustine's view of the canon of Scripture.

The same authority influenced Augustine's dealing with the Bible in another direction and in a different fashion. It has been mentioned a number of times that Augustine used the allegorical method of interpretation very extensively. Like everyone else, Augustine was a child of his times. The allegorical method was the prevalent one among all reputable students of the Bible. It had been particularly popular with Ambrose of Milan, Augustine's spiritual father. It seemed, moreover, to provide an answer to many of the rational and moral problems raised by statements in the Old Testament.[46] Augustine was a philosopher

---

44 *De Civitate Dei*, XVII, 20.
45 *Contra Gaudentium Donatistarum Episcopum*, 23.
46 *Confessiones*, V, 14; *De Doctrina Christiana*, III, x, 14.

by education and a convert from immorality. Anything which satisfied his philosophical and moral bent appealed to him.

The fact that allegorical interpretation prevailed in the Church simply meant to Augustine that such interpretation was "Catholic." It was, indeed, this interpretation, the Church's interpretation, which made him see the reasonableness of much in the Bible which he had previously considered incredible.[47] He adopted the method as his own and employed it in almost wholesale fashion in some of his commentaries on the Scripture.

It has been maintained that in the later years of his life Augustine's allegorizing tended to diminish.[48] This opinion has not been solidly substantiated. The use of allegory or figurative interpretation continues in all of his writings which have to do with Scripture, even the very last ones. In certain of them, it is true, the figurative explanation is at a minimum. For this there are evident reasons. For one thing, the anti-Pelagian writings come from the later period of Augustine's life and in them he quotes much more freely from the New Testament than from the Old. His allegorizing, as he himself has told us, was the solution mainly for problems arising from the Old Testament. Moreover, it seems to be Augustine's tendency to interpret allegorically in works which are given more largely to interpretation or which are intended for Christian instruction rather than in those which are controversial. He himself cautions against the use of allegorical interpretations in discussions with non-Christians because it could not afford convincing proof.[49] By the same token he would avoid the use of allegory in those cases where the strongest Scriptural support was needed, as it was in the arguments against Pelagianism.

Although Augustine at one time delineated four possible ways of interpreting the Old Testament,[50] he did not mean to

---

47 *Confessiones,* V, 14, "Very many passages then of those (O.T.) books having been explained spiritually, I began to condemn my own despair for having believed that no answer at all could be given to such as hated and scoffed at the Law and the Prophets."

48 Philip Schaff, *Saint Chrysostom and Saint Augustine* (New York: Whittaker, 1891), p. 90.

49 *De Unitate Ecclesiae,* v, 8.

50 *De Utilitate Credendi,* III, 5: "All of that Scripture called the Old Testament is handed down fourfold, therefore, to those eagerly bent on knowing it; according to history, according to aetiology, according to analogy and according to allegory. . . . Things are handed down according to history, when the teaching concerns what has been written or done and what has not been done, but only written as

imply that any one given passage might be interpreted in all four ways. He allowed, indeed, that a particular phrase or clause might be capable of yielding two or more meanings. He saw nothing in such a possibility at variance with the inspiration of the Scripture. As a matter of fact, he regarded it as evidence of the liberal and fruitful provision the Holy Spirit had made in the Word that the same words might be understood in several senses.[51] These several senses, however, were not to be elicited from an equal number of different *methods* of interpretation.

In actual practice Augustine seems to have used only two distinct methods himself, the literal and the figurative. At any rate these are the only ones he mentions in *De Doctrina Christiana,* the work which was devoted to the subject of Scripture interpretation. The other two types of interpretation described in *De Utilitate Credendi,* the aetiological and the analogical, are in reality but variants of the first two.[52]

There is no distinction in Augustine between what would now be called the merely figurative as over against the allegorical. One interprets according to allegory when he is taught that certain writings are not to be taken according to the letter but are to be understood figuratively. Where the sense of a statement is not clear on the face of it, but obscure, it is allegorical or enigmatical, which is the kind of expression properly called figurative.[53] Apparently in Augustine's vocabulary that which is figurative is allegorical and that which is allegorical is figurative.

Probably the greatest extreme in allegorizing comes in Augustine's dealing with the Psalms, both in his sermons and in his *Ennarrationes in Psalmos.* While he noted that the Psalms were

---

though it were done; according to aetiology, when the reason is given as to why anything has been said or done; according to analogy, when it is shown that the two Testaments, the Old and the New, are not opposed to each other; according to allegory, when one is taught that certain writings are not to be taken according to the letter, but are to be understood figuratively." (Eng. trans. quoted from *The Writings of St. Augustine,* vol. 2, in the series *The Fathers of the Church* (New York: Cima Pub. Co., 1947).

51 *De Doctrina Christiana,* III, xxvii, 38.

52 *De Utilitate Credendi* may be dated about 391 A.D. since Augustine in his *Retractiones* mentions that he wrote it the year after he was ordained as a priest. *De Doctrina Christiana* was apparently begun about 397 but not put into its final form until 426. It represents Augustine's more considered judgment, therefore.

53 *De Doctrina Christiana,* III, xi, 17.

poetry, a fact which escaped most of the medieval as well as some Reformed expositors, he seems to have felt that it would be beneath the dignity of the Holy Spirit to inspire men merely to write religious lyrics. Consequently every other word or member is made to display some unexpected reference to Christian history or theology. In Psalm 19:5 (E.V.) the sun going forth from his chamber is a reference to Christ's emergence from the virgin's womb. In Psalm 137 (E.V.) Babylon represents the unbelieving world and the demand made of the Jews to sing the Lord's song is the unbeliever's demand to God's people of a reason for believing.

Protestants, whose theological debt to Augustine is so great, have often tended to apologize for his allegorizing as if it represented a serious flaw in his otherwise great work. Augustine himself would hardly have appreciated their attitude. He revelled in his ability to find these hidden or deep meanings in the stories of the Old Testament and even claimed that in some instances he had seen meanings which had not occurred to the Biblical writers.[54]

It would be wrong, however, to assume that Augustine allegorizes just for the sake of allegorizing. In the main he takes seriously his own advice that the student must try to discover the author's real meaning, but sometimes he feels it necessary to allegorize a particular narrative because only by so doing can he derive any abiding, spiritual benefit from it. The Scripture might speak, "as it were, in carnal terms, but the meaning is always spiritual."[55] That is to say, all Scripture must lead to a divine, or spiritual end. It is significant that the great E. W. Hengstenberg advances as one of the principle reasons for holding to a figurative interpretation of the Song of Songs almost exactly the same kind of reasoning.[56]

Besides, as has already been pointed out, the figurative interpretation helped Augustine to reconcile some points of his philosophy with the Scripture. An excellent example of this is found in his handling of the Creation Story in Gen. 1. Here we find an interweaving of the Biblical and philosophical concepts. To Gen. 1:1 he attaches both a figurative and a literal meaning.

---

54 *Confessiones*, XII, 24, 33.
55 *Sermones*, XXIII, iii, 3.
56 Cf. E. W. Hengstenberg *Commentary on Ecclesiastes with Other Treatises* (Edinburgh: Clark, 1860), pp. 300-1.

"Figuratively the beginning *(principium)* is the divine Word, the eternal Son in and by whom God made all things. Literally it is the beginning of time. The world was made not in time, but with time.[57] The six days of the account are not to be understood as literal days defined by the circuit of the sun. The story is a dramatic presentation of what took place all at once and as a whole.[58] If creation took place with time, creation could not have been characterized by any temporal succession. For support of his philosophical contention Augustine could appeal to Ecclesiasticus 18:1, according to which God created all things simultaneously. Again, when Genesis represents God as speaking, we should not understand this "in a childish way, as though God exerted himself by working. For he spoke not with an audible and temporal word, but with an intellectual and eternal word, and the things were done."[59]

If Augustine ever felt the inconsistency of his wide use of allegory with the proof-text method he employs in certain of his polemic writings, he gives no indication of it. Certainly it was in accord with the view of inspiration he had espoused, for it was the door to a whole, wonderful world of meaning put there by the finger of God Himself.

It remains to be said that Augustine's reverence for Scripture as the very truth of the living God did not close his mind to the realms of thought and experience about him. Instead, the conviction that the real meaning of life had been revealed in the Bible led him to challenge the pagan philosophies of his day with a Christianized philosophy. It led him to attempt an interpretation of history in terms of the Biblical revelation. Whatever there was of philosophy in his discussions of time and eternity, of body and soul, it was of created time and created bodies and souls that he spoke. Creation out of nothing may be a philosophical concept, but it is a philosophy which is the handmaid of revelation and which stands over against the materialistic monism or the dualism in which Augustine had been nurtured. His last great effort, *De Civitate Dei,* was an attempt to provide a philosophy of history in conformity with the eternal, redemptive purposes of God. One important contribution of the great bishop to Christian thought, therefore, is

57 *Confessiones,* XIII, vi, 6.
58 *De Genesi ad Litteram,* IV, 26.
59 *De Civitate Dei,* XI, 6.

his deliberate endeavor to establish what may be called a Christian life and world view whose presuppositions would be those of the Scripture.

A more important contribution and at the same time a more successful effort on Augustine's part is his formulation of a consistent scheme of doctrine from the Scripture. No doubt his disputations with the Manichaeans, the Donatists, the Pelagian party in the Church helped him greatly not only to clarify his own thought but also to see the divine revelation as a consistent whole. All through his ecclesiastical and literary life Augustine was engaged in the defense of the truth as he saw it. Against the Manichaeans he defended the Scriptural doctrines of God and creation. Against the Donatists he defended the Scriptural doctrines, as he understood them, of the Catholic Church and the means of grace. Against the Pelagians he defended the Scriptural doctrines of man, of sin and of grace. It is small wonder that he succeeded in drawing forth from Holy Writ an integrated system of theology.

If, like others, Augustine was a child of his times, unlike most others he was also a father of the times which came after him. His exposition of Biblical dogma has left its imprint upon the Western section of the Christian Church in every century since his day. Thomas Aquinas' *Summa Theologica* owes no less to Augustine's systematic interpretation of the Bible than it does to Aristotle's philosophy. Every movement toward reform within the Roman Catholic Church has drawn to some extent upon Augustinian theology. If the Roman Church has appealed to those elements in Augustine's thought which are inconsistent with his Scriptural doctrines of sin and grace, the Protestant Reformers have appealed with much greater advantage to that segment of his thought which is consistent with the Bible. The genius of the Protestant Reformation was that in answer to the moral abuses and false doctrines which pervaded the Church of the time, it cried out with Augustine, "What saith the Scripture?"

CHAPTER III

LUTHER AND THE BIBLE*

By J. Theodore Mueller

There is no doubt that the popularity of the Bible in Christendom today is largely due to Martin Luther's deep

* When the writer of this article began his task, he kept in mind that there is as yet no complete translation of Luther's works in English and that it is not easy for English-speaking students to gain access to the great Reformer's writings in German. He therefore took his quotations from Luther's works from the following publications quite in reach of English-speaking students: (1) The St. Louis Edition of Luther's Works (St. Louis: Concordia Publishing House; a revision of the famous Walch edition; 23 volumes), quoted as follows: St. L. XIV: 491. (2) Reinhold Seeberg, *Lehrbuch der Dogmengeschichte, vierter Band, erste Abteilung, Die Lehre Luthers*, IV, 1 (Leipzig, 1933), A. Deichertsche, Verlagsbuchhandlung D. Werner Scholl, quoted: Seeberg, 101. (3) The Erlangen Edition of Luther's Works, Latin and German, quoted: E 63, 124. (4) Dr. M. Reu, *Luther and the Scriptures* (Columbus, Ohio: The Wartburg Press, 1944), quoted: Reu, 56. (5) The Weimar Edition of Luther's Works (usually used by Seeberg), quoted: W 10.3.141; Seeberg 154, if quotation is taken from Seeberg's *Die Lehre Luther's* where also at times the Erlangen Edition is quoted. This permits the reader to compare the Luther quotations in not too many works. The Weimar Edition, however, may be studied in the libraries of the foremost theological seminaries in our country. The writer took it for granted that his readers are acquainted with the modern works on Luther such as (to name only a few) those of H. Boehmer, H. Bornkamm, H. Echternach, W. Elert, Th. Harnack, K. Holl, H. Kropatscheck, J. Koestlin, K. Noesgen, M. Reu, O. Scheel, W. Walther (cf. Reu: *Luther and the Scriptures* for a fairly complete list) and the recent Luther biographies by E. Schwiebert, E. Rupp, and R. Bainton, as also the important Luther research (though not always reliable) by the Swedish School of Luther study. A good, though limited, edition of Luther's works is: *The Works of Martin Luther, Translated with Introductions and Notes*. 6 vols., (Philadelphia, 1914-32), Valuable also is the *Concordia Triglot*, containing the Confessions of the Lutheran Church, in particular, Luther's *Smalcald Articles* and Luther's *Small* and *Large Catechisms* (Concordia Publishing House), quoted: *Conc. Trigl.*, 565. Very valuable for the understanding of Luther is Dr. F. Pieper's *Christian Dogmatics* (3 vols.), and the writer's own *Christian Dogmatics* (Concordia Publishing House). Both represent Luther's doctrine of Holy Scripture from the conservative point of view.

appreciation of Holy Scripture as the infallible divine Word and the only source and norm of the Christian faith and life.

This statement does not deny the fact that other great Protestant church leaders have contributed a large and valuable share toward elevating the Bible to its proper place in the Church as the divinely inspired, inerrant principle and rule of Christian truth. But when, about 1512, Luther at Wittenberg University turned from medieval philosophy to Scriptural theology and, in particular, to the exposition of Scripture as the sole authority in religion, the newly created "Doctor of Holy Scripture" set the pace for all other Protestant church leaders in declaring Scripture to be the religious authority of Protestantism over against the authority of Roman Catholic tradition. When church historians ascribe to Luther the merit of having established the *Schriftprinzip*, that is, the axiomatic truth that Holy Scripture is the sole principle by which divine truth is truly and unmistakably known, they do this in full justice to the Wittenberg Reformer, whose alleged "liberal attitude" toward Scripture theological liberals, contrary to historical fact, in vain are trying to demonstrate.[1]

Luther's attitude toward Scripture, to be rightly understood, must be considered against the background of his heredity and environment. To appreciate Luther's personality and work, the reader must bear in mind that he was a German, with all the virtues and faults of that, in many respects, undeniably great people of Central Europe. Through his ecclesiastical affiliation with an international Church, his education and culture, his varied contacts with representative men of all nations, both by correspondence and personal acquaintance, and, above all, because of his broad vision and universal sympathies, by which he transcended local and national limitations, Luther became a cosmopolitan figure whose interests were world-wide. Personally very modest, he mightily felt the call of God to bring Christ to all nations. But to the end he remained essentially a German with his people's traits of simple-mindedness and profundity, generosity and severity, ingenuousness and ingeniousness, gullibility and astuteness, love for work and appreciation of

---

1 Cf. Mueller, *Christian Dogmatics*, pp. 116ff. Pieper, *Christian Dogmatics*, I, 276ff. Reu, *Luther and the Scriptures*, pp. 13ff. Carl F. H. Henry, *The Protestant Dilemma*, Appendix, Note B (Grand Rapids: Wm. B. Eerdmans, 1949).

relaxation, joy in fighting and delight in genial fellowship; and the people which he, first of all, served so joyously and untiringly, was fundamentally sincere, pious, and religious, very much inclined from the start to accept the gospel of Christ which the young professor proclaimed to them in its truth and purity, because they were nauseously sick of the deceit and tyranny of the papacy. Such was Luther's national background viewed in a more general way.

Viewed from the more narrow aspect of his personal heredity, Luther came from substantial middle-class stock. His parents were pious and thrifty, ambitious and industrious, fearless and independent, securing for themselves in the course of time both the esteem of their fellow men and success in business. They implanted into their children their own rugged piety, bringing them up, according to their ability, in the nurture and admonition of the Lord. Little Martin grew up in a decidedly Christian home, where he was well prepared for his later career as a teacher of the Bible.[2]

To understand properly Luther's approach to Scripture, the student must remember, moreover, that the Reformer's mind was intuitional and practical rather than academic and analytical. With all his erudition, his profundity of speculation, and his almost encyclopedic knowledge of men and events, he remained to the end of his life a "great commoner," dedicated to the welfare of the people — a man who in his entire educational and reformational work kept in mind the need of the suppressed masses. This practical, pastoral orientation greatly influenced his treatment and interpretation of the Bible, in which he saw, from beginning to end, Christ and the divine revelation of salvation through Him whom he adored as the divine Savior of the world. Luther approached the Bible not as a mere codex of precepts, rules, and principles, but as a dynamic power of God, a living, life-giving gospel message of divine love which freed him from his own long and painful fear and sorrow for sin and gave him a triumphant assurance of free and full forgiveness by grace through faith in Jesus, whom only he saw in Scripture and whom also he saw in all of Scripture. It is from this evangelical, Christ-centered view that we must study Luther's approach to the Bible. After Luther had learned to

2 Cf. Seeberg, *op. cit.*, 55ff.

know Christ as his personal Savior, he taught the Bible as a blessed child of God who in the gospel had found the Redeemer and in Him a triumphant assurance of salvation.

I. LUTHER'S APPROACH TO THE BIBLE

To appreciate Luther's painful experience of his utter sinfulness and lostness, we must examine the impelling cause that led him to enter the cloister, and the perplexing trials that made him almost despair of God until through his evangelical father confessor, Dr. John Staupitz, he experienced his first joys of divine comfort. Professor E. G. Rupp, in his recent work *Luther's Progress to the Diet of Worms,* treats this stirring subject under the heading "Mr. Fearing."[3] This indeed is a fitting title to describe the young struggling monk at this time; his life was one of unspeakable fear in view of God's wrath over sin, and it was this horrible torment of soul that moved him to seek refuge in the monastery.

Otherwise there was no rational cause to induce the young ambitious student to take up cloister life. At Erfurt University he was highly respected by professors and fellow students as a brilliant scholar. His father by this time had become rather well-to-do and desired that his promising son should become an attorney, who later might wield power and influence in an exalted government position. There is no evidence to prove that Luther confided to his parent the distress of soul in which he found himself; in fact, the frank and sharp parental rebuke of his cloister venture at a later time clearly shows that his father had not been aware of Luther's great spiritual trouble. It was not merely a terrifying accident, as the sudden death of a friend, nor the lightning striking close by as he returned from a journey, nor an accidental wound inflicted by his rapier that prompted him to enter the Augustinian cloister at Erfurt. What made Luther a monk was his indescribable fear of God's fierce wrath; he knew Christ only as a Judge, and not as a Savior; he knew only the law, not the gospel.

Dr. Rupp well describes Luther's endeavors to earn salvation by good works in this "holiest of callings" designed by the Church for those who earnestly and sincerely sought assurance of salvation.[4] He quotes Luther as saying:

3 Chicago: Wilcox & Follett Co., 1951.
4 *Op. cit.,* pp. 26ff.

There in the convent I was the most wretched man on earth, passing whole nights in weeping and feeling that everything was hopeless, which condition no one could alleviate. Thus I was bathed in my monkery and had a real "sweating sickness." Thanks be to God that I was not consumed in my fever, for I would have been in the depths of hell long ago in spite of my monastic baptism. For I no longer knew Christ except as a stern Judge from whom I wanted to flee, yet was unable to escape.[5]

Dr. E. Schwiebert explains Luther's "monastic struggle" on the basis of the following words of the terrified monk:

I always walked around in a dream, for I did not believe savingly in Christ, but believed Him to be nothing else than a stern and terrible Judge. . . . For this reason I sought other intercessors, Mary and the saints and my own good deeds and merits of faith. All this I did not do for money or possessions, but for God's own sake; yet it was all a false religion and idolatry, because I did not know Christ and I did not seek to do these things through and in Him.[6]

Dr. William Dallmann, in his popular but most valuable book, *Martin Luther,* writes of Luther, under the heading "A Slave of Superstition":

Luther picked twenty-one saints and daily prayed to three and thus made his rounds without slighting any; he scourged his body severely; he broke up his sleep during the night; he touched no food or drink for days at a stretch. . . . And yet he wailed: "Oh, when will you be pious and do enough that God will be merciful to you?" All in vain![7]

Here, then, we have the true reason for Luther's Reformation and gospel emphasis in the Bible; Roman Catholic theology had no joyous gospel message of God's free and full grace in Christ Jesus, but only "false religion and idolatry," which terrified alarmed consciences by "vain traditions of men" such as the doctrines of the uncertainty of salvation, purgatory, hopeless

---

5 *Ibid.,* p. 153; quoted from E XXXI: 279.
6 *Luther and His Times,* p. 155; quoted from E XLIX: 27.
7 William Dallmann, *Martin Luther: His Life and His Labor, For the Plain People* (St. Louis: Concordia Publishing House, 1917; 2nd ed. 1951), pp. 20f.

efforts to appease God's wrath by good works, and endless torments of body and soul.

However, there came a time when Luther could rejoice: "Thank God, we again have His Word which pictures and portrays Christ as our Righteousness."[8] Just when this assuring gospel consolation came to Luther, is not quite certain. It is usually connected with Luther's so-called "Tower Discovery" (*Turmerlebnis*) which Schwiebert dates "some time in the fall of 1514."[9] Luther himself tells us how he discovered the gospel meaning of the "righteousness of God" (Rom. 1:17) in connection with his lecture preparations on Romans in his quiet tower study. He writes:

> Then I began to comprehend "the righteousness of God" through which the righteous are saved by God's grace, namely, through faith; that the "righteousness of God," which is revealed through the Gospel, is to be understood in a passive sense, in which God in mercy justifies man by faith. . . . Now I felt just as though I had been born again, and I believed that I had entered Paradise through widely opened doors. . . . As violently as formerly I had hated the expression "the righteousness of God," so I was now as violently compelled to embrace the new conception of grace and so for me the expression of the Apostle really opened the gates of Paradise.[10]

Luther, in his report on the "Tower Discovery" goes on to say: "I then went through the Holy Scriptures." For Luther this "going through the Holy Scriptures" for the sake of the gospel message of free and full salvation in Christ became a life-long privilege and blessing. Roland Bainton in his fine book *Here I Stand* quotes Luther as saying:

> If you have a true faith that Christ is your Savior, then at once you have a gracious God, for faith leads you in and opens up God's heart and will, that you should see pure grace and overflowing love. This it means to behold God in faith that you should look upon His fatherly, friendly heart in which there is no anger nor ungraciousness. He who sees God as angry does not see Him rightly,

---

8 Schwiebert, *op. cit.*, p. 154; quoted from Reu, *op. cit.*, p. 115.
9 Schwiebert, *op. cit.*, p. 288.
10 *Ibid.*, p. 286.

but looks on a veil, as if a dark cloud had been drawn across His face.[11]

Luther's triumphant rejoicing in the gospel message of God's free and full grace in Christ thus influenced his whole use of the Bible: The God who once spoke the Bible *(Deus Locutus)* is the God still speaking in the Bible *(Deus loquens)*, and what He there speaks primarily and essentially is not law, but gospel. So to Luther the Holy Scriptures became both a divinely inspired and through the witness of the Holy Ghost a divinely inspiring message of salvation, in which Christ is all in all.

Reinhold Seeberg, in his *Lehrbuch der Dogmengeschichte* summarizes the matter as follows:

> The thought of the absolute authority of Scripture finds its culmination in Luther . . . in the inspiration of the Bible. To him the words of Scripture are the real words of God, for the Holy Spirit has comprehended His wisdom and mystery in the Word and revealed it in Scripture, for which reason he [Luther] distinguishes the "manifest external Word" (W 36, 501). The veracious God speaks in Scripture and therefore we must believingly accept what is written in it (W 40. 2, 593). What St. Paul says, the Holy Spirit says, and so whatever opposes the Word of Paul opposes the Holy Spirit (W 10. 2, 139f.). According to God's will, the Apostles were to be infallible teachers (Di, 12). They possess authority as do the prophets *(ibid.* 100). In addition, they received the Holy Ghost so that their words are the words of God (W 40. 1, 173f.). As men, they are subject to sin and error, just as Peter was at Antioch, but then the Holy Spirit corrects their failings (W 40. 1, 195f.). He moves them to speak the truth, even when they commit grammatical errors. . . . For this reason Scripture is the Word of God and not the word of man (W 5, 184; 8, 597). What is more: God is the Author of the Gospel (W 8, 584) and the Holy Spirit Himself is the Writer of Genesis (W 44, 532). Scripture therefore is the very Word of the Holy Spirit (W 7, 638; 46, 545; 47, 133).[12]

---

11 *Here I Stand, A Life of Martin Luther* (New York: Abingdon Press, 1950), p. 63.

12 Seeberg, *op. cit.,* 414f. The symbol "Di" in Seeberg's *Dogmengeschichte* stands for: Die Disputationen, Dr. M. Luthers, ed. Drews, 1896; cf. p. 55.

We have quoted Seeberg's *Dogmengeschichte* on this point with so much detail, not only because in our opinion his work represents a most scholarly and reliable treatise on this point, but also because he, while frankly stating that Luther took over the "medieval theory of inspiration,"[13] treats him fairly by disclaiming any "mechanical inspiration theory."

Again, according to Seeberg, Luther, while never developing a precise and comprehensive dogma of inspiration, in his whole teaching always presupposed the divine inspiration of the canonical books of the prophets and apostles. Luther, he declares, motivates the divine origin of Scripture, given through the operation of the Holy Ghost, from the viewpoint of its religious value, to which also Loofs agrees.[14] Just because the teaching of Scripture, in its ecclesiastical proclamation, proves itself as divinely efficacious, its origin must be sought not in man, but in the Holy Ghost. In particular, he motivates Luther's doctrine of inspiration thus:

> "Not the inspiration of the Bible is the foundation of Luther's doctrine of the Word of God, but the Word of God, experienced in the heart, is the foundation of his doctrine of Biblical inspiration. In this sense Luther writes: "The Word of God is God's Word originally and authoritatively, and not that of the Church, except passively and instrumentally."[15]

In our opinion Seeberg here does not do justice to Luther's statements on Biblical inspiration which he quotes. If Seeberg's view of Luther's motivation of inspiration were correct, Luther would have conceived of divine truth as essentially subjective, whereas in reality Luther very emphatically taught the objectivity of divine truth. According to Luther, the Bible is the inspired divine truth just because in it the Holy Ghost speaks through the prophets and apostles. There is, however, another point on which we cannot agree with Seeberg, namely, that whenever

---

13 He refers at the same time to Rohnert's *Die Inspiration der Heiligen Schrift*, 1889, p. 144ff. for more passages in Luther's writings proving that the Reformer regarded the whole Bible as God's inspired Word.

14 F. Loofs, *Dogmengeschichte*, 4, pp. 743f., 380ff., 412ff. A. Harnack, *Dogmengeschichte*, III, 4, 878f. O. Scheel, *Luthers Stellung zur Heiligen Schrift*, 1902.

15 *Verbum Dei est Verbum Dei originaliter et authoritative, non ecclesiae, nisi passive et ministerialiter;* W 30. 2, 682; Seeberg *op. cit.*, **414f.**

Luther speaks of "Scripture" or the "Word of God," he always has in mind the "doctrine of the Gospel," or "articles" having reference to it. It is true that in Luther's controversies with the nomistic and legalistic Romanists, who later in the "Decisions and Canons of the Council of Trent" declared that Scripture was given by "dictation of the Holy Ghost"[16] so that on this point no special debate was necessary, the emphasis on the gospel of Christ, in its narrow or proper sense, as the message of God's full and free grace in Christ, was central. Nevertheless, Luther's almost vehement emphasis on the gospel of Christ does not deny the inspiration of the whole Bible; in fact, Luther regarded the gospel of Christ as inspired, just because he considered the entire Scripture to be God's inspired truth and so the source and foundation of all that the Church should teach.

Such statements in Luther's writings as the following: "If I know what I believe, I know what is written in Scripture, because Scripture contains no more than Christ and the Christian faith"; or: "That is the true test by which all books are to be judged, to see whether or not they urge Christ, for the whole Bible sets forth Christ (Rom. 3:21), and St. Paul does not desire to know anything else but Christ (1 Cor. 2:2)"; or: "Whatever does not teach Christ, that is not yet apostolical, even if St. Peter or St. Paul should teach it"; or: "Whatever preaches Christ, would be apostolical, even if Judas, Annas, Pilate, and Herod should do it,"[17] were written to defend the precious gospel of salvation through faith in Christ against perverters of the divine truth who had taken out of Christianity the very core of the Bible. According to Seeberg, Luther, when speaking of "Scripture," has in mind the "whole complex of Gospel teachings, including sin," but even that fails to do justice to Luther, to whom the whole Bible was God's inspired, inerrant Word. It is indeed very significant that Seeberg does not admit Luther's identification of God's Word with Holy Scripture, that is, his manifest teaching that the Bible, as a whole and in all its parts, is the very Word of God. The claim which Seeberg here makes, is that of modern liberalism which ignores the evident historical facts.

16 *Spiritu Sancto dictante*, Sess. I, Can. 1.
17 Seeberg, *op. cit.*, 415f.; cf. W8, 236; Di 12.

In his *Christian Dogmatics,* Dr. F. Pieper treats this matter at great length,[18] and in his own *Christian Dogmatics* the writer presents an accurate summary of the chief arguments of his esteemed teacher of Christian doctrine.[19] It is Dr. Pieper's thesis, set forth comprehensively and convincingly, that the doctrine of the divine inspiration of the Bible is one clearly taught in Scripture, e.g. 2 Tim. 3:15-17; 2 Peter 1:21; 1 Cor. 2:13; John 5:39; Luke 11:28; etc., and that the doctrine of Biblical inspiration was clearly understood and consistently defended by Luther.

Dr. Pieper writes:

The alleged difference between Luther and the Lutheran dogmaticians is pure fabrication. The real difference between Luther and the dogmaticians is that the dogmaticians weakly stammer and re-echo what Luther had taught much more strongly about Scripture from Scripture. Quenstedt, for example, writes concerning Holy Scripture as the inspired Word of God: "The canonical Holy Scriptures in the original text are the infallible truth and are free from every error; in other words, in the canonical sacred Scriptures there is found no lie, no falsity, no error, not even the least, whether in subject matter or expressions, but in all things and all the details that are handed down in them, they are most certainly true, whether they pertain to doctrines or morals, to history or chronology, to topography or nomenclature. No ignorance, no thoughtlessness, no forgetfulness, no lapse of memory can and dare be ascribed to the amanuenses of the Holy Ghost in their penning the Sacred Writings" (Systema I, 112). This statement of Quenstedt has been called a "horrible assertion." But everything that Quenstedt says about Scripture is said also by Luther, including the details mentioned by Quenstedt, only that Luther states these things with incomparably greater force. To demonstrate this, we shall record here, first, what Luther says regarding the entire Scripture, and, then, what Luther says on the details concerning which it is claimed that he plainly differed from the dogmaticians.[20]

18 I, 766ff.
19 pp. 115ff.
20 *Op. cit.,* I, 277ff.

Dr. Pieper here argues against moderns who assert that there is a decided difference between Luther and the seventeenth century Lutheran dogmaticians on the subject of inspiration; in particular, that the doctrine of verbal and plenary inspiration is an "artificial theory" of the later dogmaticians, not taught by Luther and the Lutheran Confessions.[21] Against this wrong view of Luther's doctrine of inspiration, Dr. Pieper quotes such passages from his writings as: "So, then, the entire Scriptures are assigned to the Holy Ghost" (St. L. III: 1890) ; "The Holy Scriptures did not grow on earth" (St. L. VII: 2095) ; "The Holy Scriptures have been spoken by the Holy Ghost" (St. L. III: 1895) ; Scripture is "the book of the Holy Ghost" (St. L. IX: 1775) ; Scripture is "God's Epistle addressed to Men" (St. L. I:1055) . Dr. Pieper adds: "Hundreds of similar statements from Luther could be quoted."[22]

Dr. Pieper's assertion that "hundreds of similar statements from Luther could be quoted," is correct. He might have quoted also such passages as: "No other doctrine should be proclaimed in the Church than the pure Word of God, that is, the Holy Scriptures" (St. L. IX: 87) . "In the Book of the Holy Ghost, that is, Holy Scripture, we must seek and find Christ, not only in the promise [gospel], but also in the law" (St. L. IX: 1775) ; "It is our unbelief and corrupt carnal mind which does not allow us to perceive and consider that God speaks to us in Scripture, or that Scripture is the Word of God" (St. L. IX: 1800) ; "In Scripture you are reading not the word of man, but the Word of the most exalted God, who desires to have disciples that diligently observe and note what He says" (St. L. IX: 1818) . Such passages, to which many more might be added, prove that Luther truly regarded the whole Bible as the inspired Word of God.

To moderns who insist that Luther at least did not regard "certain portions" of Scripture as the inerrant Word of God, Dr. Pieper makes this reply:

21 Cf. for the liberal view T. A. Kantonen, *Resurgence of the Gospel* (Philadelphia: Muhlenberg Press, 1948), pp. 100ff. W. Pauck, *The Heritage of the Reformation* (Boston: Beacon Press, 1950), pp. 167ff. E. M. Carlson, *The Reinterpretation of Luther* (Philadelphia: Muhlenberg Press, 1948), pp. 117ff.

22 *Op. cit.,* I, 276f. Dr. Pieper usually quotes the St. Louis Edition of Luther's Works.

What Luther asserts of the entire Bible he asserts consistently also with regard to certain portions of the Scriptures, the divine authority of which has been denied. Modern theology, as it is well known, demands very vocally that the "human side" of the Bible should be duly recognized, which "human side" the later Lutheran theologians supposedly ignored. It is therefore the special contribution of modern (liberal) theology that its sense of "reality" has been so greatly developed as to bring out this "human side."

Luther, too, was well aware of the "human side" of Scripture, but only in the sense that God caused His Word to be written by men in the human tongue. Luther is horrified at people who dare assert that Scripture is not entirely and in all its parts the Word of God, because the writers, such as Peter and Paul, after all, were men. Luther remarks on I Pet. 3:15: "But if they take exception and say: You preach that one should not hold to man's doctrine and yet Peter and Paul and even Christ were men — when you hear people of this stamp who are so blinded and hardened as to deny that which Christ and the apostles spoke and wrote in God's Word, or doubt it, then be silent, speak no more with them and let them go" (St. L. IX: 1238). Again, Luther maintained that just those parts of Scripture which appear as rather "human" to us, must be identified with the Word of God. While Kahnis[23] thinks that it is hardly credible to assume that the Holy Ghost inspired David to say what he felt in his heart and expressed in the form of a Psalm, Luther says of the Psalms: "I believe that the Holy Ghost Himself wanted to take the trouble to compile a short Bible and book of illustrations for all Christendom and all saints" (St. L. XIV: 21). Those trying to assign those Psalms that describe the emotions of the human heart, not to the Holy Ghost but to David, Luther charges with having a "carnal mind" (St. L. III: 1894).[24]

In his chapter on "Luther and the Inspiration of Holy Scripture," Dr. Pieper shows that Luther regarded even the so-called "trivial things" (*levicula*) in the Bible as well as the seemingly ordinary human happenings and the "lowly things," such as

---

23 Prof. K. Kahnis, liberal Lutheran theologian at Leipzig University, d. 1888.
24 Pieper, *Christliche Dogmatik* I, 336; cf. English Edition, I, 193—367.

Jacob's marriage and domestic troubles, as divinely inspired.
Luther writes:

> God takes pleasure in describing such lowly things to
> show and testify that He does not despise or abhor the
> household, nor wants to be far away from it and from a
> pious husband, his wife, and children.[25]

He ascribes even the "atrocious tale" of Judah and Tamar
(Gen. 38) to the Holy Ghost. He writes:

> The Holy Ghost is wonderfully diligent in narrating this
> shameful, adulterous story. . . . What has induced the most
> pure mouth of the Holy Spirit to condescend to such low,
> despised, yes, and even unchaste and filthy things and
> damnable . . . to teach a lesson to the Church and
> congregation of God?[26]

Regarding the Mosaic creation report Luther says:

> If you cannot understand how it could have been done
> in six days, then accord the Holy Ghost the honor that He
> is more learned than you are. When you read the words of
> Holy Scripture, you must realize that God is speaking
> them.[27]

Concerning the chronology of Scripture, Luther holds that
whenever the chronological data of the Bible differ from those
of secular writers, the Bible is correct, and not vice versa.
He says:

> I make use of the secular writers in such a way that I
> am not compelled to contradict Scripture. For I believe
> that in the Scriptures the God of truth speaks, but in the
> histories good people display, according to their ability,
> their diligence and fidelity (but only as men), or at least
> that their [the Scriptures'] copyists have perhaps erred.[28]

Luther unfailingly asserts the inerrancy of Scripture over
against the errancy of human historians and scientists. He
writes: "The Scriptures have never erred."[29] "It is impossible
that Scripture should contradict itself; it appears so only to the
senseless and obstinate hypocrites."[30]

25 St. L. II: 537ff.
26 St. L. II: 1200ff; Pieper, *op. cit.*, p. 280.
27 St. L. III: 21.
28 St. L. XIV: 491; Pieper, *op. cit.*, p. 281.
29 St. L. XV: 1481.
30 St. L. IX: 356; Pieper, *op. cit.*, p. 382.

Dr. Pieper, moreover, demonstrates that modern liberals substitute for the inspiration of the sacred writers a sort of illumination, so that the difference between them and the non-apostolic and non-prophetic teachers of the Church is merely one of degree, not one of kind. For this reason Holy Scripture is neither inerrant nor infallible; and this, they say, is essentially Luther's doctrine of inspiration. To show how these liberals wilfully lie and deceive, Dr. Pieper writes:

> Luther holds that there is not merely a difference of degree, but a distinctive difference [one of kind] between illumination and inspiration, between the illuminated teachers of the Church and the inspired writers of Scripture. What the inspired writers of Holy Scripture teach, is out and out God's own Word; but the enlightened teachers of the Church, including Luther and his fellow Reformers, teach God's Word only inasmuch and in so far as they "repeat and preach what we have heard and learned from the prophets and apostles."[31]

In reply to such moderns as distinguish degrees in inspiration, Dr. Pieper argues:

> That means the complete surrender of the Bible concept of inspiration. . . . Inspiration is a concept which admits of no increase or decrease. Christ ascribes the same divinity to all parts of Scripture when He says, John 10:35: "The Scripture cannot be broken. . . ." Luther accepts no degrees in inspiration, for he writes: "So, then, the entire Scriptures are assigned [by God's Word and also by me] to the Holy Ghost."[32] It is true, Luther distinguishes between the various Bible books as to their relative importance for the generation and preservation of saving faith. In this sense he calls the Gospel according to St. John "the one tender, truly chief Gospel" because it occupies itself with doctrine, while the other Gospels deal more with deeds and events from Christ's life.[33]

With respect to the "arguments" that modern liberals advance to show that Luther's concept of inspiration was liberal and his "attitude" toward Scripture rather "free," Dr. Pieper points out that from beginning to end they are false, fallacious, and downright fraudulent. Thus Luther is supposed to have said that in

31 St. L. III: 1890; Pieper, *op. cit.*, p. 283.
32 St. L. III: 1890; Pieper, *op. cit.*, p. 284f.
33 *Ibid.*

Scripture there is "hay, straw, and stubble," that is, error and untruth. But long ago truthful and honest Bible scholars have proved that when using these expressions, Luther did not refer to the sacred writers setting forth the divine truth in Holy Scripture, but to explanations of the divinely inspired Scriptures.[34]

Again, there is Luther's so-called "too-weak-for-a-thrust" expression, which liberals cite to prove his "free attitude." But this "argument" is dreadfully silly; for Luther merely says that passages such as Gal. 4:11 are less convincing in a controversy with Jews than are plain passages which teach the doctrine of salvation by grace through faith in Christ, in so many clear words.[35]

To those liberals who wish to prove Luther's "free attitude" from his distinction between *homologumena* and *antilegomena,* Dr. Pieper replies that while Luther did observe this ancient distinction of the Church, he accepted and defended as divinely inspired, inerrant, and authoritative every canonical book in the Bible, both in the Old and the New Testament.[36] Dr. C. F. H. Henry ably supports this when he writes: "Whatever Luther's questions may have been about the canonicity of certain books . . . he had no question whatever about the authority and inerrancy of the books viewed as canonical."[37]

A major argument of modern liberals for Luther's "free attitude" is his emphasis on what in Scripture "urges Christ," or "deals with Christ." From this it is argued that Luther assumed "a canon within the canon." This emphasis is indeed found in Luther's writings, but it is not to deny the verbal and plenary inspiration of the Bible, but to stress the gospel of God's grace in Christ as the essential message of the Scriptures, since that very joyous news was obscured, if not entirely taken away from the people by the antichristian papacy.

Regarding the two well-known passages of Luther, which, as liberals tell us, prove Luther's "free attitude toward the Bible" beyond all doubt, namely: "Whatever does not teach Christ, is not apostolical, even though St. Peter and St. Paul should teach

---

34 Pieper, *op. cit.,* p. 287ff.
35 *Ibid.,* p. 290f. Writing in Latin, Luther says: *In acie minus valet,* that is, it is less efficient in battle; this in its German translation reads *zum Stich zu schwach,* or too weak for a thrust.
36 *Ibid.,* p. 291f.
37 *Op. cit.,* Appendix, Note B, p. 251.

it; again, whatever teaches Christ would be apostolical, even if Judas, Annas, Pilate, and Herod did teach it";[38] and: "If our adversaries urge Scripture, we urge Christ against Scripture,"[39] Dr. Pieper shows that in the first case Luther speaks hypothetically to point out the importance of Christ in Scripture, while in the second he argues against the Roman Catholic perversion of Scripture, e. g., the misinterpretation and misuse of James 2:20-26 by papists, and for the Gospel of salvation by grace through faith in Christ.[40]

In closing his rebuke of modern liberals, who shamefully pervert historical facts, misquote Luther, misrepresent his statements, refuse to read and examine Luther's writings honestly and conscientiously, but quote gleefully and uncritically what liberal purveyors of untruth have falsely written before them, in order to make Luther a champion of their own teaching, Dr. Pieper quotes as an example Kahnis, who in his *Dogmatics* asserts Luther's liberal view of the Bible and then, having quoted a number of Luther's statements, says: "We are not verifying these statements . . . , but for verification direct the reader to the compilations mentioned."[41] And such procedure liberals call scholarship!

As Dr. F. Pieper taught Christian doctrine in the Lutheran Church — Missouri Synod — for more than half a century, so Dr. M. Reu was the outstanding professor of Dogmatics in the American Lutheran Church; and as Dr. Pieper in his *Christian Dogmatics,* so Dr. Reu in his *Luther and the Scriptures* defends the Wittenberg Reformer's Biblical doctrine of inspiration against the misinterpretations, by which moderns try to make it appear that Luther on this point was a theological liberal. In his excellent monograph Dr. Reu champions the following theses, namely, that Scripture was the sole authority of Luther; that Luther's preface to the Epistle of James does not prove a different attitude; that Scripture remained Luther's sole authority of the Christian faith till the end of his life; that Luther never admitted any error in Scripture; that Luther considered even those parts of the Bible that do not concern our salvation as inerrant; that Luther ascribed this absolute inerrancy to the

---

38 St. L. XIV: 129; Pieper, p. 293.
39 St. L. XIX: 1441.
40 Pieper, *op. cit.,* p. 293f.
41 *Ibid.,* p. 296f.

original drafts of the Bible; and that Luther did not teach a mechanical theory of inspiration. Luther indeed believed in verbal and plenary inspiration, but not in a mechanical dictation theory.

There is one point, however, in Reu's excellent treatise that might receive clarification. He declares that not Luther, but the later dogmaticians were on the road to a mechanical, or dictation inspiration. In justification of the much maligned later Lutheran dogmaticians, however, it must be said that they too taught that the sacred writers wrote "cheerfully," "willingly," and "intelligently" and so disclaimed a "mechanical" or "dictation theory" of inspiration.[42] Dr. Reu, however, is right when, in explanation of the fact that neither Luther nor the Lutheran Confessions developed a dogma of inspiration, he writes: "The Bible is the Word of God. That was apparently considered sufficient information for the common people."[43] This was indeed sufficient since the doctrine of Biblical inspiration was not in controversy; and so it is sufficient today if theologians would only believe and teach what these words declare.

As we close this first part of our treatise, we wish to call attention to Dr. H. Echternach's essay on *The Lutheran Doctrine of the Autopistia of Holy Scripture,* which he read at a Free Conference of Lutheran theologians at Berlin-Spandau in 1951 and which appeared since in an English translation by the writer in the *Concordia Theological Monthly.*[44] Dr. Echternach approaches the doctrine of Biblical inspiration in a novel and arresting way, and his essay is a valuable contribution to the defense of the conservative Christian view of inspiration. In it he writes:

> The infallibility of Scripture was the consensus of the Church, irrespective of denominational lines, until long after 1700 A.D.[45]

42 Quenstedt (1617-1685), for example, who usually is looked upon as an extreme example of ossified Lutheran dogmatism and for his nice classification of Lutheran doctrine has received the sobriquet "bookkeeper of Lutheran orthodoxy," emphatically asserts that the sacred writers did not write in a trance as the ancient soothsayers, but wrote "cheerfully," "willingly," "intelligently," thus openly rejecting the idea of a mechanical inspiration.

43 Reu, *op. cit.,* p. 131.

44 April, 1952, pp. 241ff.

45 *Ibid.,* p. 260.

> Lutheran theology, however, refused to surrender its
> doctrine of inspiration also for another reason. It was
> aware of the heinousness of false doctrine, something the
> moderns have lost. . . . The 17th century still knew
> something of "being constrained by truth" and of the
> moral implications of religious knowledge. It therefore rec-
> ognized that both in the secular and the ecclesiastical
> realm every error is blasphemy and soul-murder.[46]

What Dr. Echternach here writes is valid; for from Luther's
day to the present time Lutheran orthodoxy has adhered to the
Biblical doctrine of verbal and plenary inspiration despite all
attacks of liberals and destructive higher critics. When the
Formula of Concord laid down the rule: "We receive and embrace with all our heart the Prophetic and Apostolic Scriptures
of the Old and the New Testament as the pure, clear fountain
of Israel, which is the only true standard by which all teachers
and doctrines are to be judged,"[47] it only re-affirmed what
Luther taught concerning the verbal and plenary inspiration of
the Bible under his great slogan *Sola Scriptura,* that is, Scripture
alone shall be the source and norm of the Christian faith
and life.

II. LUTHER'S TREATMENT OF THE BIBLE

We shall concern ourselves in this part of our treatise not
with such minor considerations as Luther's view of the
homologumena and *antilegomena,* which he asserted against the
Roman Catholic tendency to ignore ancient church decisions
and to add to the canonical books of Scripture the Apocrypha
and tradition, but with what Luther taught regarding the
attributes of Holy Scripture and points deserving emphasis in
connection with these.

The authority of the Bible. Luther's confession at Worms:
"Here I stand!" meant his absolute disavowal of the Roman
tradition and his loyal adherence to Scripture as the sole authority in religion. Dr. Reu interprets it to mean: "On Scripture
I stand."[48] Nor was this a new doctrine for Luther. As Seeberg
shows, he had learned already from his Erfurt professor,
Trutvetter, that "only to the canonical writings do we owe faith,
to all others judgment" and that all doctrines must be proved

46 *Ibid.,* p. 265.
47 *Conc. Trigl.,* p. 851.
48 *Op. cit.,* p. 36.

from passages of Scripture.[49] It is from the viewpoint of this normative authority of Holy Scripture as the only rule of faith that Luther could write:

> Therefore we let bishops and church councils decide and establish what ever they desire; wherever we have on our side the Word of God, we shall decide and not they, whether it is right or wrong, and they should yield to us and obey our word.[50]

So also Luther writes in the Smalcald Articles from the viewpoint of the divine authority of Scripture: "It will not do to frame articles of faith from the works and words of the holy fathers. . . . We have another rule, namely, that the Word of God shall establish articles of faith, and no one else, not even an angel."[51] From the viewpoint of the normative authority of Scripture Luther states that a single Scripture passage renders the whole world too small for him, that is, a single Scripture passage forbids him to let his thoughts and speculations soar beyond and outside Scripture. For Luther it was axiomatic that whenever Scripture had spoken, the matter was decided.[52] For proof of this we might quote many clear and unmistakable passages from his writings.

Already in his *Lectures on the Psalms* (1513-1515),[53] Luther says: "The Scriptures are divine; in them God speaks and they are His Word."[54] In the *Lectures on the Psalms,* as Dr. Reu shows, he "regards the expressions 'God speaks,' and 'Scripture speaks' as convertible."[55] The same may be said of Luther's *Lectures on Romans* (1515-1516), which teem with statements to that effect. In Luther's famous polemic *Concerning the Babylonian Captivity of the Church,* which appeared in 1520, he declares decisively that the Church must submit to Scripture, and not vice versa. He writes:

49 *Mit Gespruchen der Schrift,* Seeberg, 83.
50 Seeberg, 426.
51 *Conc. Trigl.,* p. 467.
52 *Scriptura locuta, res decisa est.*
53 Luther was created Doctor of Sacred Scriptures on Oct. 19, 1512, and took over the Lectura in Biblia, that is, the prescribed course in Biblical exegesis, which obliged him to expound Scripture. Apparently Luther immediately prepared his lecture notes on the Psalms and began his lectures on them in the spring of 1513.
54 W III, 41, 6; 451, 26; Reu, *op. cit.,* pp. 17 and 137.
55 Reu, *loc. cit.*

The Church has no power to establish new divine means of grace, as some foolishly say that everything that the Church ordains is of no lesser authority than that which is ordained by God, since she is guided by the Holy Spirit. For the Church comes into being through the Word of promise [the Gospel] by faith. . . . God's Word stands incomparably high above the Church. About this Word it, as a creature, cannot resolve, order, or execute, but can only be resolved, ordered, and executed.[56]

On April 18, 1521, Luther gave his famous reply at Worms:

Unless I am convinced by testimony from Scripture or evident reasons[57] — for I believe neither the Pope nor the councils alone, since it is established that they have often erred and contradicted themselves — I am conquered by the writings [i. e., passages from Scripture] cited by me, and my conscience is captive to the Word of God. Therefore I will not and cannot recant anything since it is neither safe nor honest to do anything against conscience.

Dr. Reu remarks that this heroic confession concerning the Scriptures before the ecclesiastical and secular powers of his day once for all established the Sola Scriptura, that is, the principle that Scripture should be the only authority in theology.[58]

Against the objection that Luther's confession shows that at this time he still accepted also reason and conscience as normative of his faith, Dr. Reu rightly argues that to Luther at Worms "conscience" meant "conscience bound by God's Word," and "reason" the "logically correct deductions" from clear Scripture passages.[59] This explanation is correct, for Luther already in his early fight against Aristotle and his place in theology, had ruled out human reason as an authority in matters of faith. Seeberg regards Luther's words as a challenge to his opponents to prove his teachings either as unscriptural or as illogical deductions from Scripture.[60] In other words, for his evangelical teachings Luther claimed, positively, agreement with Scripture; negatively, agreement with logic in deducing truths from Scripture.

It is needless to prove that by "conscience" Luther meant his conscience as bound by clear Scripture passages. For Luther to

56 *Ibid.*, p. 27. W 6, 561.
57 *Convictus testimoniis Scripturae aut ratione evidente.*
58 Reu, *op. cit.*, pp. 29 and 145.
59 *Ibid.*, pp. 28ff.
60 Seeberg, *op. cit.*, 413ff.

confess the full evangelical truth at Worms was a matter of conscience, since, as he himself says, he was "captive to the Word of God." Neither reason nor conscience per se, but solely the canonical books of Scripture determined for Luther what he should teach and confess, since God's Word was to him the supreme, indeed, the only authority in religion.

The Efficacy of the Bible. To Luther, however, the canonical Scriptures were not only the normative authority of faith and life, but also the causative authority, that is, the living, powerful divine Word which engenders faith and works, and in the regenerate true sanctification. In other words, Luther regarded the divine Word of Scripture as the efficacious means of grace, by which the Holy Spirit works faith in men and keeps them in the true faith to the end. In many respects this causative authority of the Bible is central in Luther's theological thought and reformatory work. Against his Romanist and enthusiastic opponents he consistently defends the divine Word as both the normative and the causative authority of the Christian faith and life.

For Luther to emphasize the causative authority, or the efficacy, of the divine Word was only natural since here was a point where he found himself at variance with both Roman Catholic and Protestant theologians. But his emphasis on the efficacy, or power, of the divine Word was not merely a matter of polemics. At this point, too, Luther's conscience was "captive to the divine Word," and his doctrine of the efficacy of the divine Word was based on such passages as Rom. 10:17: "Faith cometh by hearing, and hearing by the Word of God"; John 6:63: "The words that I speak unto you, they are spirit and they are life"; Rom. 1:16: "The gospel is the power of God unto salvation"; and many others. This does not mean that Luther ascribed to the divine Word a magical power, but, since the divine Word is the means by which the Holy Ghost operates, it is efficacious because of that very divine operation. Luther, of course, also realized the problem of "Why some, and not others?"[61] But he never tried to solve the problem since here, as in many other articles of faith, he was confronted by a mystery, the comprehension of which must be left to the perfect understanding of heaven (Rom. 11:33-36; 1 Cor. 13:9-12). Nor

61 *Cur alii, alii non? Cur alii prae aliis?*

did he develop or formulate the doctrine of the efficacy of the divine Word into a dogma as this was done later by the Lutheran dogmaticians. Nevertheless, there is nothing that the later Lutheran dogmaticians have taught regarding the Word and Sacraments as means of grace which Luther did not teach clearly and fully before them. The later Lutheran dogmaticians merely systematized what Luther set forth on this point.

Luther's "Back to the divine Word!" therefore did not mean a return to the divine Word as to a mere divine legal codex, but a turning to the living, powerful, divine means by which the Holy Spirit performs His saving work in men. Seeberg puts this doctrine in the following words: "The Word, which interprets itself is [according to Luther] the sole authority of the Christian Church; but it becomes such authority [to believers], because the testimony of the Holy Spirit makes us sure inwardly of the truth of its teachings."[62] That means that the divine Word is both the objective divine truth and that it makes us subjectively sure of the objective divine truth through faith wrought by the Holy Spirit through the Word. In further explanation of this point Seeberg says: "The right understanding of the Scriptures therefore is wrought in the soul by the same Spirit from whom Scripture came forth." For this he cites Luther's saying: "The Holy Spirit must address us through the Word of God."[63] This does not mean that Luther took a quasi neo-orthodox view of Scripture, nor had Barth a right to quote him in his favor. To Barth the "Word of God" is no more than a subjective spiritual experience; to Luther the Bible is the objective divine truth, which must be accepted as it stands. Luther says: "The content of Scripture is true and certain per se, but we perceive this fact only inasmuch as by its objective operation we experience it subjectively." Again: "Personal [divinely wrought] experience makes me sure of Scripture."[64] Or: "Everyone is certain concerning the Gospel who has the witness of the Holy Spirit within himself that it is the Gospel. He who believes is made certain; he who does not believe remains uncertain."[65]

62 Seeberg, *op. cit.*, 411.
63 *Spiritus Sanctus muss uns ansprechen Verbo Dei.* W 29, 580. Seeberg, *op. cit.*, 411.
64 Luther: *Die selb experientia macht mir die Schrift gewiss.* Seeberg, *op. cit.*, 418.
65 W 30. 2, 688. Seeberg, *op. cit.*, 418.

Against enthusiasm or spiritualism, that is, the separation of the operation of the Holy Spirit from the Word, or the immediate operation of the Holy Ghost in the hearts of men without the divine Word, Luther maintained that the Holy Spirit operates savingly in men only through the divine Word. He writes:

> Since God has now permitted His holy Gospel to go forth, He deals with us in two ways: first, outwardly, and second, inwardly. Outwardly He deals with us through the oral Word [oral, that is, the proclaimed Word, which Luther emphasized since the Roman Catholic Church had practically ceased preaching the gospel], or the Gospel and through visible signs, as Baptism and the Lord's Supper. Inwardly He deals with us through the Holy Spirit and faith . . . but always in such a way and in this order that the outward means must precede the inward means, which come afterwards through the outward means. So, then, God has willed that He will not give to anyone the inward gifts [of the Spirit and faith] except through the outward means.[66]

Seeberg rightly interprets Luther's doctrine of the causative authority, or efficacy, of Scripture thus:

> The indissoluble connection of Word and Spirit proves itself also by this that the Spirit grants to anyone nothing else and nothing more than that which the Word, heard by him, says. He goes no farther than the Word goes. The Holy Spirit therefore does not enlarge the area of revelation, but puts into the hearts of men only what the words declare.[67]

This doctrine Luther asserted time and again in his popular Confessions as, for example, in his explanation of the Third Article of the Apostles' Creed, where he writes:

> I believe that I cannot by my own reason or strength believe in Jesus Christ, my Lord, or come to Him; but the Holy Ghost has called me by the Gospel, enlightened me with His gifts [faith, spiritual understanding, regeneration, etc.], sanctified and kept me in the true faith.

In the Smalcald Articles he writes:

> And in these things which concern the spoken, outward Word, we must firmly hold that God grants His Spirit of

---

66 W 18, 136; 33, 189f.; 45, 522. Seeberg, *op. cit.*, 381f.
67 Seeberg, *op. cit.*, 383.

grace to no one except through or with the preceding outward Word.

Again:

> Therefore, we ought and must constantly maintain this truth that God does not desire to deal with us otherwise than through the spoken Word and the Sacraments. It is the devil himself whatsoever men extol as spirit (divine, spiritual truth) without the Word and Sacraments.[68]

Luther therefore taught both the normative and the causative authority of the divine Word. To him the divine Word, or Holy Scripture, was the living voice of God, "God speaking to men," threatening the impenitent sinner by the law, and consoling terrified consciences by the gospel; outside this divine Word there is no saving faith and no salvation.

The perspicuity of the Bible. In his polemics against Romanism and enthusiasm Luther stoutly maintained and defended the perspicuity or clarity of Scripture. Although he left no systematically formulated dogma on this point, nevertheless, whatever formulation on this doctrine took place in later orthodox Lutheran dogmatics, had its roots in Luther's teaching on this point. It is true, Luther admitted that Scripture is not clear everywhere, especially not in all its historical and prophetic parts; yet to Luther the Bible was most clear with respect to all doctrines necessary for salvation. Therefore less clear matters must be interpreted in the light of the lucid; and, above all, Scripture must be at all times its own interpreter.[69] Again, for the clear understanding of the Bible there must be kept in mind the Scriptural distinction between the law and the gospel, in order that divine wrath and divine grace, repentance and remission of sins might be savingly proclaimed to men; for men must know both the divine message of God's fierce wrath over sin and the divine message of His exceeding grace in Christ Jesus. In other words, there must be proclaimed to men first the total corruption of natural man through Adam's fall, in order that they might accept by faith, wrought by the Holy Ghost, salvation by grace alone through faith in Christ's vicarious satisfaction.

---

68 Part III, Art. VIII; No. 3 and 10. *Conc. Trigl.,* p. 497. Cf. for the "Third Article," *Conc. Trigl.,* p. 545. Cf. for Luther's emphasis on the Means of Grace his *De Servo Arbitrio.*
69 *Scriptura Scriptura interpretatur. Scriptura sua luce radiat.*

Concerning the clarity of Scripture, Luther, in his exposition of Psa. 37, comments very aptly:

> If anyone of them [the papists] should trouble you and say: "You must have the interpretation of the Fathers since Scripture is obscure," then reply: "It is not true! There is no clearer book upon earth than the Holy Bible, which in comparison to all other books is like the sun in its relation to all other lights." They say such things only because they want to lead us away from Scripture and elevate themselves to the place of masters over us, in order that we might believe their sermons based upon their own dreams. . . . It is indeed true, some passages in Scripture are obscure, but in these you find nothing but what is found elsewhere in clear and plain passages. . . . Do not permit yourselves to be led out of and away from Scripture, no matter how hard they [the papists] may try; for if you get away from Scripture, you are lost; then they will mislead you as they please. But if you stay in the Bible, you have won the victory. . . . Be absolutely certain that there is nothing else than the same clear sun behind it. So if you find an obscure passage in Scripture, do not be alarmed, for certainly the same truth is set forth in it which in another place is taught plainly. If you cannot understand the obscure, then adhere to the clear.[70]

A comparison of Luther's expressions on the perspicuity of Scripture shows that he speaks of the clarity of the Bible in a threefold way, namely, its grammatical clarity, its spiritual clarity, and its essential clarity. The first means that the matters which Scripture treats are set forth in words and expressions so very clear that even an unbeliever or atheist can understand grammatically what they say. Thus even an intelligent Mohammedan can understand grammatically the gospel message of John 3:16. The spiritual clarity of Scripture flows from faith in Christ; in other words, the Bible is spiritually clear only to those who believe in Christ as their Savior. Luther writes: "Take Christ out of the Bible, and what more then will you find in it?"[71] The unbelieving Mohammedan thus cannot understand John 3:16 savingly, because he does not believe in Christ. To him the whole gospel remains a stumblingblock and foolishness, until through the Holy Spirit his eyes are opened to

70 St. L. V: 334ff. Cf. Mueller, *Christian Dogmatics*, p. 139f.
71 St. L. XVIII: 1681ff.

behold the wonders of God's love in His precious gospel. The essential perspicuity of Scripture refers to the understanding of the mysteries of the faith, of which St. Paul speaks in 1 Cor. 13:9-12. The Bible thus is grammatically clear to all men of sound mind; it is spiritually clear to all who believe in Christ; it is essentially clear to the saints in heaven, who see God face to face.

Luther's insistence on the reading of the Bible by laymen was based on his doctrine of Scripture's perspicuity; he translated it into the language of the people just because he was convinced that the Bible is God's clear book for all men.

The sufficiency of the Bible. From the beginning of the Reformation to the end of his reformatory work Luther with great vigor taught the sufficiency, or perfection of the Bible. Against both Romanists and enthusiasts he defended the truth that the Bible is the only source and norm of faith and life, just because it is sufficient for salvation. Luther, of course, readily admitted that the Bible does not contain all things, secular and spiritual, which men might want to know. But it was his first and foremost principle of theology that the Bible teaches everything necessary for salvation. He therefore rejected all "supplementation" of Scripture, either through tradition, or papal decretals, or new revelations, such as the enthusiasts boasted, or even deductions of reason from philosophy or science. Rome had made the Bible a restricted norm, that is, one dependent on the interpretation of the Church. Luther exalted the Bible as the absolute norm, not dependent on anyone or anything outside the Holy Spirit who gave it to men by divine interpretation and who Himself interprets it. For Luther "private judgment" meant that the Christian must let Scripture interpret itself.

What Luther says on this point is worth hearing even today. He writes: "In teaching Christian doctrine we must not declare anything which Holy Scripture does not teach."[72] Again: "All Christian articles [of faith] must be of such a nature that they are not only certain to the Christians themselves, but also are so confirmed by manifest and clear Scripture passages that they can stop the mouths of all [adversaries], so that they can say nothing against them."[73] Or: "The apostles proved all their

72 St. L. XIX: 593.
73 St. L. XVIII: 1747.

teachings from Scripture. So we too must exercise ourselves in it that it is to us the norm of all things."[74]

These quotations from Luther show that he regarded the Bible as the divinely inspired, infallible Word of God, which is authoritative, demanding faith and obedience; efficacious, working faith and salvation in men; and clear and sufficient in all doctrines necessary for salvation. This point becomes clear, especially in his interpretation of Scripture to establish his specific Reformation doctrines.

A Note on Luther's Interpretation of the Bible

To understand Luther's fundamental principle in interpreting and applying Holy Scripture, the reader must bear in mind two important facts. The first is that Luther had come to the saving knowledge of the gospel the hard way. He obtained true and abiding consolation from God's message of salvation in Christ Jesus only after a long and difficult struggle for assurance of personal salvation. There was nothing morbid about this great soul wrestling; it was the natural result (found also in others at that time) of an awakened conscience that left him trembling at God's wrath and punishment in a church in which there was no longer any pure gospel message of free and full pardon in Christ. The question that troubled Luther, was, as he himself says: "How can I find an appeased God?"[75] The consoling and quickening reply came to him when the Holy Spirit through the divine Word enabled him rightly to understand Rom. 1:16, 17, and, in particular, the "righteousness of God from faith to faith," as the precious imputed righteousness of Christ which the believer secures for himself by grace through faith. This right understanding of the gospel message changed Luther's entire life and work. Born again by faith in Christ, Luther perceived everywhere in Scripture God's matchless grace and ineffable love in Christ. God, who, before Luther's conversion, had meant to him only terror, now meant to him nothing but saving, redeeming, gracious love. The message which he now found in the Bible, as its central theme, was: God is love and Scripture is His book of love. This conception of God as pure Love left no place for any legalism; his whole concept and interpretation became evangelical; it made him primarily a

---

74 St. L. IX: 915.
75 *Quomodo inveniam Deum placatum?* Seeberg, *op. cit.*, 49.

gospel messenger who had passed out of death into life to preach eternal life to men.

The second point which the reader must bear in mind in this connection is Luther's childlike, reverent, devout conviction that the Word of his loving Father in Christ must be taken seriously, so that it must always be accepted and expounded, "as the words declare." There must not be any rationalizing of the precious teachings of the dear Father in heaven addressed to His children on earth in need of forgiveness. Man's conceited reason must be silent where God speaks in His saving grace, whether one feels it or not, whether one understands it or not. What God says is always true, always saving, always to be taken as the words read; for God is love and what He speaks in love is always true, always saving. "A little word of God makes the whole world too narrow for me!" He might well have said, "It fences me in; it bids me obey and worship and give thanks." To Luther the gospel was a precious gift of love, which he must obediently receive and gratefully pass on to others, and also for which he must live or die.

Chapter IV

CALVIN AND THE HOLY SCRIPTURES

By Kenneth S. Kantzer

Down through the centuries, Calvin has become known as the Doctor of Predestination. Whatever element of truth may adhere to this judgment of history, it is certain that John Calvin would have been the first to repudiate the title. If he had been consulted, he would unequivocally have pronounced in favor of a very different degree, Doctor of Sacred Scripture.[1]

No man ever strove more zealously to demonstrate by the labors of his life exactly where lay the focal point of his thought and energy. His voluminous commentaries on the books of the Bible, his letters, sermons, and articles — all Biblical "tracts for the times" — and his *magnum opus, The Institutes of the Christian Religion* spread through fifty-nine huge Latin tomes.[2]

In the introduction to his famous *Institutes,* he avowed that his purpose in writing this summary of doctrine was "to prepare and train students of theology for the study of the Sacred Volume" by providing them with "the sum of what God has been pleased to teach us in His Word." The "system" of theology which he erected is proved from the Scriptures and is

---

1 Both Ernst Troeltsch and R. Seeberg find the key to Calvin's theology in his doctrine of predestination or providential control of all things. Doumerge and Otto Ritschl prefer to consider the Sovereignty of God as the foundation upon which Calvin built his system of thought. See Peter Barth, "Fünfundzwanzig Jahre Calvinforschung 1909-1934," *Theologische Rundschau,* August, 1934, pp. 246-67 and T. H. Parker, "A Bibliography and Survey of British Study of Calvin, 1900 to 1940," *Evangelical Quarterly,* XVIII, 1946, pp. 123-31. Both Barth and Parker defend the view set forth above.

2 John Calvin, *Ioannis Calvini Opera Quae Supersunt Omnia (Corpus Reformatorum).* Edited by Eduardus Cunitz, Eduardus Reuss, Paul Lobstein, *et. al.,* 59 vols (Brunsvigae: C. A. Schweischke et filium, 1863-1900). These Latin works by no means exhaust the productive pen of the Geneva reformer. Besides the various editions of his works and a few additional items published only in French, or in translations, there are yet numerous documents still lying unpublished.

simply "set forth as in a mirror" in all his commentaries on the Bible.[3] Even if the content of Calvin's system of thought were focused upon the doctrine of predestination or of sovereignty, Calvin himself would have argued that this is true, not as an ultimate philosophical position, but only because Scripture teaches that this is so.[4]

In his own estimation, Calvin was first and foremost an interpreter of Scripture. Just before his death, as he looked back across the years, he was able to say to his fellow pastors in Geneva, "Concerning my doctrine, I have taught faithfully, . . . and God has given me the grace to write. I have done this as faithfully as possible and have not corrupted a single passage of Scripture or knowingly twisted it."[5] Calvin regarded his life's work as the faithful exposition and systematization of the teaching of the Bible.

The Need for Special Revelation

Calvin's doctrine of Scripture can be understood only against a background of his doctrine of natural revelation.[6] According

---

3 Preface to the various editions 1536, 1539, 1545, 1559 of John Calvin, *Institutes of the Christian Religion*, Henry Beveridge, trans. (Edinburgh: Calvin Translation Society, 1845), I, 3-33. See also J. G. Lorimer, "The Orthodox Faith Superior to Modern Opinions," *Commentaries on the Book of Joshua*, Henry Beveridge, trans. (Edinburgh: Calvin Translation Society, 1852-1853), p. 441.

4 Hermann Bauke came very close to the truth when he wrote, "Calvin war kein Philosophenschüler, noch weniger Philosoph im deutschen Verstande. Darin irren die Lutheraner und die deutschen Forscher . . . Er hat kein philosophisches System, keine speculativen Prinzipien und geht nicht metaphysischen Problemen nach. Man verbaut sich sofort sein Verständnis, wenn man ihn als Philosophen mit philosophischem Grundprinzip und philosophischen Problemen annimt." *Die Probleme der Theologie Calvins* (Leipzig: J. C. Hinrichs, 1922), p. 37. Whatever qualification of Bauke's position is needed will be made below in the discussion of the relationship which, according to Calvin, exists between faith and reason.

5 *Corpus Reformatorum*, IX, 893b.

6 No exhaustive work which sets forth Calvin's doctrine of Scripture and especially of inspiration has yet appeared either in English-speaking lands or on the continent. William Young adds ("The Inspiration of Scripture in Reformation and in Barthian Theology," *The Westminster Theological Journal*, Nov. 1945, pp. 141ff.), "A comprehensive study of Calvin's position referring to all relevant passages in the commentaries, homilies, and other works as well as the *Institutes*, is a great *desideratum* of reformed theology."

to the thought of Calvin, man's knowledge of God[7] may be divided into two parts, knowledge of God as creator and knowledge of God as redeemer. The former knowledge is primarily concerned with man as a human being originally created in the divine image. The latter is a knowledge of man as sinner fallen from his original state and righteously condemned by God. The sources for this double knowledge of God are again twofold: the natural revelation and the special or supernatural revelation, the latter of which for all practical purposes may be equated with the written Scriptures.[8]

By His revelation in nature God presents to man evidence altogether adequate to establish both the existence of a divine being and also the essential attributes of the God of the Bible, including His mercy and goodness. These evidences are so overwhelmingly conclusive that no rational mind can fail to be convinced.[9]

7 "Knowledge of God" is defined as "that by which we not only see that there is some God, but also apprehend what is for our interest and conducive to his glory, what in short it is fitting to know concerning him," *Institutes*, I, 51. Calvin further defines the phrase by insisting that knowledge of God rightly so-called must be *full* and *complete* (John Calvin, *Commentary on the Book of the Prophet Isaiah*, William Pringle, trans. [Edinburgh: Calvin Translation Society, 1850-1853], IV, 98; John Calvin, *Commentaries on the Epistle of Paul the Apostle to the Hebrews*, John Owen, trans. and ed. [Edinburgh: Calvin Translation Society, 1853], p. 264.), *certain* (John Calvin, *Commentaries on the Catholic Epistles*, John Owen, trans. and ed. [Edinburgh: Calvin Translation Society, 1855], p. 137; *Institutes*, I, 85; II, 104), *deeply rooted and permanent* (John Calvin, *Commentary on the Book of Psalms*, James Anderson, trans. [Edinburgh: Calvin Translation Society, 1856-1859], III, 349-50; *Hebrews*, pp. 138, 264, 265), *pure and undistorted* (*Institutes*, I, 161; John Calvin, *Commentaries on the Book of the Prophet Daniel*, Thomas Meyers, trans. [Edinburgh: Calvin Translation Society, 1852-1853], I, 378; *Psalms*, II, 232), and includes *acquaintance* as well as *information* (*Institutes*, I, 51, 74, 139; John Calvin, *Commentaries on the Four Last Books of Moses, Arranged in the Form of a Harmony* [hereafter called *Pentateuch*], William Bingham trans. [Edinburgh: Calvin Translation Society, 1852-1855], I, 365; John Calvin, *Commentaries on the Twelve Minor Prophets*, John Owen trans., [Edinburgh: Calvin Translation Society, 1856-1858], I, 430). Neglect of this definition has prevented most students of Calvin from understanding his views on natural revelation.

8 *Institutes*, I, 51, 84, 85.

9 "Both heaven and earth contain innumerable proofs!" John Calvin, *Institutes of the Christian Religion*, John Allen trans. (Philadelphia: Presbyterian Board of Publications, 1813), I, 58. The order of the universe furnished full "proof of the existence and perfections of God" (*Psalms*, II, 310) and is intended to "serve to bring us unto

Unfortunately for man, his mind does not naturally function in a rational manner when he thinks about God. Because of sin, man deliberately refuses to consider God, or if perchance he does turn his attention Godward, his mind immediately wanders into the most pernicious errors.[10] For man without supernatural illumination, the natural revelation of God to all only serves negatively to leave him without excuse for his ignorance and sin[11] and positively to lead him into servile fear of God and brazen idolatry.[12]

God." John Calvin, *Sermons of Master John Calvin, upon the Book of Job,* Arthur Golding, trans. (London: Lucas Harrison and George Byshop, 1574), p. 159. Lothar Binde ("Die Frage der Gotteserkenntnis bei Calvin dargestellt auf Grund der Institutio Religionis Christianae von 1559" [Heidelberg: Inaug. diss., 1932, p. 11) writes "Könnte der Mensch diese Offenbarung vernehmen, er würde zu voller Erkenntnis Gottes gelangt sein und besässe den Weg zur Seligkeit." In recent years Calvin's teaching regarding a natural theology or a rational case for theism has become the subject of heated theological dispute. See Brunner versus Barth (Emil Brunner and Karl Barth, *Natural Theology,* Comprising "Nature and Grace," by Professor Dr. Emil Brunner and the reply "No!" by Dr. Karl Barth, Peter Fraenkel, trans. [London: The Centenary Press, 1946]) and their respective seconds, Günter Gloede (*Theologia Naturalis bei Calvin* [Stuttgart: W. Kohlhammer, 1935]) and Edward A. Dowey (*The Knowledge of God in Calvin's Theology* [New York: Columbia University Press, 1952]) for Brunner, and Peter Barth (*Das Problem der Natürlichen Theologie bei Calvin, Theologische Existenz Heute,* ed. Karl Barth and Ed. Thurneysen [München: Chr. Kaiser, 1935]) for Karl Barth. Barth accuses Brunner of Thomism (*loc. cit.,* pp. 87ff) and Brunner replies that Calvin was still more a Thomist than is he (*loc. cit.,* pp. 27ff.). For a critical evaluation of these various interpretations of Calvin's views on natural revelation see the author's "The Knowledge of God and the Word of God in John Calvin" (Unpublished Ph.D. dissertation, Harvard University, 1950).

10 *Institutes,* I, 59, 315; John Calvin, *Commentary on the Gospel According to John,* William Pringle, trans. (Edinburgh: Calvin Translation Society, 1857), I, 379. *Psalms,* III, 141; *Isaiah,* III, 226; *Minor Prophets,* I, 507-8; *Job,* 477, 567, 646; *et passim.*

11 "The most illiterate and stupid cannot exculpate themselves by the plea of ignorance." *Institutes,* Allen translation I, 58. *Institutes,* II, 355; *et passim.*

12 Peter Barth (*op. cit.,* p. 26) writes, "Dieses wird ihm aber nun nur zu einem Quell des Goetzendienstes und des Aberglaubens." See John Calvin, *Commentaries on the Book of the Prophet Jeremiah and the Lamentations,* John Owen, trans. (Edinburgh: Calvin Translation Society, 1850-1855), II, 10; *Minor Prophets,* III, 40; *Institutes,* I, 79.

By a special illuminating grace of God, it is true, even the unbeliever may to a certain extent evaluate the case for theism.[13] The natural world can even lead the elect *towards* true faith in God.[14] In the case of anyone who already possesses true faith, evidence from nature may serve to confirm the believer's faith in God as creator.[15] Natural revelation alone, however, can never provide a complete system of theology,[16] it can never bring a sinner to salvation or true faith in God as creator or redeemer.[17] It can never be the primary ground for a believer's faith in God as creator (though it may be a supplementary ground).[18]

13 Unregenerate men are enlightened so that they possess many correct ideas about God including his existence (*Isaiah*, III, 397-398; *et passim*), his attributes (*Institutes*, I, 172; and *Psalms*, III, 467; *et passim*), and his will (*John*, I, 33, 38, 112; *Institutes*, I, 429; *et passim*). Though these ideas are correct, the unregenerate do not, according to Calvin, possess true knowledge in the full sense of that word (see above, footnote 7, for Calvin's definition of the knowledge of God).

14 "It is a step whereby we come nearer unto God." John Calvin, *Commentary on the Acts of the Apostles*, Christopher Fetherstone, trans., Henry Beveridge, ed., (Edinburgh: Calvin Translation Society, 1854), II, 134. See also *Psalms*, IV, 470, and *Acts*, I, 140, 141; II, 16. This represents a point of controversy in the interpretation of Calvin's views on natural revelation. Peter Barth flatly denies that in Calvin's teaching natural revelation can in any sense lead man to God (*op. cit.*, pp. 6-26).

15 Etienne Gilson (*Christianity and Philosophy* [New Haven: Yale University Press, 1951], p. 50) maintains that the denial of any validity to reason with respect to the things of God is a mark of "authentic Calvinism." See also Gerrit Hendrik Hospers, *The Reformed Principle of Authority: the Scripture Principle of the Reformation Set Forth in the Light of Our Times* (Grand Rapids: The Reformed Press, 1924), p. 68. Calvin's own view of the confirming power of rational evidences is abundantly clear. They "have a twofold advantage to prepare the mind for faith, and, when it has been formed by the Word, to confirm it still more" (*John*, I, 100, 107). He adds elsewhere: "Then since God manifests himself to us partly by his Word, and partly by his works, he is not satisfied unless in regard to both of these we ascribe to him what is his due, and thus embrace whatever has proceeded from him" (*Institutes*, II, 510).

16 *Psalms*, II, 235; *Institutes*, I, 86; II, 261; *John*, I, 30; John Calvin, *Commentaries on the Epistles to Timothy, Titus, and Philemon*, William Pringle, trans. (Edinburgh: Calvin Translation Society, 1856), p. 305.

17 John Calvin, *Commentary on the Epistle of Paul to the Romans*, Frances Sibson, trans. (Philadelphia: Whethern, 1836), p. 71; *Isaiah*, III, 397; *Daniel*, I, 232, 236; *Institutes*, I, 396.

18 *Psalms*, III, 141-42; IV, 470; *Romans*, pp. 449ff.; *Institutes*, I, 228.

In no sense could God be judged as arbitrary or ungracious were He to abandon sinners to their perverse ignorance of the knowledge of God. Because of His infinite love, however, God is not satisfied merely to leave men without excuse. He comes to the sinner with "another and better help" to "guide him properly to God." This second help, above and beyond the natural revelation, is the Word of God embodied in the written Scriptures, the Bible.[19]

The advantage for sinful men in this new source of revelation is threefold. Scripture serves first to republish the knowledge of God as creator which men ought to have gleaned from natural revelation but which, because of the blindness of sin, they did not secure there. "For as the aged or those whose sight is defective, when any book however fair is set before them, though they perceive that there is something written, are scarcely able to make out two consecutive words but when aided by glasses, begin to read distinctly, so Scripture, gathering together the impressions of deity which till then lay confused in our minds, dissipates the darkness and shows us the true God clearly." Special revelation therefore provides a "surer and more direct means" to the knowledge of God as creator, and in doing so it repeats the content of natural revelation by giving the perfect and divine interpretation of the works of God rather than the sinful and fallible interpretations made by "our depraved intellect."[20]

A second advantage also accrues from the revelation in Scripture. In it we find not only the repetition of what is revealed in nature but additional information about God as creator. The special revelation, therefore, embellishes the natural by telling us of God as triune and of details concerning creation, angels, providence, and man.[21]

A final benefit of special revelation is the knowledge of God as redeemer. It was necessary, held Calvin, "in passing from death unto life that they should know God, not only as Creator

19 *Institutes*, I, 83ff.
20 *Ibid.*, pp. 83, 84, 87.
21 Book One of the *Institutes*, Chapters 9 through 28, deals exclusively with the Scriptural doctrine of God as creator. See also John Calvin, *Letters of John Calvin*, Jules Bonnet, ed., David Constable, trans. (Edinburgh: Thomas Constable and Co., 1855-1857), II, 199.

but as a Redeemer also, and both kinds of knowledge they certainly did obtain from the Word."[22]

In Calvin's thought all such knowledge of God as redeemer must come from special revelation. The necessity of special revelation for knowledge of God as redeemer is *absolute* because Christ is not even revealed in nature. The knowledge of God as creator must also come from Scripture; but in this latter case Scripture is only relatively necessary owing to our sin. Ideally, if man had never fallen into sin, natural revelation would be sufficient to bring men to God. For the sinner, even the specially illuminated sinner, however, natural revelation may only lead towards a true faith in God or it may confirm a true faith primarily grounded in Scripture. It cannot actually lead man unto a true knowledge of God either as creator or redeemer. Only the Bible can do this.

If someone asks why man ought to trust the Scripture when he cannot trust the power of his own sinful reason, Calvin has a ready answer. In the Bible we do not have the word of fallible human beings. We do not even have the testimony of perfect finite beings. The ultimate authority of Scripture, on the contrary, is founded upon its being spoken by God. As the Word of God it can be given the absolute trust due to God Himself, who is truth. "Hence," Calvin argues, "the highest proof" for the authority of Scripture is uniformly taken from the character of Him whose Word it is. The prophets and apostles boast not their own acuteness or any qualities which win credit to speakers nor do they dwell on reasons; but they appeal to the sacred name of God in order that the whole world may be compelled to submission.[23] The faithful ought thus "to embrace the Word of God as they know that they have not to deal with men the credit of whom is doubtful and inconsistent, but with Him who is the true God, who cannot lie, and whose truth is immutable."[24]

The Case for Scripture as Revelation

Immediately after his endeavor to ground the authority of Scripture in its derivation from the omniscient, immutable God, Calvin writes, "The next thing to be considered is, how it

22 *Ibid.*, I, 84. See also *John*, I, 218.
23 *Ibid.*, p. 93.
24 *Minor Prophets*, III, 273.

appears not probable merely, but certain; that the name of God is neither rashly nor cunningly pretended."[25] His solution to this problem constitutes one of the most perplexing and controversial issues in the history of theological literature. Although Calvin nowhere discusses in complete fashion the proofs for the divine authority of Scripture, in the opening chapters of the *Institutes* he sets forth sufficient data to indicate accurately the direction of his thought. He admits frankly that "the subject well deserves to be treated more at length." He defends his cursory survey of the proofs for the divine authority of Scripture by referring to the plan of his work as a whole.[26]

The argumentative defense of the Scripture is easy to construct, Calvin avers. In Chapter 8 of the *Institutes* he briefly outlines his argument, dividing it into four parts. He lists first a number of rather general proofs. He refers to the subject matter of Scripture, which displays admirably the system of divine wisdom contained in it. He turns next to the dignity of the divine content "by which our hearts are still more firmly assured." He touches in passing upon the majesty of Scripture which "makes a deeper impression because of its unpolished simplicity almost bordering on rudeness." He pauses to dwell for a moment upon the "truth-character" or "power of truth" to be found in Scripture. No human writings are "at all capable of affecting us in a similar way." It is "manifest that in the Sacred Volume there is a truth divine, a something which makes it immeasurably superior to all the gifts and graces attainable by man."[27] These internal evidences are manifest to whoever will read the Scriptures. If the skeptics will but turn to the pages of the Bible and read, "willingly or unwillingly, they

25 *Institutes,* I, 93.

26 *Ibid.,* p. 90. In these early chapters of the *Institutes,* Calvin really presents us with an apologetic treatise of no mean proportions. Although it developed gradually through the various editions of his "sum of the Christian philosophy," it soon became standard for theologians in both the Lutheran and Reformed traditions. See Julius Köstlin, "Calvins Institutio nach Form und Inhalt, in Ihrer Geschichtlichen Entwicklung," *Theologische Studien und Kritiken, eine Zeitschrift für das gesamte gebiet der Theologie . . .,* 1868, p. 411.

27 *Institutes,* I (Chapter 8), pp. 98-100. Both the "impression of majesty" and the "power of truth" are qualities of divinity residing directly in the Scriptures. No one, therefore, needs to look for any evidences outside of the Scriptures themselves in order to be convinced that they are the Word of God.

will find a thousand sentences which will burn into their consciences as with a red hot iron."[28]

Not only are there internal evidences available to all who read; but entirely apart from any external supports for its authority, they alone are adequate to establish the divine authorship of the Scriptures. They alone are sufficient to produce an impression of divinity upon the mind of any fair-minded observer. "For," claims Calvin, "the truth is vindicated in opposition to every doubt when, unsupported by foreign aid, it has its sole sufficiency in itself." The Holy Scriptures, therefore, are self-authenticating.[29]

From these internal evidences of its divine authority, Calvin turns next to the special proofs from the Old Testament. He treats of the antiquity of the volume, of its miracles and predictions, and of God's providential care in preserving the books.[30] Turning to the New Testament evidence, he dwells upon the harmony of the Gospel writers, the simplicity of the writings, and the evidence for a supernatural call on the part of the apostles and particularly the apostle Paul.[31] Finally Calvin adduces various proofs from church history. He evaluates cautiously the argument derived from the consent of the Church; he notes universal agreement upon the doctrine of Scripture, an agreement even more remarkable because of the continual divergences from the truth on many other matters;[32] and he remarks finally upon the constancy of the Christian martyrs, whose witness to the invisible power of the Scripture "is no

28 *Ibid.*, p. 108. This effect of Scripture upon the conscience is confused by Pannier with the witness of the Spirit (Jacques Pannier, *Récherches sur la Formation intellectuelle de Calvin*, [Paris: Librairie Alcon, 1931]).

29 *Institutes*, I, 79. Hospers (*op. cit.*, pp. 67-68) misses by a nuance the point of Calvin when he writes: "Holy Scripture is autopistic . . . . We may indeed refer to the characteristics of Scripture, to the majesty of the style, etc.; but these are not the grounds of his faith: they are merely properties and characteristics which in course of time were discovered through believing thought." For Calvin, the majesty, etc., perceived immediately in Scripture rendered it autopistic or self-evidencing apart from external evidences. These internal evidences are completely valid as proofs. They do not, however, represent the primary ground of faith for the elect.

30 *Institutes*, I, 100-107.

31 *Ibid.*, pp. 107-8.

32 Calvin takes no notice of the obvious disagreement between Protestants and Roman Catholics over the apocrypha. His point is that all agree to the divine authority of Scripture.

small proof."[33] There are other reasons, neither "few nor feeble," Calvin concludes, "by which the dignity and majesty of the Scriptures may be not only proved to the pious but also completely vindicated against the cavils of slanderers."[34]

In Calvin's thought miracles represent one of the most imposing evidences for the authority of Scripture. He adduces numerous miracles and predictions from Old and New Testament history in order to prove that the writers of Scripture were true prophets of God.[35] The crowning miracle in his apologetics is the resurrection of Christ. By this miracle as well as by other miracles recorded in the four Gospels, Calvin establishes both the authority of Christ and His true deity. He writes, "And, indeed, he who, after having received these striking proofs, which are to be found in the gospel, does not perceive Christ as God, does not deserve to look even at the sun and the earth, for he is blind amidst the brightness of noonday."[36]

Although he does not discuss it at length in his apologetic section of the *Institutes,* Calvin emphasizes constantly the value of experience in confirming the truth of Scripture. Through the experience of life, even the unregenerate "shall at length really find whose word is firm."[37] For the regenerate, of course, experiential evidences to confirm the Scriptures are of continuous occurrence.[38]

For Calvin, therefore, the validity of the rational arguments to establish the authority of Scripture is beyond question. He summarizes his own convictions:

33 *Ibid.,* pp. 108-9.

34 *Ibid.,* p. 109. Karl Barth writes disparagingly of these "proofs" as of no significance to the reformed "Fathers." See Karl Barth, *The Word of God and the Word of Man,* Douglas Horton, trans. (Boston: Pilgrim Press, 1928), pp. 242ff. At this point, however, Barth ought not to claim Calvin as his father.

35 God will "clearly point out true prophets by miracles." *John,* I, 377. Cf. also *John,* II, 88, 281, 282; *Acts,* 1, 71, 530; II, 286; John Calvin, *Commentary on the Epistle of Paul the Apostle to the Corinthians,* John Pringle, trans. (Edinburgh: Calvin Translation Society, 1858), II, 382, 383, 393; *Catholic Epistles,* p. 383; *Jeremiah,* IV, 540; John Calvin, *Commentaries on the First Twenty Chapters of the Book of the Prophet Ezekiel,* Thomas Myers, trans. (Edinburgh: Calvin Translation Society, 1849-1850), II, 53-59; *et passim.*

36 *John,* II, 282. See also *John* 1, 421; *Acts,* 1, 36, 94, 530; *Romans,* p. 46; *Catholic Epistles,* p. 159; *Corinthians,* I, 12; II, 613; *Institutes,* I, 102ff.; and many other passages.

37 *Jeremiah,* IV, 560.

38 *Isaiah,* IV, 98; III, 277: *Pentateuch,* I, 142; *Jeremiah,* III, 232; IV, 162; *Minor Prophets,* II, 136; *et passim.*

It is true, indeed, that if we choose to proceed in the way of argument, it is easy to establish, by evidence of various kinds, that if there is a God in heaven, the law, the Prophecies, the Gospels, proceeded from Him. Nay, although learned men, and men of the greatest talent, should take the opposite side, summoning and ostentatiously displaying all the powers of their genius in the discussion; if they are not possessed of shameless effrontery, they will be compelled to confess that the Scripture exhibits clear evidence of its being spoken by God, and, consequently, of its containing his heavenly doctrine . . . if we look at it with clear eyes, and unbiased judgment, it will forthwith present itself with a divine majesty which will subdue our presumptuous opposition, and force us to do it homage.[39]

True, were I called to contend with the craftiest despisers of God, I trust, though I am not possessed of the highest ability or eloquence, I should not find it difficult to stop their obstreperous mouths; I could, without much ado, put down the boastings which they mutter in corners, were anything to be gained by refuting their cavils.[40]

Unfortunately for man, all the evidence in the world can fall on his ears without accomplishing its goal. Despite the availability of altogether convincing evidences for the full authority of Scripture, man's sin prevents him from evaluating these evidences as he ought. "Thus our own corruption alone prevents us to receive Christ since he gives us full proof for believing in His power."[41] Jesus gave "striking proofs" of His divinity "but either our stupidity or our malice hinders us from perceiving God in His works and Christ in the works of God."[42]

This is not to say that the evidences for the supernatural authority of Scripture are without value whatsoever. Such evidences frequently lead to a "special faith" which correctly interprets some particular aspect of the divine revelation.[43]

---

39 The following significant words are purposely omitted in this quotation: "Still, however, it is preposterous to attempt, by discussions, to rear up a full faith in Scripture." See below, The Testimony of the Holy Spirit.
40 *Institutes*, I, 93-94.
41 *Catholic Epistles*, p. 260.
42 John Calvin, *Commentary on a Harmony of the Evangelists, Matthew, Mark, and Luke*, William Pringle, trans. (Edinburgh: Calvin Translation Society, 1856-1859), II, 96; cf. also *Harmony*, p. 107; *Jeremiah*, I, 31 and II, 80.
43 *Corinthians*, I, 402, 420; cf. also *Daniel*, I, 237ff.

Many unregenerate men even acknowledge the fact of Christ as
the Son of God and the Scripture as God's Word. This "historical faith," in so far as its content is concerned, cannot be
distinguished from true faith.[44] In preaching the gospel, moreover, both Paul and our Lord, Himself, set us examples to show
us the necessity of presenting these evidences to unbelievers.[45]
In the case of the non-elect, this historical faith or special faith
thus engendered will, of course, never lead to salvation. It will
serve only to bring further condemnation upon those who stub-
bornly refuse to exercise true faith. God, however, will be
justified by leaving the unregenerate still more without excuse
for their lack of faith.[46] In the case of the elect, on the other
hand, the evidences for Christ and His Word serve a twofold
purpose: (1) They "prepare the mind for faith" and thus lead
to true and saving faith. (2) They confirm the true believer in
the certainty of the faith which he already possesses on other
grounds.[47]

One thing only these evidences cannot do. They cannot of
themselves produce the right kind of faith in Scripture. "It is
foolish," Calvin therefore warns, "to attempt to convince the
infidel that the Scripture is the Word of God." All the evidences

---

44 *Institutes,* II, 106-7, 177-78.

45 "Someone, however, will object thus: 'What! Will a man's doctrine,
then, be exempted from all investigation, so soon as he makes it
his boast, that he has Christ as his authority?' . . . every objection
of this nature Paul anticipates, when he says that Christ has wrought
efficaciously in them by his ministry; . . . we see, that he does not
merely boast in words, but proves in reality that Christ speaks in
him, and convinces the Corinthians before requiring them to give
him credit." *Corinthians,* II, 393. See also *Minor Prophets,* III, 65;
Acts, II, 130 and 131; *et passim.*

46 *John,* II, 43; *Acts,* I, 220; *et passim.*

47 For the elect, "Miracles have a two-fold use. They are intended
either to prepare us for faith or to confirm us in faith." *John,* I,
448. Schweizer interprets Calvin in similar fashion. (Alexander
Schweizer, *Die Glaubenslehre der Evangelisch-reformierten Kirche
dargestellt, aus den Quellen Belegt* [Zürich: Orelli, Fussli und
Comp., 1884], I, 185). Warfield (Benjamin B. Warfield, *Calvin and
Calvinism* [New York: Oxford University Press, 1931]) ascribes to
Calvin the view that while these proofs are insufficient of themselves to produce faith, they are the ground of faith once the Holy
Spirit has illuminated the mind of the elect to evaluate them
properly. Calvin indicates rather that they can never be *the* ground
for true faith but only *a* confirming ground. See the discussion
of the witness of the Spirit.

in the world, no matter how ably presented, are insufficient for this task.[48]

The ultimate accomplishment for the eternal blessing of man, therefore, is the same in the case of the second help given to men in special revelation, as it was in the case of the first revelation given in nature. In both instances the evidence is overwhelming. Any fair mind ought to come to the full and certain conviction of the knowledge of God as creator from nature and to the full authority of Scripture and of its doctrine from the supernatural evidences attesting the truth of special revelation. In both the natural and the special revelations, however, despite the full validity of their rational support, man, because of his sin, will not and cannot act upon this evidence and enter into a true knowledge of God.

THE WITNESS OF THE SPIRIT

Calvin finds the key to his defense of the divine authority of Scripture in the testimony of the Holy Spirit. By the rational arguments for theism and for special revelation, man could at best arrive only at a human judgment as to the truth of God. Such a mere *fides humana* is a product of the sinful human intellect and is liable to all the disabilities of its source. To know God rightly man must renounce the sufficiency of his sinful human reason and seek the ultimate ground of his faith in a divine reason, a *fides divina*. He comes to recognize the Scriptures to be the Word of God not merely upon the grounds of his own judgments but primarily upon the grounds of God's perfect wisdom provided for man. This decision of God is available to man in the witness of the Holy Spirit.

> In vain [Calvin argues in the *Institutes*] were the authority of Scripture fortified by argument or supported by the consent of the Church or confirmed by any other helps, if unaccompanied by an assurance higher and stronger than human judgment can give. Till this better foundation has been laid, the authority of Scripture remains in suspense.[49]

---

48 *Institutes*, I, 109. Following the example of Paul and Christ, we are to *present* evidences to the infidel; but we dare not pretend to *convince* the infidel. God does that! The evidences are sufficient so far as their own light is concerned; but so far as our blindness is concerned, they are insufficient. Cf. also *Corpus Reformatorum*, XLIV, 24.

49 *Institutes*, I, 98.

This *fides divina* or the divine alternative to human understanding is, of course, not "natural" to man. Its origin must be traced to the immediate activity of God. From its inception to its conclusion, it is entirely a supernatural work of God.[50]

Because this knowledge is divinely wrought and is not the product of mere human understanding, moreover, it is characterized by all the attributes lacking in any mere *fides humana*. The omniscient God brings by His judgment a full knowledge about Himself to the human mind. He imposes this knowledge upon the mind so that full certainty is obtained. God wills to make this witness of the Spirit deeply rooted, involving the whole nature of man. He chooses, also, to seal it permanently upon the hearts of His elect. All the characteristics which render human faith inevitably inadequate for the spiritual needs of man are, in short, eliminated; and instead, the believer by the grace of God finds himself possessor of a divinely wrought knowledge which provides a full, certain, permanent knowledge, adequate for all the moral and spiritual needs of men.[51] The distinguishing characteristics between a *fides humana* and the *fides divina*, however, do not constitute the latter a proper kind of faith. Rather the distinguishing features of saving faith are only the consequences naturally expected from a faith wrought by God as over against what could be expected from the product of the mind of sinful men.[52]

One of the most intriguing and yet one of the most baffling problems in the study of Calvin's doctrine of Scripture is that of the precise nature of the testimony of the Holy Spirit. The diversity of interpretations upon this point is almost as great as the number of those who have sought to set forth the reformer's

50 The recipients of this *fides divina*, quite naturally in the thought of Calvin, are only the elect. He writes: "God doth illuminate no man with the spirit of faith whom he doth not also regenerate unto newness of life." *Acts*, II, 245. See also *Acts*, pp. 166-67; *Institutes*, I, 96, 116-17; *Hebrews*, pp. 100, 138; *Harmony*, II, 107; *Corinthians*, II, 216-17, *Isaiah*, II, 277.

51 Cf. *Institutes*, I, 44; *et passim*.

52 Note the following passage from the *Institutes*, 1, 94: "For as God alone can properly bear witness to his own words so these words will not obtain full credit in the hearts of men until they are sealed by the inward testimony of the Spirit." Schweizer analyzes Calvin in similar fashion: "Alle andern, nur menschlichen Zeugnisse haben nur untergeordneten Wert, da sie alle zusammen keine absolute Zuversicht, immer nur persuasionem humanam begründet . . ." *op. cit.*, p. 207. Cf. also *Romans*, p. 404; *Corinthians*, I, 110; *John*, II, 42-43; *Institutes*, II, 321; *et passim*.

views. The result of this Babel has been to obscure the doctrine which almost all scholars and, indeed, Calvin himself recognize to be the very key to his defense of his faith.

This testimony, Calvin makes plain, is not to be understood as a further internal revelation of the Spirit intended to bear witness that the external revelation in Scripture, is, as a matter of fact, true. As Pannier and numerous other writers have pointed out, this would merely involve Calvin in a continuous circular argument. If a revelation is needed to validate the revelation in Scripture, then a further revelation again is needed to validate this revelation.[53] Calvin writes unequivocally, "Hence the office of the Spirit promised to us is not to form new and unheard of revelations . . . but to seal on our minds the very doctrine which the gospel recommends."[54]

Many of his interpreters have discovered in Calvin's witness of the Spirit an appeal to the religious consciousness. Lobstein praises Calvin for having introduced a "radical revolution in the domain of dogmatic theology" by his appeal to the human religious consciousness as the final authority in spiritual matters.[55] Closely related to this view of Calvin's thought is that which makes the heart, the seat of human affections, serve as his final court of appeal. The faculty by which man knows is not the intellect which provides a rational judgment but the heart which calls for a decision. "The feeling of the presence of God in the Scripture, the testimony of His Spirit in our hearts, God perceptible to the heart not to the reason, there is the whole faith of Calvin, there is the whole secret of his apologetic."[56]

---

53 Pannier, *op. cit.*, pp. 95ff.
54 *Institutes*, I, 111-12. Cf. also, *John*, II, 101.
55 P. Lobstein, *La connaissance religieuse d'àpres Calvin* (Paris: Lausanne, 1909), pp. 76-79. See also Paul Wernle, *Der Evangelische Glaube nach den Hauptschriften der Reformatoren, III, Calvin* (Tübingen: J. C. B. Mohr, 1919), pp. 179-80.
56 Pannier, *op. cit.*, p. 85. Fritz (Johannes Fritz, *Der Glaubensbegriff bei Calvin und den Modernisten* [Freiburg: Herder, 1913], pp. 13, 18, 81), a severe critic of Calvin, declares: "Calvins Glaubenslehre ist antiintellektualistisch und irrationalistisch; Glauben ist ihm nicht ein festes Fürwahrhalten auf Grund vernünftiger Einsicht in die Bürgschaft für die Göttlichkeit der biblischen Offenbarung, sondern eine reine zuversicht des Herzens." "Der ethischpsychologische Akt, durch den Calvin sich der Autorität der Bibel unterwerfen will, ist ein Gemüts-oder Gefühlsakt, kein Denk-oder Erkenntnisakt." "Der Glaubensbegriff Calvins ist psychologisch unhaltbar, denn er ist rein subjectiv."

In numerous passages, of course, Calvin asserts the importance of the heart to a true faith in Christ or in the Scriptures.[57] Any ultimate appeal to the religious consciousness or to the heart would, however, represent a complete reversal of Calvin's flow of thought. His basic contention is that he is making an appeal not to anything in man, whether that be in man's intellect or feelings or inner consciousness. Rather, Calvin is making his appeal directly to God.

Frequently Calvin has been interpreted as teaching that the witness of the Spirit is a divine act upon the soul which stands as a sign or testimony to the truth of the gospel. The Spirit, hence, produces within the soul of men a new body of evidence which witnesses to the validity of the Christian experience of salvation. By a logical deduction, then, Calvin finds support for the authority of Scripture which bears to him its transforming message.[58] Another suggests that, according to Calvin, the witness partakes of the nature of "an immense postulation" or of a basic presupposition consciously chosen.[59]

---

57 *Institutes*, II, 105, 136-37; *et passim*.

58 See Percy Austin, *Letters to a Fundamentalist* (London: Student Christian Movement Press, 1930), p. 76ff. Austin writes: "Calvin . . . based everything on the reality of spiritual experience, the presence of Christ himself with his people, and the witness of the Spirit in the believing soul." Both Stearns (Lewis F. Stearns, *The Evidences of Christian Experience* [New York: Charles Scribner's Sons, 1890], pp. 200ff.) and DeWitt (John DeWitt, "Testimony of Holy Spirit to the Bible," *Presbyterian Reformed Review*, VI [1895], 80-82) set forth this same idea; but Stearns in particular is careful to distinguish it from Calvin's own view. Doumerge, interestingly enough, cites DeWitt's analysis of the Reformed view and ascribes it to Calvin (Emile Doumerge, *La Pensée religieuse de Calvin*. Vol. IV. *Jean Calvin, les hommes et les choses de son temps* [Lausanne: G. Bridel and cie, 1899-1927], p. 67).

59 See both Hospers, *op. cit.*, p. 49; and Henry Meeter, *Calvinism, An Interpretation of its Basic Ideas* (Grand Rapids: Zondervan, c. 1939), p. 45. Of this interpretation Karl Barth writes: "The astonishing statement that the Bible is his Word has been called an axiom. But it is such only in its logical form. In content its certainly is wholly unlike the self-evidenced certainty of mathematical axioms. It expresses rather the self-evidenced *revelation* which God gives simultaneously to his Biblical witnesses and to those who accept their witness" (Karl Barth, *The Word of God and the Word of Man*, p. 244). This quotation is imbedded in quite an uncalvinistic context, but the passage selected above contains a real insight into the thought of Calvin. See also Klaiber, "Die Lehre der altprotestantischen Dogmatiken von dem testimonium Spiritus Sancti," *Jahrbücher für Deutsche Theologie* (1857), p. 4.

In opposition to all theories which appeal ultimately to a human judgment lie the unequivocal declarations of Calvin himself, that the witness of the Spirit is a divine judgment ensconced within the believer's mind by the immediate activity of the Spirit without the necessity of human testing or human judgment. In the early chapters of the *Institutes* Calvin sets forth his doctrine of the testimony of the Holy Spirit in its clearest and most fully elaborated form. He writes:

> If, then, we would consult most effectually for our consciences, and save them from being driven about in a whirl of uncertainty, from wavering, and even stumbling at the smallest obstacle, our conviction of the truth of Scripture must be derived from a higher source than human conjectures, judgments, or reason; namely, the secret testimony of the Spirit.

> Scripture carrying its own evidence along with it, deigns not to submit to proofs and arguments, but owes the full conviction with which we ought to receive it, to the testimony of the Spirit.[60]

> Enlightened by him, we no longer believe, either on our own judgment or that of others, that the Scriptures are from God; but, in a way superior to human judgment, feel perfectly assured — as much so as if we beheld the divine image visibly impressed on it — that it came to us by the instrumentality of men, from the very mouth of God. We ask not for proofs or probabilities on which to rest our judgments, but we subject our intellect and judgment to it as too transcendent for us to estimate.

> Such, then, is a conviction which asks not for reason; such, a knowledge which accords with the highest reason, namely, knowledge, in which the mind rests more firmly and securely than in any reasons; such, in fine, the conviction which revelation from heaven alone can produce.

> Then only, therefore, does Scripture suffice to give a saving knowledge of God when its certainty is founded on the inward persuasion of the Holy Spirit. Still, the human testimonies which go to confirm it will not be without

---

60 The French adds, "For though in its own majesty it has enough to command reverence, nevertheless, it then begins truly to touch us when it is sealed in our hearts by the Holy Spirit." Cited in *Institutes*, I, 95, f.n. 1.

effect, if they are used in subordination to that chief and highest proof, as secondary helps to our weakness.[61]

The testimony of the Spirit, it is immediately evident, is a work of the Holy Spirit. It is an act of God by which He gives certainty to man. There is no appeal to any part of man whether to intellect, will, or emotions. There is no new evidence provided for man to judge. Rather, there is a divinely originated and energized and a divinely formulated judgment within, though not stemming from, the human intellect.

This testimony, moreover, is an illumination of the mind or an opening up of the mind to see the truth, as well as a fixing of this truth firmly and securely upon the human mind. Warfield, hence, is quite right when he insists that the believer's trust in the authority of Scripture is not thus a blind conviction.[62]

61 *Institutes*, I, 93-110; See also *Institutes*, I, 180-81; *Job*, p. 667; *Harmony*, II, 193: John Calvin, *Commentaries on the Epistles of Paul to the Galatians, and Ephesians*, William Pringle, trans., (Edinburgh: Calvin Translation Society, 1854), p. 207-8; *Letters*, II, 53; *Psalms*, V, 256-57. "Faith will not be satisfied with any human testimonies, but where the inward confirmation of the Spirit has already taken place, it allows them some weight in the historical knowledge as facts. By the historical knowledge I mean that knowledge which we obtain respecting events either by our own observation or by the statements of others" (*Harmony*, I, 6). Not all students of Calvin have grasped accurately this aspect of his thought, but Meeter declares, "After we have faith, these rational arguments to establish the authority of Scripture all seem strong—although they are not the real grounds of our faith" (*op. cit.*, pp. 44ff.). This statement by Meeter reflects correctly the general flow of Calvin's thought. In order to be precisely accurate, however, it ought to read, "the primary ground" instead of "the real grounds."

62 Unfortunately Warfield misconceives the subtle nuances of Calvin's thought, and contends strenuously that this illumination merely enables the human mind to see the validity of the proofs for the authority of Scripture so that by these evidences the intellect is convinced that the Scripture is the Word of God. "It is," he maintains, "through the *indicia* of that divinity that it is brought into its proper confidence in the divinity of Scripture." In treating of the *indicia*, however, Calvin himself distinguishes the *indicia* from the witness. Warfield admits, "He sometimes even appears to speak of them (*i.e.* the *indicia*) rather as if they lay side by side with the testimony of the Spirit than acted along with it as co-factors in the production of the supreme effect. . . . Of the Spirit he does not appear explicitly to speak" (*op. cit.*, pp. 84-90). As a matter of fact Calvin is quite explicit. The part played by the *indicia* is "preparatory" and "confirmatory." The sinner is led towards true faith by consideration of the *indicia*. The saint is confirmed in his true faith by *indicia*. True faith, however, does

It is rather a work of illumination subjectively to enable the sinner to see that which previously he had been unable to see — namely, the objective truth of God. This "seeing" of the truth, however, is not due to the Spirit's enablement of the human mind now for the first time to draw the correct conclusions on the basis of a proper evaluation of the evidence. It is rather the Spirit's working immediately upon the mind and heart of the elect to form within the human soul and to seal upon it His own divine judgment as to the truth and authority of Scripture.[63]

The object to which the Holy Spirit bears witness is presented in various fashion by Calvin. God Himself is frequently indicated to be the object of the Spirit's testimony. Although to a certain extent God may be known by other means, Calvin speaks of the knowledge of God in the full sense as possible only by the illumination of the Holy Spirit. "For the right knowledge of God is a wisdom which far surpasses the comprehension of man's understanding; therefore to attain it no one is able except through the secret revelation of the Spirit."[64]

The person of Christ also becomes an object to which the Spirit testifies. Occasionally Calvin indicates that some particular truth about Christ, such as the resurrection from the dead, is

---

not terminate on these *indicia*. True faith terminates not on any human judgment whatsoever but on the immediate "sight" given by God.

63 In his *Das Gewissheitsproblem,* Karl Heim argues that Calvin's thought underwent a radical change through the years. In his earlier works Calvin set forth the witness as an independent substantiation of the Christian faith. Later, as a result of his disputations with the Anabaptists, Calvin modified his original thesis by identifying the testimony with the *indicia* or impressions of divinity and by subordinating the witness more and more to the written Scripture (Karl Heim, *Das Gewissheitsproblem in der Systematischen Theologie bis zu Schleiermacher* [Leipzig: J. C. Hinrich, 1911]). A careful survey of Calvin's chapters in the apologetic section of the various editions of the *Institutes* and of relevant material in the commentaries and other works will scarcely substantiate the view that his treatment was so confused as Heim would try to make out. Calvin's emphasis upon the *indicia* in his earlier works, even in the preface to his first edition of the *Institutes,* and his unequivocal emphasis upon the primacy of the testimony of the Holy Spirit in the later editions of the *Institutes* provide a consistency of Calvin's thought extending throughout his lifetime as a productive theologian.

64 *Hebrews,* pp. 191-92. Cf. also *Institutes,* I, 80-81; *Acts,* II, 18; *Psalms,* IV, 460.

known by the witness; but more often it is Christ Himself, as a person, who becomes the object of knowledge.[65] Christ as a person, however, is never separated by Calvin from truth about Christ. For him faith in Christ was more than intellectual assent to the truth, but it never was divorced from such assent. Rabaud is quite right when he insists that for Calvin the *doctrine* of Christ is an "essential object of revelation."[66]

Occasionally Calvin indicates that within the Scripture as a whole, there is an inner core which represents pre-eminently the object to which the Spirit testifies. By the Spirit man can know the truth of many doctrines; but the truth of the gospel is primary and all other truths are secondary to it. Referring to the testimony of the Holy Spirit, Calvin writes, "We point to the promise of mercy as its special object."[67]

Not only does the witness of the Spirit enable man to know the truth of the gospel but it also enables him to know with certainty that his own response to the gospel has been satisfactory and that he, in spite of his sin, is accepted with God. The Spirit, in short, witnesses to the sinner the fact of his own forgiveness and adoption into the family of God. "The Holy Spirit," Calvin writes, "becomes the witness of adoption." Only by the testimony of God Himself can man know with certainty that he is a son of God.[68]

---

65 See *Catholic Epistles,* p. 259; also p. 383 (resurrection is the object); *Romans,* p. 86 (resurrection is the object); *Institutes,* II, 105; *et passim.*

66 Edouard Rabaud, *Histoire de la doctrine de l'inspiration DES SAINTES ECRITURES dans les pays de langue Francaise de la Réforme à nos jours* (Paris: Fischbacher, 1833), p. 61. See *Institutes,* II, 978ff,; *et passim.* Emil Brunner, to the contrary, insists that there is no object of revelation, rather "revelation consists in the meeting of two subjects." God himself is the revelation; being at one and the same time the revealer and the revealed. It is a "Someone" not a "something" which really becomes the object of the testimony of the Spirit ("Nature and Grace," *loc. cit.,* pp. 8, 33, 37, *et passim).* Karl Heim expounds Calvin in the same way (Karl Heim, *op. cit.,* p. 98, *et passim).*

67 *Institutes,* II, 130. See also *Institutes,* I, 251-52; II, 102-3; *Corinthians,* II, 200; *et passim.*

68 *Institutes,* II, 105-6. *Romans,* pp. 178-79. Cf. also *Romans,* p. 218; *Galatians and Ephesians,* p. 120; *Corinthians,* II, 216-17. Otto Ritschl distinguishes between the Lutheran and Calvinistic interpretations of the testimony of the Spirit. For the Lutheran this testimony is to the rest of the soul; but for the Calvinist it is to the authority of

In his appeals to the witness of the Spirit, however, Calvin refers most frequently to the Scriptures. By the Spirit's testimony alone sinners are enabled to see that this book has come from God. "Enlightened by him [the Spirit] we no longer believe either on our own judgment or that of others, that the Scriptures are from God; but, in a way superior to human judgment, feel perfectly assured — as much so as if we beheld the divine image visibly impressed on it — that it came to us, by the instrumentality of men, from the very mouth of God." The Spirit thus becomes witness not just to the truth of Scripture, but to its divine origin, to the historical act by which God had dictated His truth to men who served as instruments to record and bear to us the divine message.[69]

Doumerge holds that in Calvin the attestation of the inspiration of the Scripture is indirect. "The direct object . . . of the Holy Spirit is the divinity of the truth offered in Christ." He further explains, "Even the facts of salvation in their character

---

Scripture. Ritschl's interpretation of the Lutheran position is essentially correct, but his understanding of Calvin fails to include the many-sided facets of Calvin's apologetic. For the Swiss reformer the testimony of the Spirit applied both to the objective truth of Scripture and its doctrine but also to the sinner's subjective response to this truth. Cf. Otto Ritschl, *Dogmengeschichte des Protestantismus* (Leipzig: J. C. Hinrichs, 1908), I, 179.

69 *Institutes*, I, 111-12. Dowey (*op. cit.*, p. 124) distinguishes between the witness to the Scriptures as the Word of God and the witness to a pedigree of inspiration. The former he discovers in Calvin, the latter he does not. Calvin, of course, never conceived of such a distinction and claims the immediate testimony of the Spirit for both. The Bible is the Word of God because He long ago spoke it to man through the instrumentality of His prophets. The element of truth in Dowey's interpretation lies in this: man acknowledges that the Bible is and has been the Word of God only when the Spirit now works through it upon the soul of man to establish an acknowledgement of its divine origin in man's heart and mind. Again and again Calvin reflects this aspect of the Spirit's work. "The same Spirit, therefore, who spoke by the mouth of the prophets, must penetrate our hearts in order to convince us that they faithfully delivered the message with which they were divinely entrusted" (*Institutes*, I, 94-95). Cf. also, "The same Spirit, who spoke through Moses and the prophets, now testifies to our hearts, that he has thus employed them as his servants to instruct us" (*Timothy, Titus, and Philemon*, pp. 248-49). Dowey, of course, is quite right when he insists that the witness of the Spirit does not produce true faith upon the basis of a rational judgment as to prophetic authorship or as to any other explanation of its origin which might be considered as proof of the inspiration of Scripture.

as naked facts are not the object of this testimony. Scripture is attested as a divine judgment indirectly in that it is the instrument of the gospel; it is attested directly only as a human judgment."[70]

Calvin, as has been noted, looked upon the gospel as the primary object of the Spirit's witness; but he emphatically asserts that the Spirit also testifies directly and immediately to the divine authority of Scripture. For Calvin the inspiration of the Bible, the doctrine it sets forth, and especially the basic doctrine of the gospel, are all immediately given by a divine judgment. They are all equally and completely known only by the Spirit's direct witness in the soul of man.[71]

Dorner, with his usual insight, catches precisely the spirit of Calvin. "He is far from applying the *testimonium spiritus sancti* only to the form and origin of Scripture, or to Christian truth which makes upon him the impression of divine truth; but certainly the form and subject matter of the Holy Scriptures are taken together by him as if the testimony of the Holy Ghost to the subject-matter and its truth were also forthwith a testimony to the fact of inspiration."[72]

The testimony of the Holy Spirit, to summarize Calvin's teaching on this crucial doctrine, is a divine judgment of the truth and authority of the Holy Scriptures and of its essential message. The Spirit brings this divine judgment to the elect and seals it on their hearts and minds. This witness is not a nebulous awareness of the divine presence nor an unintelligible religious idea. It is neither a blind faith by which man desperately wills to believe what he does not know nor a rationally grounded faith terminating upon objective evidence. For Calvin, the witness of the Spirit conveys an immediate sight or awareness

---

70 Doumerge, *Op. cit.*, p. 70.
71 In some passages Calvin seems almost to declare that the acceptance of the Scriptures as the Word of God is essential to salvation. His thought is not that belief in inspiration is a condition of acceptance with God; but rather that he who has been truly regenerated will certainly recognize the voice of God in the Bible. Cf. *John*, I, 251, 252; *Jeremiah*, I, 280.
72 J. A. Dorner, *History of Protestant Theology*, George Robson and Sophia Taylor, trans., (Edinburgh: T. & T. Clark, 1871), I, 389-90. Calvin writes: "The true conviction which believers have of the Word of God, of their own salvation, and of religion in general does not spring from . . . human and philosophical arguments, but from the sealing of the Spirit" (*Galatians and Ephesians*, p. 208).

of precise propositional truth and at the same time an overt appreciation of and acquaintance with the divine person. Above all it is an act of God upon the whole soul by which man secures all the ultimate benefits of both general and special revelation, of God and His Word, of Christ and His salvation.

THE METHOD AND EXTENT OF INSPIRATION

The most amazing of all controversies regarding Calvin's doctrine of Scripture is centered in his view of the method and extent of inspiration. To Doumerge,[73] Briggs,[74] and Strong,[75] could be added the names of a long list of scholars who have claimed for Calvin a freer view of Scripture than the rigidly orthodox verbal type of inspiration. The evidence from Calvin, however, is so transparent that any endeavor to clarify his position seems almost to be a work of supererogation.

The method of inspiration as outlined by Calvin is a direct dictation by God to the prophet or apostle who authors the Scripture. "The Holy Spirit," declares Calvin, "dictated to the prophets and the apostles" the writings of Scripture so that exactly what He wished was contained in the final production.[76] This dictation did not refer primarily to the divine message received in the mind of the prophet but rather to the written document of which the Scriptures consist.

> God . . . was pleased to commit and consign his word to writing . . . he commanded also the prophecies to be committed to writing, and to be held part of his word. To these at the same time were added historical details, which are also the composition of prophets but dictated by the Holy Spirit. The whole body, therefore, composed of the

---

73 *Op. cit.*, pp. 73ff.

74 Charles Briggs, *The Bible, Church, and Reason* (New York: Scribners, n.d.), p. 24.

75 A. H. Strong, *Systematic Theology* (Philadelphia: The Judson Press, 1907), I, 217. See also the comment of Paul T. Fuhrman, *God-Centered Religion; An Essay Inspired by Some French and Swiss Protestant Writers* (Grand Rapids: Zondervan Publishing House, 1942), p. 85. "Calvin has not written one word that may be invoked in favor of literal inspiration."

76 *Jeremiah*, IV, 229.

Law, the Prophets, the Psalms, and Histories formed the
word of the Lord to his ancient people. . . .[77]

The Spirit of God has thus spoken "by the mouths of the
prophets" and "demands that we shall listen to him in their
writings."[78] In the final analysis, God is the true author of the
books of the Bible.[79]

In the production of the written Word of God, the part
played by the human author is relatively insignificant. He
brings "forth nothing from his own brain," but his highest duty
is faithfully to deliver "what the Lord has commanded" without
adding anything whatsoever of his own. The content of Scripture
does not proceed from the mind of its human writers, but rather
comes directly from the mind of God.[80] Accordingly Calvin
refers to the writers of Scripture as "clerks"[81] and "penmen."[82]
They were "sure and authentic amenuenses of the Holy Spirit;
and, therefore, their writings are to be considered as the oracles
of God. . . ."[83] In Scripture the Holy Spirit has spoken by means
of His "organs and instruments."[84] They are "mouths" for God
Himself.[85] Calvin stands unequivocally for the view that the
entire body of written Scriptures was dictated by the Spirit of

---

77 *Institutes*, III, 163. Calvin's works abound with references to the
"dictation" of Scripture. See *Daniel*, I, 79; II, 184, 188; *Pentateuch*,
I, xiv; IV, 107; *Psalms*, II, 166; III, 163, 205; John Calvin, *Commentaries on the Epistles of Paul the Apostle to the Philippians,
Colossians, and Thessalonians*, John Pringle, trans. and ed., (Edinburgh: Calvin Translation Society, 1851), p. 23; *Jeremiah*, I, 331;
John, I, 22; *Hebrews*, p. 358; *Catholic Epistles*, pp. xix, 40; and
many other passages.
78 *Galatians and Ephesians*, p. 243.
79 *Minor Prophets*, II, 205, 206. See also, *Pentateuch*, III, 328; *Minor
Prophets*, III, 347; *Genesis*, I, 59; *Institutes*, I, 264 (written Scripture
gives "the meaning of the Holy Spirit"); *Timothy*, II, 248-49 ("God
is . . . the author of it."); *Jeremiah*, I, 34 ("The words were his,
but . . . he [Jeremiah] was not the author of them . . . he only
executed what God had commanded.")
80 *Minor Prophets*, I, 42, 43, 325. See also *Minor Prophets*, pp. 328, 347;
III, 197; *Ezekiel*, II, 8; *Jeremiah*, I, 34, 331; IV, 326, 329. Even the
wit and humor of the Bible is in reality the wit and humor of
the Holy Spirit (*Philippians*, p 87).
81 *Harmony*, I, 127.
82 *Psalms*, III, 205.
83 *Institutes*, III, 166.
84 *Philippians*, p. 87; *Minor Prophets*, III, 197.
85 *Minor Prophets*, III, 347; *Ezekiel*, II, 8; *Jeremiah*, IV, 326; *Genesis*,
I, 59; *et passim*.

God. His teaching is so clear and he reiterates his point so frequently, no other conclusion is possible.[86]

It must be admitted, nevertheless, that this is a very peculiar kind of dictation which Calvin finds in Scripture. He refers to the epistles of Paul as expressing Paul's own judgment as well as the judgment of the Spirit.[87] Peter in writing his letter recorded the "testimony" of his own mind.[88] Calvin expressly distinguishes between the inspiration of Balaam who mechanically produced that which did not come from his own soul and the inspiration of the true prophets. The Biblical writers were never thrown into "ecstasies" nor were they "carried away" by a "heavenly afflatus." Rather "God illuminated their senses before he guided their tongues."[89] Each of the Gospel writers followed his own method of writing and "wrote freely and honestly."[90] God dictated four Gospels so that we might have four different viewpoints.[91] In many cases, the prophets had learned by natural means the facts which they set down in Scripture. In other instances they gleaned their information through tradition or observation.[92] God sharpened the memory of the prophets so that they might recall their past experiences and thus be able to record the Scripture.[93] David and other prophets wrote of their own experiences and in composing their Scriptures had spoken out of the depths of their own hearts.[94] The writers of Scripture used varying styles each according to his own personality and all were used by the Holy Spirit in his dictation of the written Scripture.[95]

86 So Calvin has been interpreted by many writers including Davies and Young (Rupert E. Davies, *The Problem of Authority in the Continental Reformers: A Study in Luther, Zwingli, and Calvin* [London: Epworth Press, 1946], pp. 114ff.; William Young, *op. cit.*, pp. 1-38).

87 *Corinthians*, I, 271.

88 *Catholic Epistles*, p. 363.

89 *Pentateuch*, IV, 204.

90 *Harmony*, I, xxxviii, xxxix, 127, 410.

91 *John*, I, 22.

92 *Genesis*, I, 58; *Harmony*, I, xxxix.

93 *Jeremiah*, IV, 329.

94 *Pentateuch*, IV, 203.

95 *Harmony*, I, 127; *Institutes*, I, 99; *Catholic Epistles*, p. 363; *Hebrews*, p. xxvii.

Rabaud, and others, therefore, have rightly concluded that Calvin never conceived of the inspiration of the prophets in any mechanical fashion.[96]

Some students of Calvin, among them Warfield, have argued that the reformer does not really teach a true dictation theory of inspiration. Rather, so he explains, Calvin means only to imply that the written Scriptures, which the prophets and apostles composed in the full exercise of their human powers of intellect and emotion and will, are just as much the Word of God as though every word had been immediately dictated.[97]

Whether the forcefulness of the reformer's vocabulary can be adequately accounted for by such an interpretation may be open to question; but the broad outlines of Calvin's psychology of inspiration are very transparent. According to him the human authors of Scripture were controlled by God in every detail of what they wrote. The words of Scripture are, therefore, God's divinely chosen words and in this sense are dictated. In ordinary dictation, however, the secretary is active only to recognize and to copy words originating outside of the mind of the secretary. This sort of dictation is by no means consistent with Calvin's view of the method of inspiration. As he interprets the facts, the sacred authors are active with their minds and whole personalities in the selection both of ideas and words. Scripture really originates in the mind of God, who is its ultimate author in the sense that He sovereignly controls the mind and personality of the men He has chosen to write Scripture. By this means, God

96 "Mais l'action de Dieu ne transforme pourtant pas, de l'avis de Calvin, les auteurs sacrés en machines" (*op. cit.*, 56-57). Binde likewise insists that the method of inspiration in Calvin's thought was dictation but not a mechanical dictation. The latter "appears to me definitely not to be the case" (*op. cit.*, p. 20). See also Young (*loc. cit.*, p. 26), "Dictation in Calvin's sense of the term is not mechanical, inasmuch as it does not exclude conscious rational and voluntary human agency."

97 Warfield, *op. cit.*, p. 63-64; see also Dowey, *op. cit.*, pp. 101-3; and Davies, *op. cit.*, pp. 116f. Calvin's rather loose usage of the word "dictate" corroborates the suggestion that he did not conceive of dictation in any mechanical sense. For example, he refers constantly to the dictates of nature. The natural order dictates: *Pentateuch*, III, 18, 193; *Jeremiah*, IV, 318. Human reason dictates: *Ezekiel*, I, 315. Common sense and experience dictate: *Institutes*, I, 60. Natural feelings dictate: *Galatians and Ephesians*, p. 121. On the basis of these passages and of the usage of the word *dictate* in late medieval thought, it becomes evident that Calvin employs the word as the equivalent of produce, affirm, or prescribe.

inspires the writers of Scripture (better breathes out through them as instruments) to speak to man exactly His chosen words which He wills. When, in Calvin's thought, the prophet is referred to as an instrument, he is by no means an instrument which simply passes on words mechanically given to him. Rather, because of God's sovereign control of his being, he is an instrument whose whole personality expresses itself naturally to write exactly the words God wishes to speak. Only in this large and comprehensive sense are the words of Scripture dictated by God.[98]

This double sense of "dictation" is clearly brought out by Calvin's comments regarding Mark and the second Gospel. In other passages he frequently describes the true authors of Scripture as mere "clerks" and "amenuenses"; but writing of Mark's relation to Peter, he says, "It is even believed that he wrote the gospel, as it was dictated to him by Peter, and thus merely performed the office of an amenuensis or clerk." In such a case, of course, Peter would be the real author of the second Gospel. In Calvin's thought, clearly, there is a sense in which the true human author of Scripture was merely an amenuensis to whom God dictated; there is also another sense in which he was by no means a mere amenuensis, and the Scriptures were not written by a method of dictation. In ordinary dictation, the secretary does not handle his subject,[99] plan the work,[100] select the facts,[101] intend to indicate the order of the material,[102] choose,[103] or neglect uninteresting detail.[104] In the dictation of Scriptures, as Calvin understands it, the prophet did all these things.

The extent of inspiration, as taught by Calvin, is necessarily involved in his idea of the method of inspiration.[105] All the words of Scripture have been dictated or produced by God through the instrumentality of the human author of Scripture. Every word is from God. Mark, for example, committed nothing

---

98 Hospers, *op. cit.,* p. 115; Otto Ritschl, *op. cit.,* pp. 59-60.
99 *Harmony,* I, xxxviii.
100 *Genesis,* I, 86.
101 *Pentateuch,* IV, 285; I, 227-28; *Harmony,* II, 429.
102 *Harmony,* I, 85.
103 *Harmony,* I, 133; *Psalms,* II, 276; *Harmony,* I, 216, 258.
104 *Pentateuch,* III, 294; *Harmony,* I, xxxix; II, 433.
105 See Bauke, *op. cit.,* p. 51.

to writing which was not of God.[106] The words of Jeremiah, the human author, are in every detail the words of God.[107] Calvin expressly declares that he never distinguishes the word of God from the words of the prophet Haggai.[108]

In the titles which Calvin gives to Scripture this irrefragable identity between the word of God and the word of the prophet is very plain. He refers continuously to Scripture, as the "sure and infallible record,"[109] as the "unerring standard,"[110] as "the pure Word of God,"[111] and as "the infallible rule of his holy truth."[112]

In all his writings Calvin presents a consistent picture of his views on the extent of inspiration. The suggestion that Calvin set forth in his commentaries a much looser view than he holds in the *Institutes* is utterly without foundation. The merest glance at Calvin's commentaries will demonstrate how seriously the reformer applied his rigid doctrine of verbal inerrancy to his exegesis of Scripture.[113]

---

106 See also *Institutes*, I, xviii, 4: "Our wisdom ought to be nothing else than to embrace in gentle docility, and without any exception, whatever is handed down to us in the Sacred Scriptures." Cf. also *Institutes*, III, xxi, 3: "The Scriptures are the school of the Holy Spirit, in which nothing is omitted which it is necessary and useful to know and nothing is taught except what it is of advantage to know."

107 *Jeremiah*, II, 279; IV, 334.

108 *Minor Prophets*, IV, 341. "For the word of God is not distinguished from the words of the prophet, as though the prophet had added anything of his own."

109 *Job*, p. 744.

110 *Institutes*, I, 149.

111 *Institutes*, III, 166; *Minor Prophets*, II, 177.

112 *Hebrews*, p. xxi. Other expressions found scattered through the writings of Calvin are: "the true standard of righteousness," *Institutes*, II, 402; "free from every stain or defect," *Minor Prophets*, I, 506; "the unerring certainty (of the Word of God)," *Psalms*, II, 429; "the certain and unerring rule," *Psalms*, V, 11; "unerring light," *Psalms*, IV, 480; "infallible Word of God," *Institutes*, II, 58 and III, 309; "has nothing belonging to man mixed with it," *Timothy*, p. 249, and also *Acts*, I, xxix, 6; "inviolable," *Minor Prophets*, III, 200, and *John*, I, 420; "infallible oracles," *Catholic Epistles*, p 131;"the only rule of perfect wisdom," *Institutes*, III, 178;"nothing corrupt or impure or adventitious," *Minor Prophets*, I, 328; "a decree steadfast and irreversible," *Psalms*, II, 429; "contains nothing but what was revealed by the Spirit of God," *Isaiah*, I, 36.

113 For a contrary view, see August Bénézech, "Theorie de Calvin sur l'Ecriture sainte," (Thèse, Faculté de theologie protestante de Paris, 1890), p. 15. Fullerton (Kemper Fullerton, *Prophecy and Authority, A Study in the History of the Doctrine and Interpretation of Scrip-*

Doumerge finds evidence for a looser view of inspiration in the French *Institutes* of 1560, as over against the Latin *Institutes* of 1559. The particular text cited by Doumerge, however, proves only that the French edition, in that one sentence, does not quite so clearly pronounce upon a verbal infallibility as does the Latin *Institutes* of 1559. If this passage stood alone, it would still be the part of discretion to trust the Latin edition of 1559 as over against the carelessly translated French edition. This single passage, however, is really quite irrelevant to the issue. Calvin sets forth his view so clearly in a multitude of other passages in both the Latin *Institutes* of 1559 and the French *Institutes* of 1560, to say nothing of his other works produced continuously through the years of his active life, that it is the merest folly to draw any conclusion from such a shaky foundation.[114]

Other attempts to discover a looser view of inspiration in Calvin's teaching fall flat upon examination. Schweizer, for example, labels Calvin's view "dynamic."[115] Pannier sums up the conclusion to which many interpreters of Calvin's thoughts have come. He asserts, "Calvin has not written a single word that can be invoked in favor of a literal inspiration."[116] The

---

ture [New York: Macmillan Company, 1919], pp. 182, 183) argues that only Calvin's failure to draw out and elaborate his "very high theory of inspiration" prevented his noting "the essential disagreement between his theory of inspiration and his exegetical results."

114 The Latin edition reads: "illi fuerunt certi et authentici . . . Spiritus Sancti amenuenses et idea eorum scripta, pro Dei oraculis habenda sunt"; but the French translates "amenuenses" as "les notaires jurez du Saint-Esprit" and "Dei oraculis" as "les écritures authentiques."
    Note that the French edition by no means casts any doubt upon a high view of inspiration; it may possibly be interpreted as a trifle less bald and explicit in its implication than the Latin version. Doumerge (*op. cit.*, pp. 73-74) in arguing against a "verbal and literal" inspiration finds the key to Calvin's view in an inspiration of doctrine and, accordingly, interprets Calvin as allowing errors in Scripture with respect to non-doctrinal details. He bases most of his case against the interpretation that Calvin held to verbal inerrancy upon the reformer's free treatment of Scripture in his commentaries. See pp. 76-79.

115 Schweizer, *op. cit.*, pp. 200ff.

116 Pannier, *op. cit.*, p. 200. See also Samuel Berger, *La Bible au seizième siècle: étude sur les origines de la critique Biblique* (Paris: Sandoz and Fischbacher, 1879) p. 118: "Il n'y a pas, dans toute l'Institution chrétienne, un seul mot pour définir l'autorité (bien moins encore l'infaillibilité) de la Parole de Dieu. Nous entendons Calvin au contraire, dans ses commentaires, s'exprimer avec une grande liberté. . . ." Even milder attempts to interpret Calvin such as that by

only foundation they are able to adduce in support of this interpretation, however, is the strong argument which Calvin makes against the mechanical view of the apostles and prophets as mere robots.

Various students of Calvin including both Doumerge and Pannier have adduced long lists of mistakes and errors which, so they affirm, Calvin allows in the Holy Scriptures.[117] Upon analysis, however, these so-called mistakes generally turn out to be what Calvin considered "textual errors." He holds that only the autographs were truly inspired of God; and, therefore, they alone partook of inerrancy. "Nor does any reverence prevent us from saying that, as it sometimes happens in minor matters, a wrong number may have crept in from the carelessness of scribes." In all extant manuscripts Calvin is quite willing to admit mistakes.[118]

Where he is confident that he has before him the correct text originally produced by the prophet, however, he never once allows for a true error in judgment. To conceive of the idea that Scripture should teach an error of any kind is "utterly blasphemous." To suggest that any interpretation implies an error in the teaching of the apostle is the *reductio ad absurdum* of any position. In every detail the words written by the prophets were written by God and are, therefore, inerrant down to the very last jot and tittle.[119]

The method by which Calvin tries to harmonize his view of the inerrancy of Scripture and the facts which he himself observes in the pages of Scripture is sometimes amazing. There are, of course, no contradictions in the written Scripture; for "it is certain that the Spirit cannot be at variance with him-

---

D. J. DeGroot ("Calvijn en de Heilige Schrift," *Gereformeerd Theologisch Tijdschrift* [Holland, 1933], pp. 1-22 [Section I] and pp. 87-113 [Section II]), who ascribes to Calvin an "organic" view of inspiration, is somewhat beside the point. There is, no doubt, considerable justification for the idea that according to Calvin all Scripture is to be fitted into its functional place assigned by God. As far as inspiration is concerned, however, Calvin considered the Bible as a written book in which every word was divinely produced.

117 Doumerge, *op. cit.*, pp. 76-78. Bénézech, *op. cit.*, pp. 29-39. See also Berger, *op. cit.*, p. 118.
118 *Pentateuch*, II, 304. See also *Acts*, I, 263-64, 297; *Joshua*, pp. 206-7; *John*, II, 297; *Harmony*, III, 272; *et passim*.
119 *Institutes*, II, 408.

self."[120] To hold to one least contradiction would be to "upset true religion."[121] If after all his industrious labor at bringing divergent passages together the problem of harmonization still seems to his mind insoluble, Calvin will only remind us that after all it is God who seems to contradict Himself.[122]

In similar fashion Calvin treats the historical facts of Scripture. If the chronology of Matthew is not precisely the same as that of Mark, Calvin argues that there can be no contradiction because the Holy Spirit is not interested in chronological order. In such instances the Scriptures do not teach any order; and, therefore, they obviously cannot teach contradictory order, nor can they be mistaken as to the order of events which they describe. In a passage where Luke does indicate the order, he is right and Josephus must be wrong.[123] If a number is not precisely accurate, Calvin reminds us that we must not find fault if God prefers to give us round numbers.[124] If Luke speaks "improperly," it is the Holy Spirit who speaks thus.[125]

Even the ethical teaching of the Old Testament is everywhere defended as from God. The Psalmist "errs," "displays intemperateness," and "spoke less advisedly than he ought to have done"; but still the Bible is true, for the writer is accurately and truly describing his own feelings.[126] The Psalmist is correct in referring to Solomon's wives as a sign of God's blessing, but he does not mean to teach that polygamy is approved by God.[127] The apparent cruelty and the imprecations of the Old Testament are the imprecations stemming from the Holy Spirit. With respect to these difficult passages, Calvin warns, therefore, that

120 *Institutes*, II, 406.
121 *Institutes*, II, 404; *Minor Prophets*, I, 506.
122 "God sets a kind of contradiction in his Word" (*Pentateuch*, III, 340).
123 "Mark . . . appears to differ more openly both from Matthew and from Luke in the narrative; . . . but I reconcile them in this way . . . Anyone who will consider how little care the evangelists bestowed on pointing out dates will not stumble at this diversity" (*Harmony*, III, 9, 10).
 Calvin passes readily from Luke's failure to observe the succession of events to "the Spirit of God has disregarded" (*Harmony*, I, 258). In another passage he writes: "The Evangelists were not very exact as to order of dates . . . so that the difficulty is soon removed" (*Harmony*, II, 89-90). See also *Jeremiah*, IV, 560; *Harmony*, I, 449, 357, 238, 239, 250; II, 429, 433; III, 259; *Pentateuch*, III, 294.
124 *Pentateuch*, I, 230.
125 *Acts*, II, 134.
126 *Psalms*, II, 88; III, 410, 415, 445.
127 *Psalms*, II, 185-186.

we must not be more fastidious than the Holy Spirit but ought rather to adore His mysterious judgments.[128]

In the realm of science the Scripture is completely true in all its judgments. "The Holy Spirit," Calvin explains, "had no intention to teach astronomy; and, in proposing instruction meant to be common to the simplest and most educated persons, he made use by Moses and the other Prophets of popular language."[129] Nevertheless, in the sense in which they intended their words, the prophets always speak the truth. Upon investigation Calvin discovers some sense in which the Biblical statement is true. If the Bible speaks of the lands beyond the sea as islands, that is because it is referring to those territories by the word commonly used in that day. By no means does it mean that the Biblical writer is committing himself to the scientific judgment that all lands beyond the seas are islands.[130] One of the charges levelled by Calvin against Servetus was that he held that the land of Palestine was unfertile, whereas the Bible declares that it is a land which flowed with milk and honey.[131] Even the most trifling error in memory on the part of the apostle is beyond the realm of possibility.[132]

In his treatment of the Old Testament quotations recorded in the New Testament, Calvin extends himself to the utmost to be consistent with his position. It is true, he concedes, that the New Testament writers "do not study verbal exactness in their quotations from the Old Testament."[133] They are not interested in words as mere words, but it is the idea or the meaning of the Old Testament for which the New Testament writers strive precisely and to which they adhere without fail.[134]

---

128 *Pentateuch*, II, 404; *Psalms*, III, 67. "David did not rashly, or un-advisedly, utter curses against his enemies, but strictly adhered to what the Spirit dictated" (*Psalms*, II, 285-86).
129 *Psalms*, V, 184-85. See also *Harmony*, I, 129; *Genesis*, I, 86.
130 *Jeremiah*, I, 88. See also *Psalms*, II, 372-73. Here Calvin suggests that David "borrows his comparison from a popular and prevalent error" but of course does not commit his own judgment to this erroneous superstition.
131 *Corpus Reformatorum*, VIII, 497.
132 *Harmony*, I, 91; *Jeremiah*, IV, 329.
133 *Psalms*, II, 289. "In this respect the apostles were not squeamish" (*Isaiah*, IV, 364).
134 "We must always have a regard to the end for which they quote passages, for they are very careful as to the main object, so as not to turn Scripture to another meaning; but as to words and other

It is impossible, however, that any New Testament writer should ever really twist any passage of Scripture from its intended meaning. If a writer of Scripture were ever to give a wrong interpretation of another passage of Scripture, such a circumstance would "disturb the whole religion of Christ." Only the ungodly would dare to suggest such a thing.[135]

Interestingly enough Calvin argues that quotation of the Old Testament by the New Testament is no guarantee of the correct text of the Old Testament. The New Testament writer, however, never uses the incorrect element in the quotation to prove his point. Luke, for example, in quoting an inaccurate text from the Septuagint, is merely using the commonly accepted version with which folks are familiar. The point which Luke wishes to make, nevertheless, is derived from that part of the Septuagint text which is absolutely correct.[136]

The critical views of Calvin are quite conservative; but he displays an understanding of the essential problems involved. He rejects the traditional authorship of the book of Joshua[137] and the Pauline authorship of the book of Hebrews.[138] He willingly admits the possibility of Antiochian Psalms.[139] He reckons that the book of Jeremiah was not written as we now have it by Jeremiah but is in reality a compilation of numerous individual messages of Jeremiah put together by the Scribes and not necessarily in the order in which Jeremiah gave them.[140]

---

things which do not bear on the subject in hand, they use great freedom" (*Hebrews*, pp. 227-80). ". . . the Evangelists never torture Scripture into a different meaning, but apply it correctly in its native meaning" (*Harmony*, I, 133-34). Cf. also *Institutes*, II, 548; *Isaiah*, IV, 364; *Pentateuch*, IV, 373; *Psalms*, II, 288-89; *Harmony*, I, 236; Fullerton concurs in this view of Calvin's exegesis (*op. cit.*, pp. 151, 154, 155).

135 *Minor Prophets*, I, 386-87.

136 *Acts*, I, 263-64. See also *Isaiah*, IV, 364.

137 *Joshua*, p. xvii. That this judgment as to the authorship of the book affects his view of its inspiration no whit is evident in his comment: "The doctrine herein contained was dictated by the Holy Spirit for our use. . . ." (*Joshua*, pp. xvii-xviii).

138 *Hebrews*, p. xxvi.

139 *Psalms*, III, 159; cf. also V, 84.

140 *Jeremiah*, IV, 564-65; V, 293.

Second Peter, however, if it is to be considered canonical at all, must have been written by the apostle Peter. Calvin's conclusion in the realm of historical criticism is in this case determined for him by his view of the inerrancy of Scripture. The epistle directly claims that Peter is its author; and, therefore, if it is canonical and consequently inerrant, it must have been written by Peter. Calvin explains the divergent style of this letter by suggesting that Peter dictated it in substance to a scribe, who then wrote it out for Peter. In any case the letter in its final form was set forth upon the basis of Peter's authority as an apostle.[141]

Calvin's views of the canon underwent some slight development during his lifetime. In the *Psychopannychia* and in the first edition of the *Institutes,* he cited Baruch as written by a prophet of God. This is corrected in later editions. From 1539 on, he adheres rigidly in all his writings to the sixty-six books of the Protestant canon and explicitly rejects all Roman Catholic additions.[142]

In his rejection of the Roman Catholic apocrypha Calvin appeals to the authority of Jerome and holds that these books were added late in the history of the Church in order to bolster Romish inventions which had no foundation in the true Scripture.[143]

Although some students of Calvin have argued that he did not accept the canonicity of certain books of both the Old and New Testament, the evidence is conclusive against this view. Most serious objections have been raised against his acceptance of the books of Revelation and the Second and Third Epistles of John. Doubt as to his view of the Apocalypse has risen because it stands significantly as the only New Testament book of any size on which he has not commented and also because on one occasion he remarked to a friend that he did not understand the book. Scattered throughout his writings, however, are innumerable references to the book of Revelation as the fully inspired

---

141 "If it be received as canonical, we must allow Peter to be the author, since it has his name inscribed . . ." (*Catholic Epistles,* pp. 276-77, 363).

142 "Psychopannychia" in John Calvin, *Tracts Relating to the Reformation,* Henry Beveridge *et. al.* trans. (Edinburgh: Calvin Translation Society, 1844-1851), III, 455; and *Corpus Reformatorum,* I, 82 and 906; V, 205, 227.

143 See "Council Antidotes," *Tracts,* I, 70ff.

Word of God; and whether he understood the book or not, he certainly considered it to be canonical.[144]

Much has been made of the fact that Calvin in several places refers to the canonical Epistle of John intending by that title only the First Epistle. Some have thought that he was thus explicitly ruling out as uncanonical the Second and Third Epistles.[145] As a matter of fact, on numerous occasions Calvin quotes the Second Epistle as by the apostle John and as the authoritative Word of God. The apparent lack of references to the Third Epistle can best be explained on other grounds than that he held it to be uncanonical.[146]

The tests of canonicity are nowhere developed by Calvin with sufficient fullness so that his views can be pinpointed with any degree of certainty. He understands clearly that the Bible is really a library of ancient books. For him the problem of canonicity must be attacked piecemeal, book by book. In his commentaries, therefore, he ordinarily devotes a short paragraph or more to the canonicity of each book which he considers. He recognizes that he must validate each separate book as given by God if it is to be received as the authoritative Word of God.[147]

---

144 *Institutes*, II, 249; *et passim*. For the contrary view see Pannier, *op. cit.*, pp. 111, 113, 202, 203. Here Pannier argues that Calvin rejected the canonicity of the Song of Solomon, Revelation, and 2 and 3 John. The charge with respect to the Song of Solomon is ridiculous in the light of Calvin's refusal to ordain a man because he was in doubt on this point. See *Letters*, I, 379. The evidence with respect to Revelation has just been pointed out; as to the question regarding 2 and 3 John, see below.

145 "Ce mot (canonique) exclut, dans la pensée de l'auteur, les deux autres épîtres attribuées à cet apôtre" (Berger, *op. cit.*, 120).

146 Cf. *Pentateuch*, II, 40; *Job*, p. 740; *Daniel*, II, 34; *et passim*. That the term of "canonical" as applied by Calvin to 1 John did not imply any adverse judgment against 2 and 3 John is proved by the use of the term itself. Calvin, following the medieval western church, used it as a synonym for "catholic" in referring to the so-called general epistles of the New Testament. See B. F. Westcott, *The Epistles of St. John* (London: Macmillan Co., 1892), pp. xxvii, xxix. Calvin's frequent citation of 2 John as Scripture makes abundantly clear that he did not intend to rule out that epistle. See *Galatians and Ephesians*, p. 234; *Institutes*, II, 432; *et passim*. This destroys also the only plausible argument against Calvin's acceptance of 3 John, and its extreme brevity coupled with the nature of its contents adequately explains the omission of references to it. See Davies, *op. cit.*, p. 109.

147 See *Catholic Epistles*, pp. 264, 276, 363, 427-29.

The test by which each individual book is recognized as divinely inspired is, according to most students of Calvin, the inner testimony of the Holy Spirit.[148] The evidence for this interpretation of Calvin is twofold. It rests first upon a passage in the *Institutes* where Calvin introduces a long series of questions including the question: "Who [can] persuade us that this book is to be received with reverence and that one expunged from the list?" He concludes that only the Spirit of God can give us certainty in such matters.[149] Warfield may be right, however, when he declares that we must not push Calvin into meaning that the witness of the Spirit is directly answering all the "cavils" which Calvin heaps up in this passage.[150] The second bit of evidence is the direct statement in the Gallican Confession of 1559 that the witness of the Spirit determines the canon. This again may not be taken as conclusive evidence regarding Calvin's view, for as Pannier has pointed out, Calvin was not the author of this particular section dealing with the canon, but on the contrary it was added later without his authorization.[151]

The strongest evidence that Calvin does not consider the witness of the Spirit as finally determining the extent of the canon is to be found in his introductions to the various books of the Bible. In spite of the fact that he takes up very explicitly the means by which we can know that these books are canonical, he never refers to the witness of the Holy Spirit. He sets forth

---

148 Bénézech (*op. cit.*, p. 46), Köstlin (*op. cit.*, p. 417), and Pannier (*op. cit.*, p. 203) argue that Calvin recognized each book as from God by the witness which the Holy Spirit bore directly to the book. In each case this testimony was never given to parts of a book; but if a book was recognized as canonical, it was always recognized *en bloc* as inspired of God. Rabaud, (*op. cit.*, pp. 62 and 63) and J. A. Cramer (*De Heilige Schrift Bij Calvijn* [Utrecht: A. Oosthoek, 1926], pp. 67-68), argue for the same position with this slight change that the witness of the Spirit to the authority of Scripture is directly to the content of Scripture and only indirectly to the units of the books.

149 *Institutes*, I, 89.

150 Warfield, *op. cit.*, pp. 93-94.

151 Pannier, *op. cit.*, pp. 206-7. The fourth article of the Gallican Confession reads: "We know these books to be canonical, and the very sure rule of our faith, not so much by the common accord and consent of the church, as by the testimony and inward illumination of the Holy Spirit, which enables us to distinguish them from other ecclesiastical books" (Philip Schaff, *The Creeds of Christendom* [New York: Harper & Brothers, 1877], III, 361-62).

his conclusions, moreover, with a lack of certainty that is totally incompatible with what he says in other contexts about the witness of the Holy Spirit. In these introductory comments Calvin lays down three types of tests for the authority of Scripture. The first is prophetic authorship. Although apparently he does not consider it necessary to know what particular apostle wrote each book, he always insists upon the prophetic or apostolic authorship of any book held to be canonical.[152] A second test is to be found in the testimony of the Church or perhaps in God's preservation of certain of the prophetic writings in the Church. "Those which the Lord judged to be necessary for his church have been selected by his providence for everlasting remembrance."[153]

This testimony of the Church, however, does not seem to be elaborated in his thought as an independent test of canonicity, but rather its testimony is given indirectly to the authenticity and apostolic or prophetic authority of the author. It attests not so much the inspiration as the proper pedigree of the inspired book.

Finally, in these prophetic books there are evident certain marks of divinity that proclaim them of divine authority. Usually these marks are referred to by the title the "Majesty" of divinity. In Calvin's understanding of the matter, if a book bears the majesty or marks of divinity, it must then have been producd by inspiration and, therefore, must be accepted as the authoritative Word of God. The two lines of thought are interchangeable. If a book was produced by a chosen prophet of God, it must be reckoned as inspired. On the other hand, if a book bears upon its pages the marks of divinity, it must have been given by God through a prophet. By this latter means Calvin makes his final decision with respect to the canonicity of the Epistle of Second Peter.[154]

In spite of the want of precision in his outline of the tests of canonicity, Calvin is unambiguously clear in his conclusions

---

152 *Institutes*, II, 176; *Catholic Epistles*, pp. 276, 427. *Galatians and Ephesians*, p. 243. Of Mark's identity Calvin writes, "It is of little importance to us provided only we believe that he is a properly qualified and divinely appointed witness who committed nothing to writing but as the Holy Spirit directed him and guided his pen" (*Harmony*, I, xxxviii).
153 *Galatians and Ephesians*, p. 249.
154 *Catholic Epistles*, p. 264.

regarding the inspiration of the sixty-six books which he ultimately accepts as canonical. Considered "in the lump" as one
book, the Holy Scripture, they present us from cover to cover
with the inerrant words of God. They establish their right to be
considered as the very words of God by internal and external
evidences which are overwhelmingly convincing to any sound
mind. The supreme testimony to their divine authorship and
authority comes in the immediate testimony of the Holy Spirit
to the believing soul working in conjunction with but not itself
resting upon these human evidences or any mere human judgment. Upon this testimony of God, the Bible in its entirety, is
seen to be the Word of God, written by His inspiration and
therefore inerrantly true and completely authoritative in all
its parts.

The Use of Scripture

In order for it to accomplish its purpose in the redemption
of human souls, the Word of God must be rightly interpreted
and correctly applied to life. Mere "reading or hearing" of the
words of Scripture is not enough. This task of rightly interpreting the Bible, unfortunately, cannot be performed by the natural
man working with only his unaided human resources. Left to
follow his own sinful inclinations, man without the Spirit of
God will inevitably press Scripture into whatever shape he
pleases and thus render void the truth of God. Man needs the
special supernatural illumination of the Holy Spirit in order to
understand the Scripture just as much as he does to see in the
first place that it is the Word of God. Only thus can sinful man
discover in the words of the Scripture the true meaning of
the Spirit.[155]

The Bible, therefore, is by no means perspicuous to all. "It is,
indeed, obscure to the unbelieving," who do not possess the
Spirit of God. With respect to the doctrine of salvation, however,
it is so abundantly clear that only the sinner's willful blindness
prevents his seeing its obvious meaning.[156]

---

155 We dare not "rely on our own acumen to understand the Scriptures
   but on the Spirit" (*Pentateuch*, I, 92). See also *Harmony*, I, 39 and
   40; *Catholic Epistles*, pp. 386-89, *Romans*, p. xxvii; *Psalms*, III, 388;
   et passim.
156 *Catholic Epistles*, 389.

Even for the regenerate, Scripture is not immediately under-standable in all its parts.[157] To him who faithfully applies him-self to the Word of God and studies it with proper humility and a discerning spirit, however, even the detailed teaching of the book will eventually be unfolded. The Holy Spirit, working in our hearts and minds, can and will make plain all that man needs to know for the good of his eternal soul.[158]

The correct interpretation of Scripture to which the Holy Spirit leads the reverent student is, moreover, never secured through fanciful allegories.[159] Rather "the true meaning of the Scripture is the natural and obvious meaning of the words."[160] "We must," Calvin warns, "be ever on our guard against wresting Scripture from its natural meaning."[161] For him, a proper method of interpretation means adherence to what would be called today the grammatical-historical method of exegesis. He discovers the true meaning of the Spirit through the analysis of the historical situation in which the prophet or apostle produced his writing.[162]

By no means does Calvin insist upon a wooden, literal method of interpretation. "Any man would make himself ridiculous by attempting to restrict the Spirit of the Law to the strict letter of the words." The choice between a figurative or literal interpreta-tion of a passage of Scripture depends upon "the pure and genuine meaning of the lawgiver."[163]

---

157 But in another passage he adds, "nothing is required of them but diligent study." *Pentateuch* I, 412.

158 In Calvin's mind this does not, of course, preclude the use of com-mentaries or of human guidance in the study of Scripture. "Pious Doctors," inquiring into the truth of Scripture, are able to throw light on many a dark passage. Cf. "Antidote to the Decree of Council of Trent," *Tracts,* III, 74. Calvin wrote his own com-mentaries to lead the student into the truth. The Spirit uses means; but these means are successful in bringing the reader into true light only as the Holy Spirit illuminates the mind and unveils the truth. See also *Acts* I, 354.

159 *Institutes,* II, 191; *Pentateuch,* II, 139, 140, 335; *Galatians and Ephe-sians,* p. 135. Occasionally Calvin will not repudiate altogether the allegorical method but will leave the question open "for anyone to accept it or not" (*Acts,* II, 64). See also *Harmony,* I, 436.

160 *Galatians and Ephesians,* p. 136.

161 *Psalms,* II, 388.

162 See Irwin H. De Long, "Calvin as an Interpreter of the Bible, "*The Reformed Church Review* (April, 1909), p. 656.

163 *Institutes,* I, 437.

Calvin's doctrine of Scripture is climaxed by his view of the Bible as the immediate and contemporary voice of the Spirit. Through the words of Scripture, which God spoke by His Spirit to the prophets, He now speaks directly to the souls of men. Calvin does not conceive of this present speech in deistic fashion. The Bible is not the Word of God merely in the sense that it presents a certified record of what God spoke in the past. It is that and much more. Calvin conceives of this communication by the Spirit in the Word as a present supernatural work. He never rebukes the enthusiasts for claiming an immediate "voice" of the Spirit of God. He rebukes them only because they claim this immediate voice separated from the written Word. God "speaks" today and God speaks in and through the words written by Him long ago as He today unfolds the true meaning of those words and applies that truth to the heart and mind of man.[164]

The Word of God, rightly interpreted and rightly applied by the Spirit of God, is the absolute rule of life. "Scripture," Calvin declares, "is the school of the Holy Spirit, in which as nothing useful and necessary to be known has been omitted, so nothing is taught but what is of importance to know." Scripture is the final court of appeals. If religion is based on Scripture, it is approved of God. If it is not based on Scripture, it is not approved of God. True obedience to God in matters of the Spirit requires not only complete subjection to the revealed will of God, but also demands that we must not add one whit to the law of God. "There is no true religion before God," he

---

164 *Institutes,* I, 113, 114, 169. To the objection that it is insulting to the Spirit to be subject to the Scripture Calvin replies that Scripture is not a word to be distinguished from the Holy Spirit. It is not disgraceful to the Holy Spirit to be in all respects consistent with Himself (*Institutes,* I, 112). Calvin could never be called a mystic but many facets of his thought reflect the essential mystical nature of his faith. "It is," he avers, "no less unreasonable to boast of the Spirit without the Word, than it would be absurd to bring forward the Word itself without the Spirit" ("Reply to Cardinal Sadolet's Letter," *Tracts,* I, 37). Even the minister who faithfully executes his commission by speaking only what God puts into his mouth, may trust that the Holy Spirit joins His immediate power to the voice of His messenger (*Psalms,* IV, 199); cf. also *Hebrews,* p. 103. A delicate balance between a bloodless rationalism and a fanatical mysticism has always been a characteristic of authentic Calvinism.

concludes, "except it be formed according to the rule of his Word."[165]

Calvin's loyalty to the written Scriptures knows no bounds. For him the words of the Bible are the very words of God spoken through the prophets and apostles of long ago and now bringing unerringly to the souls of men the immediate voice of the living God with all the authority of the supreme Sovereign of the universe.

165 *Institutes,* II, 165, 532; *Pentateuch,* I, 345; *Acts,* II, 129-30; *John* I, 160, 161, 242; *Job,* 706-07; *Genesis,* I, lii; *Minor Prophets,* I, 450; *Jeremiah,* III, 185. Again and again Calvin warns against seeking "to know more than God has revealed" (*Pentateuch,* I, 329; III, 423; *Institutes,* I, 193; II, 530-31; *Letters,* IV, 160; *Jeremiah,* V, 429; *Romans,* p. 219; *Minor Prophets,* IV, 196; *John,* II, 143; *Psalms,* II, 130).

Chapter V

JOHN WESLEY AS AN INTERPRETER OF SCRIPTURE

By George A. Turner

The far-reaching influence of the Wesleys upon English life and letters is generally recognized. This influence in the areas of science, literature, politics, theology, the sacraments and social progress has been carefully explored in many highly specialized and competent studies. Little, however, has been written on the specific subject of Wesley as an interpreter of the Bible. Several definitive volumes have been written on the use of the Bible by other leaders in the Church universal but none here, in spite of the fact that few men in Christian history appealed more constantly and effectively to that body of writings which the Christian Church holds uniquely sacred. Certain it is that the Bible was the dominant influence in early Methodist thought. Indeed it is generally recognized that the evangelical revival of the eighteenth century did much to restore the Bible to its former prominence in English life.[1] In

1 Cf. A. C. McGiffert, *Protestant Thought Before Kant* (Scribner's, 1912), pp. 172f. "The authority of the Bible was made more of by them than for a long time before. In opposition to the current recognition of the sufficiency of human reason, they delighted to belittle it, and to denounce its claims as presumptuous and irreligious. But they appealed in opposition to it, not to the Spirit in the hearts of all believers, as the Quakers did, but to the written and infallible word. It is due to evangelical influence, and not to scholasticism or the Protestantism of the Reformation period that the authority of the Scriptures has meant so much to English and American Christians of modern times. In German pietism the Bible was employed chiefly as a devotional book. But in evangelicalism its significance as a divine revelation, authenticating the orthodox faith over against deism and scepticism, became especially prominent. Interpreted evangelically, it was made a doctrinal and moral authority of the most binding character. To venture to criticise its statements, to question its authority, to raise doubts as to the authenticity of any part, to set one's own judgment above it, to treat it as in any way ill-adapted to present conditions, all this was intolerable to a genuine Evangelical."

this short monograph only a preliminary survey can be attempted in a field which merits more extended research. The present purpose, therefore, is to consider Wesley as an interpreter of Scripture, a study which touches upon the varied aspects of homiletics, theology and exegesis. After a preliminary orientation, attention will be directed to the primary source materials; then to the subject's early acquaintance with the Bible; then to the three phases of his work as preacher, apologist and expositor; and finally to the principles of interpretation he followed.

I The Scriptures in Early Methodist Thought

Wesley was one with other Protestants in recognizing in the Scriptures the charter of religious freedom and vitality; the chief distinctions were in matters of emphasis. The Methodists stood midway between the Calvinists and the Friends in their general view of the Bible. To the Calvinists the Bible was the written Word through which the Holy Spirit speaks. There was little stress upon the witness of the Spirit except in connection with the printed page. The Christian thus comes into direct contact with God, not through the sacraments (as with the Lutherans and Anglicans), nor in silence (as with the Friends), nor through the direct inspiration of the Spirit (as in many ecstatic sects), but through the Scriptures as illuminated and made personally applicable by the Holy Spirit. In both Reformed and Friends churches the Spirit's work is more that of illumination than of purifying and energizing. They follow the Johannine, while the Evangelicals follow the Pauline emphasis on the Spirit's work. The close relationship between the Spirit and the Word in Reformed theology is illustrated in the words of Calvin: "The very office of the Holy Spirit is to confirm within us what God promises by His Word." And again, "The Word cannot enter into our spirits unless the Spirit of God, who is the inner master, gives us access to it by his illumination."[2] For the Friends, on the other hand, the Spirit may be received without the medium of the written Word to a greater extent than in most communions. Here the stress is upon the immediacy of the Spirit, upon insight or an

---

2 J. Calvin, *Institutes* of 1551, II, 32; cited by P. R. Fuhrmann, "Calvin, the Expositor of Scripture," *Interpretation*, April, 1952, pp. 194f.

intuitive grasp of the truth. In line wtih the pattern set by George Fox, the devout Friend waits in silence for the "Inner Light" or "openings" brought about by the Spirit. As their chief theologian expressed it,

> From these revelations of the Spirit of God to the Saints have proceeded the Scriptures of truth, . . . they are and may be esteemed a secondary rule, subordinate to the Spirit . . . . Because they proceeded from the Spirit therefore also the Spirit is more originally and principally the rule. . . .[3]

Barclay assumed that everyone's claim to the immediate inspiration of the Spirit is to be taken at face value as on a par with the writings generally accepted as being uniquely inspired by the Spirit. The ideal is sound but the emphasis too subjective.

Wesley agreed with the Quakers that the Spirit of God is the real source of all divine truth, being prior to its historical preservation in a Book. He differed, however, from Barclay's statement that these divine revelations are not to be subjected "to the outward testimony of the Scriptures or of the natural reason of man, as to a more noble or certain rule or touchstone." Instead, Wesley insisted that the Scriptures are "the touchstone whereby Christians examine all, real or supposed, revelations."[4] Wesley was thus more in line with Calvin than with the Quakers in this respect, as is apparent in Calvin's declaration: "Without the spirit, the Word is a dead letter; without the Word, the Spirit flutters as an illusion."[5] Wesley therefore differed little in his view of the Bible from other Protestant groups. The differences in emphasis that existed arose from differing views of the Spirit and His work rather than views of the Bible as such. In his attitude toward the Scriptures, as in so many other respects, Wesley was in "the middle of the road," within the broad stream of Protestantism.

The disciples of John Wesley have seldom studied their Bibles as diligently as have the disciples of John Calvin. The chief reason for this is probably glimpsed in the remark of an Amsterdam merchant after appraising Count Zinzendorf, leader

---

3 Robert Barclay, "Theses Theologicae," cited by P. Schaff, *The Creeds of Christendom*, 3rd ed., III, 791.
4 J. Wesley, *Letters* (Standard Edition, J. Telford, ed.), II, 117.
5 Fuhrmann, *loc. cit.*

of the *Unitas Fratrum,* to which the Wesleys owed so much. He distrusted the Count because his theological position was not prominent and because he emphasized that Christ was within the believer as "a sort of living Bible."[6] This appraisal of Zinzendorf and the Pietists is, to a lesser degree, true of Methodists in general. The stress upon the inwardness of religion makes for vitality, but it also tends to subjectivism and facilitates distorted emphases. Calvinism needs the vitality and subjective effects for which Methodism has stood, and the latter needs to take more seriously a thorough acquaintance with the written Word as the indispensable avenue to the living Word; in short, to be more objective.

The sources for a study of Wesley as an expositor are extensive. In order of importance, probably, they are: his sermons, his *Notes* on the New Testament, special treatises such as "An Earnest Appeal to Men of Reason and Religion," *Plain Account of Christian Perfection, Original Sin,* and his *Letters.* Wesley's influence upon his contemporaries and the confidence of these contemporaries in him as a Bible interpreter can be felt by a perusal of contemporary literature, as is done in several important bibliographies.[7] Indispensable also to a thorough knowledge of Wesley as an expositor are the glimpses afforded by his *Journal.*

II. Wesley's General View of the Scriptures

Revelation. That the Bible is the unique revelation of God was one of the two most fundamental convictions in Wesley's theological outlook. In the rare moments of agnosticism, two convictions remained with him: there is a God, and God has revealed Himself in a Book. Wesley believed that God and man dwell in two different spheres, that while man can learn much through his natural faculties he cannot gain a knowledge of spiritual things by his own efforts alone. Such knowledge must come from God by means of a revelation. Man's response to this revelation is in the nature of faith, defined by Wesley

---

6 John Stockers, cited by G. Tennant, *Some Account of the Principles of the Moravians* (London, 1743), p. 14.

7 *E.g.,* T. B. Shepherd, *Methodism and the Literature of the Eighteenth Century;* (London: Epworth Press, 1940); George Osborne, *Outlines of Methodist Biography* (London, 1809); Richard Green, *Anti-Methodist Publications issued during the Eighteenth Century* (1902).

as "the eye and ear of the new-born soul," by which the believer perceives "both the existence and the presence of Him in whom 'he lives, moves, and has his being'; and indeed the whole invisible world."[8] In his view of the Bible as revelation, Wesley was in line with the classic view of Augustine and the Reformers, but out of line with the rationalists of his day. Even when writing to Deists who did not believe the Scriptures, he attempted no *apologia* for the Bible as such. To these he appealed by reason and conscience; to those who did accept the Scriptures, no defense was needed. The place which the Bible occupied in his conception of revelation is clear in the oft-quoted "Preface" to his *Sermons* which appeared in 1746.

> I am a spirit come from God, and returning to God . . .
> I want to know one thing, the way to heaven . . . God Himself has condescended to teach me the way . . . He hath written it down in a book. O give me that book! At any price, give me the book of God! I have it: here is knowledge enough for me. Let me be *homo unius libri*. Here then I am, far from the busy ways of men. I sit down alone: only God is here. In His presence I open, I read His book; for this end, to find the way to heaven.[9]

In this passage is revealed both Wesley's attitude toward the Scriptures and his method of interpretation. The Bible to him is a book of which the most characteristic thing is that God is the author. Of secondary importance is the matter of date, authorship and motive of the various contributors. On another occasion Wesley set forth in greater detail his general viewpoint regarding the sacred writings.

> Concerning the Scriptures in general, it may be observed, the word of the living God, which directed the first patriarchs also, was, in the time of *Moses,* committed to writing. To this were added, in several succeeding generations, the inspired writings of the other prophets. Afterward, what the Son of God preached, and the Holy Ghost spake by the apostles, the apostles and evangelists wrote. . . . Every part thereof is worthy of God; and all together are one entire body, wherein is no defect, no excess.

8 J. Wesley, "An Earnest Appeal to Men of Reason and Religion," *Works* (1st American ed.), V, 6.
9 J. Wesley, "Preface," *Sermons* (3d Amer. ed.), I, 6.

An exact knowledge of the truth was accompanied in the inspired writers with an exactly regular series of arguments, a precise expression of their meaning, and a genuine vigour of suitable affections . . . .

All the elegancies of human compositions sink into nothing before it: God speaks not as man, but as God. His thoughts are very deep: and thence his words are of inexhaustible virtue. And the language of his messengers also is exact in the highest degree: for the words which were given them accurately answered the impression made upon their minds: and hence *Luther* says, "Divinity is nothing but a grammar of the language of the Holy Ghost." To understand this thoroughly, we should observe the *emphasis* which lies on every word; the holy *affections* expressed thereby, and *tempers* shown by every writer.[10]

Inspiration. Wesley believed in the full inspiration and inerrancy of the Bible. His view would now be described as pre-critical, as would the view of most eighteenth-century writers. The problem of authority which Luther faced was less acute in Wesley's day than the problem of indifference in the Church. Thus Wesley was less bold than Luther in determining the relative value of different books of the Bible; to him they were all equally inspired and hence authoritative. Living as he did midway between the sixteenth and twentieth centuries, he did not feel the need of establishing the authority of the Bible or defending it from destructive critics. Jean Astruc, "the father of Pentateuchal criticism," published his views on the authorship of Genesis in 1753, but there is no evidence that it was noticed by Wesley and his colleagues. To him, therefore, as to the majority of Jews and Christians, of that day at least, the Bible in its totality was God's Word to man mediated through human instrumentality—a pre-critical view.[11] He

10 J. Wesley, "Preface," *Explanatory Notes Upon the New Testament,* pp. 10, 11, 12.

11 W. E. Sangster, recognizes that Wesley wrote in pre-critical times and that "if one part seems more illuminating than another, the explanation is to be sought in one's need, apprehension, or present interest, and not in the Scripture itself." *The Path to Perfection* (Abingdon-Cokesbury, 1943) pp. 35f.
E. H. Sugden, on the other hand, appealing to Wesley's introduction to his commentary on Joshua and to his New Testament *Notes,* says, "Wesley was a critic, both higher and lower, before those much mis-understood terms were invented." *Standard Sermons,* I, 21. Sugden apparently bases his judgment on these words of

did, however, recognize that some truths in the Bible are more important than others, and hence he possibly believed in different degrees of inspiration.

Criticism. At the same time, Wesley was not reactionary in his attitude toward Biblical scholarship. He hailed Bengel, "father" of New Testament textual criticism, as "that great light of the Christian world," and gladly welcomed his contribution to scholarship. He recognized in the celebrated exegete of German pietism not only a top-ranking scholar, but one who combined sound learning with Christian commitment and devotion. So favorably impressed was he with Bengel's learning and piety that he laid aside his plans for a commentary on the New Testament and instead translated Bengel's *Gnomon Novi Testamenti,* making abridgments and changes as he thought best. [12] He did not, however, agree with those who believed that because the Biblical writers were human they made mistakes. "Nay, if there be any mistakes in the Bible there may as well be a thousand. If there be one falsehood in that book it did not come from the God of truth." [13] However, his candor is seen in his recognition of the possibility of error in the genealogies (Notes on Matt. 1:1). To state it more precisely, Wesley was a "lower" (textual) but not a "higher" critic. He readily adjusted his beliefs to the evidence, but he instinctively reacted against any rationalistic bias inimical to evangelical faith.

Moderation. Wesley's attitude towards the Bible, as in so many other things, was characterized by moderation. Repeat-

---

Wesley: "It seems the substance of the several histories was written under divine direction, when the events had just happened, and long after put into the form wherein they stand now, perhaps all by the same hand." Wesley is referring to the historical books from Joshua to Esther; he regarded the Pentateuch as the work of Moses as the same passage indicates. To classify Wesley as a "critical" scholar represents a vain attempt to "modernize" him. Cf. F. Hildebrand, *From Luther to Wesley* (London: Lutterworth, 1951), pp. 25f.

12 See A. W. Harrison: ". . . he was no expert in textual criticism. He accepted the findings of a man in whom he could trust, and when he differed from him he did so not for any technical reasons but because of the possible effect of the change on the plain, unlettered men to whom his life-work was given." "The Text of Wesley's Translation of the New Testament," *Proceedings of the Wesley Historical Society,* IX, 1913-14, p. 113.

13 J. Wesley, *Journal,* VI, 117.

edly he states one common interpretation and then contrasts it with another alternative view. His own position is often one which embraces both. It was therefore characteristic of him to refuse an "either-or" position in favor of "both-and."[14] This was due perhaps to his breadth of perspective and also to his eclectic temperament. It must not be supposed, however, that Wesley's conclusions were always gained by resolving conflicting positions to their common denominators. At times he was an extremist in defending his position—for example his view of original sin—but he was naturally inclined to find the middle way between extreme views, especially in matters of secondary importance, possibly in view of the dictum that "truth seldom lies in extremes."

Catholicity. As a servant of the Word, Wesley manifests a catholicity of spirit in most of his work. He laments, partly mournfully, partly scornfully, the strife in Christian nations, cities, families, and churches, and pleads for universal peace and brotherhood.[15] That this subject was important to Wesley may be judged from the fact that he devotes two major sermons to the subject, one entitled, "A Caution Against Bigotry," and another on a "Catholic Spirit." In these, tolerance which is the result of Christian love, rather than of uncertainty or indifference, is urged with evangelical fervor. The importance of intention and sincerity are stressed as over against uniformity of faith and order. Like the German Pietists, the Methodists minimized the importance of opinions as compared with personal integrity, and felt that purity of doctrine was less important than purity of life. The only condition for membership in the Societies was a desire "to flee from the wrath to come." Wesley made much of this characteristic of the Methodists and claimed for them uniqueness in it.[16] In matters of belief which he considered important, Wesley was far from tolerant, however. He was convinced that the "acid-test" of

14 *E.g.*, "Some have supposed that He designed . . . to point out several stages of the Christian course . . . others, that all the particulars here set down belong at all times to every Christian. And why may we not allow both the one and the other? What inconsistency is there between them?" *Standard Sermons,* I, 321.
15 *Standard Sermons,* II, 355.
16 "I do not know any other religious society . . . wherein such liberty of conscience is allowed, since the age of the Apostles. Here is our glorying; and a glorying peculiar to us. What Society shares it with us?" J. Wesley, *Journal* (Standard Edition), VII, 389.

whether a person was a Christian was whether he believed in original sin.[17]

III. WESLEY AS INTERPRETER

Early preparation. Wesley was trained in the parsonage by his efficient mother with a generous portion of Bible reading. At school, Biblical languages were a prominent feature of the curriculum—Hebrew, Greek, and Latin. At his first school—Charterhouse, to which he went at the age of fourteen—he soon gained recognition for his proficiency in Hebrew. His skill in Greek was such that while at Oxford he and Charles conducted daily devotions in Greek, using not only the Greek New Testament but reading also in the early church fathers. Later he was able to say that he had examined every word carefully in the Greek New Testament. It is said of him that he could correct a wrong quotation from the New Testament by quoting from memory the Greek.[18] Throughout his life he translated books from Latin into English, as his work on Bengel's *Gnomon* exemplifies. While at Oxford he adopted a schedule of study which he kept for years, the results of which continued throughout his long life. It was the classics on Monday and Tuesday, logic and ethics on Wednesday, Hebrew and Arabic on Thursday, metaphysics and philosophy on Friday, oratory and poetry on Saturday, and Divinity on Sunday.

Such were the literary tools for Bible study which he acquired at an early age. Not only did he have a natural aptitude for languages, but he lived in an age when classical learning rather than manual arts was the normal thing.[19]

Homo Unius Libri. After this period of classical training there came a time when Wesley became, to use his own words, "homo unius libri"—a man of one book. He was then twenty-six years of age.

In the year 1729, I began not only to read, but to study the Bible, as the one, the only standard of truth,

---

17 "All who deny this, call it 'original sin,' or by any other title, are but Heathens still, in the fundamental point which differences Heathenism from Christianity." Sermon, "Original Sin," *Standard Sermons*, II, 223.

18 See G. C. Cell, "Introduction," *The New Testament*, tr. by John Wesley, p. 219.

19 See W.C.S. Pellowe, *John Wesley, Master in Religion* (n.d.), pp. 78-85.

and the only model of pure religion. Hence I saw, in a
clearer and clearer light, the indispensable necessity of
having "the mind which was in Christ" and of "walking
as Christ also walked;" . . . in all things.[20]

As Wesley's foremost biographer says of the Oxford Methodists,

> They had one, and only one, rule of judgment, with
> regard to all their tempers, words, and actions—namely,
> the oracles of God, and were one and all determined to
> be Bible Christians. The book which, next to the holy
> Scripture, was of the greatest use to them, in settling their
> judgment as to the grand point of justification by faith,
> was the Book of Homilies.[21]

Since they were Englishmen, their Bible study was pre-eminently practical; since they were pietists, their Bible study was
primarily for the purpose of devotion. Unlike many pietists,
however, they used the Bible also as their authoritative rule
of doctrine. Near the close of his life John Wesley stated his
daily schedule, which was surprisingly like that discipline set
up as a young man. This spiritual, mental, and physical discipline lay at the base of all his study and exposition as *homo
unius libri.*

As a preacher. As an interpreter of the Bible, Wesley's most
characteristic role was that of preacher — not exegete like
Bengel, nor teacher like Calvin, but evangelist. Unlike Calvin,
it was not his custom to take a Bible book and expound it
systematically. This is partly due to the different ages in which
they lived but mostly to the fact that Wesley was not a pastor
but an evangelist. The prophetic and hortatory mode was more
characteristic of him than the didactic. Furthermore, Wesley
lived not in the century of the Reformation but in that of the
evangelical revival. He was predominantly a textual preacher
rather than an expositor. While he did not ignore the context,
he seldom made use of it. Often the text was only a "pretext,"
the context being ignored and the verse used as a motto for
a topical discourse.[22]

20 J. Wesley, *A Plain Account of Christian Perfection* (Summers, ed.,
   1882), p. 7.
21 L. Tyerman, *Life and Times of J. Wesley,* I, 73.
22 Thus, Jehu is mentioned in the text (2 Kings 10:15) of the sermon
   entitled "A Catholic Spirit" only to be discarded like Agrippa in
   "Almost Christian."

The people to whom he was preaching were more the object of his attention than the people to whom the various Bible authors addressed themselves. He seldom took time to elucidate the historical setting of the passage and the original intent of the writer but pressed the text into service for the immediate objective — that of the spiritual quickening of his hearers. Most of his life he preached to the common people in the open air, his purpose being to arrest attention and bring conviction and repentance rather than information. It is rare that a person with such a mastery of the tools and discipline of research, and with such mental curiosity, should be so exclusively evangelistic. It probably is to be explained as owing to the spiritual urgency of the situation rather than to the lack of capacity for or inclination to a more labored and methodical exposition, after the fashion of a Maclaren, Morgan or Jowett.

A notable exception to this is the series of sermons in which Wesley expounds Jesus' Sermon on the Mount — thirteen of them, or almost one fourth of Wesley's "standard" sermons. These are fully expository. In them Wesley takes pains to get at the original setting and to observe the original sense of the words and clauses before making application to the immediate situation. On occasion also he calls upon his linguistic training in the Hebrew, Greek or Latin to clarify the sense. He repeatedly elucidates the context by an appeal to history. He utilizes historical background, for instance, in describing the scribes and Pharisees of Matt. 5:20. In short, this series of sermons, in spite of the fact that they were preached by an itinerant on different occasions, reflect solid exposition which includes exegesis, textual criticism and historical background to make the meaning clear. Sometimes, as in the first sermon of the series, the familiar homiletical device of using the interrogative pronouns — who, what, whom, and how — is employed to direct attention repeatedly to the text.

Here, as in all his Bible exposition, Wesley is more than an interpreter; he never fails to emphasize the *relevancy* of the passage to his hearers and the *importance* of a proper response to the Word of the living God. He does not content himself with stating principles and leaving to the hearers the responsibility of making the application. Always uppermost are the inner spiritual needs of the audience, which create a directness

and urgency so that even these expository sermons are evangelistic in the best sense of the term. They are designed not
merely to inform but to convert. The appeal is through the
intellect to the conscience. Attention is not gained or kept by
a series of stories and illustrations; there are no jokes or
humorous anecdotes, no attempt to be entertaining. There is
often eloquence but no rhetoric for rhetoric's sake. Wesley
expressly repudiated any attempt at ornamentation — his model
for style was the simplicity and directness of the First Epistle
of John. All is subordinate to the objective of confronting the
hearer with the demands and promises of God. At times, in
condemning the popular sins of the day, Wesley overstates the
case. Sometimes his language is too absolute and uncondi-
tional. In most cases, however, he does not permit his
earnestness to distort the facts or oversimplify the case. The
general impression his sermons convey is that the tools and
training of a scholar have been subordinated to the note of
evangelistic urgency, which accentuates the ring of authority
with which he speaks.

Another characteristic of Wesley's sermons is the amazing ease
with which Biblical quotations and allusions come from his
lips. His years of reading the Bible had woven its phrases into
the very texture of his thought. His mind was thoroughly
impregnated with the Scripture. For example, in connection
with his observations on "blessed are they that mourn" there
is a paragraph of average length in which he is not comment-
ing closely upon the passage but elaborating on its general
application, but there are allusions to some thirteen different
Biblical passages from various parts of both Old and New
Testaments. These are not parallel passages in which a relationship is pointed out, but are spontaneously woven into
Wesley's mode of self-expression. To illustrate this phenomenon
it may be justifiable to quote the paragraph verbatim. The
Scripture references inserted in the quotation are not Wesley's
but those of the present writer to show how rich in Biblical
allusion is Wesley's utterance.

> Sure it is, that this "affliction," for the present [cf. 2 Cor.
> 4:17] " is not joyous, but grievous; nevertheless, afterward
> it bringeth forth peaceable fruit unto them that are ex-
> ercised thereby" [Heb. 12:11]. Blessed, therefore, are they
> that thus mourn [Matt. 5:4 — the passage under consider-

ation], if they "tarry the Lord's leisure" [source of quotation unknown], and suffer not themselves to be turned out of the way, by the miserable comforters [cf. Job 16:2] of the world; if they resolutely reject all the comforts of sin, of folly, and vanity [cf. Eccles. 1:2]; all the idle diversions and amusements of the world; all the pleasures which "perish in the using" [Col. 2:22], and which only tend to benumb and stupefy the soul, that it may neither be sensible of itself nor God. Blessed are they who "follow on to know the Lord" [Hos. 6:3], and steadily refuse all other comfort. They shall be comforted by the consolations of His spirit [cf. 2 Cor. 1:4]; by a fresh manifestation of His love; by such a witness of His accepting them in the Beloved [Eph. 1:6], as shall never more be taken away from them [cf. Luke 10:42]. This "full assurance of faith" [Heb. 10:22] swallows up [cf. 1 Cor. 15:55] all doubt, as well as all tormenting fear [cf. 1 John 4:18]; God now giving them a sure hope of an enduring substance [cf. Heb. 11], and a "strong consolation through grace" [Heb. 6:18]. Without disputing whether it be possible for any of those to "fall away, who were once enlighted, and made partakers of the Holy Ghost" [Heb. 6:4], it suffices them to say, by the power now resting upon them, "Who shall separate us from the love of Christ?" [Rom. 8:35] [23]

It is when Wesley is describing the inner struggles of the soul that his expression is the most replete with quotation and allusion, when he has the greatest freedom of utterance.

As an apologist. The best examples of Wesley's accuracy as an interpreter of the Scripture are afforded when he is not preaching but rather elucidating some disputed theological position such as in his treatises on perfection and original sin.

The tract entitled *Plain Account of Christian Perfection* seeks to lay a solid Biblical basis for the most characteristic and the most controversial of the Wesleyan doctrinal emphases. The *Plain Account,* according to W. E. Sangster, contains 195 quotations from the Bible, of which 23 are from the Old and 172 from the New Testament, the latter being divided mostly among the Synoptics, Paul and John.[24] There are some 70 quotations from Paul's writings and about 34 from those of

---

23 J. Wesley, "Sermon XVI," *Standard Sermons,* I, 331.
24 W. E. Sangster, *op. cit.,* p. 36.

John. The First Epistle of John contributed 20 texts to Wesley's presentation. In harmony with these statistics is the generalization which comes to the reader of Wesley's sermons and treatises that he leaned most heavily on 1 John and almost as heavily upon Paul. Thus, while Wesley in theory believed that all of the Bible was equally inspired, his theological emphasis is primarily Johannine and Pauline.

In this treatise, where the apologetic note is uppermost, the method is that of citing proof texts rather than surveying the broad sweep or general tenor of a particular Bible book. This, of course, was the prevailing mode of the eighteenth century. The Scriptures are surveyed deductively or topically — that is, a proposition made and texts cited in defense of it. Part of the treatise deals topically with the prayers of the apostles for full deliverance from sin and perfection in righteousness. Sometimes the failure to interpret the context greatly weakens the argument, as when Heb. 6:1 is used as something of a motto rather than the focal point in an extended passage.

Wesley's omissions are significant. Many texts which could have been cited effectively in support of his case are ignored or slighted. He failed, for instance, to employ Rom. 6 and the Thessalonian letters in defense of his position. Some segments of New Testament theology would have strengthened his case but are unused, such as the Pauline phrase "in Christ," and the close relationship between the *parousia* and holy living.

On the other hand, it is hard to find instances of texts being distorted in support of a position. Good judgment is apparent throughout Wesley's use of Bible evidence. A basic intellectual integrity is also apparent. One does not get the impression that the writer is ignoring contrary evidence or bending ambiguous passages to his purpose. On the whole, the evidence is handled with a remarkable degree of honest-mindedness. The treatise is more "plain" and practical than comprehensive, reflecting the fact that its author was a busy preacher rather than a leisurely scholar.

The treatise on *Original Sin* affords an excellent opportunity to see Wesley at work as an interpreter of Scripture. He follows a strict historical-literal sense less in degree than the Presbyterian clergyman whose ideas he was combating.[25] There is in

25 John Taylor, *The Doctrine of Original Sin* (London, 1741).

Wesley a greater tendency to look at the question theologically than exegetically. In other words, Wesley tended to interpret a disputed passage by the Scripture as a whole without strictly limiting himself to a literal-historical interpretation. He was as apt to explain an Old Testament passage by an appeal to Paul, for example, as to consider it in the light of its own context. Because sin is universal, he argues, its cause must lie at the very beginning of racial history. As is often done, the prevalence of sin is regarded as owing to the transmission of depravity from one generation to another. To Wesley, in contrast with John Taylor, the moral argument is as influential as strictly factual literalism. Often a quotation from a classical writer is adduced to confirm or illustrate a generalization drawn from the Scriptures. Wesley followed the Epistle of Hebrews and Augustine in believing that all sinned "in the loins of Adam" — that is, they incurred guilt as well as pollution by an act for which they had no responsibility — the "Realistic Theory" of original guilt. The argument with Wesley, as with Paul, Augustine and Luther, aimed to accentuate the sinfulness and impotence of man in order to underscore the importance of God's free grace. In *most* instances it is not apparent that a moral concern or theological "interest" led Wesley astray or warped his judgment. He compares very well with his contemporaries in this respect. He does not study the Scriptures inductively, at least he does not present it in that manner. Instead, he follows the more customary and lucid method of a deductive approach in which the proposition is made and pertinent passages cited in support. As compared with Taylor, his approach is more theological and experiential and less severely literal. His interpretation of Paul is more Pauline than is that of Taylor.

Wesley appears in a somewhat poorer light as an apologist than he does either as a preacher or an exegete, so far as his use of the Bible is concerned. He was a formidable foe in apologetics and his manner of use reveals an honest, effective mind. It is only in his grasping of a Bible writer's own thought and purpose, as seen in his failure to relate proof text to context that Wesley's method is weak. But, as has been noted, that was the universal practice for two centuries of Protestant history. While he often slighted the immediate context, he was careful to interpret a particular verse by the general tenor of Scripture as a whole.

As an expositor — his exegesis. In considering Wesley's role as as exegetical student of the Bible, one does well to consult his *Notes* on the Old and New Testaments. The *Notes* on the New Testament were published in 1754 and were, as previously noted, largely a translation of the *Gnomon* of Bengel. The *Notes* on the Old Testament appeared in 1765, and were for the most part an abridgment and revision of Matthew Henry's *Commentary* on the Old Testament. In both cases, Wesley's purpose was severely practical; he wrote for the busy but eager laymen who needed something less labored and technical than the works of Bengel and Henry afforded. History has decided that the New Testament *Notes* are among the most important elements of Wesley's literary legacy. They, along with the Standard Sermons, form the only doctrinal pattern which Methodism has adopted, with the exception of Wesley's revision of the Articles of Religion, added later.

In both Old and New Testament work, Wesley's purpose was identical with that of Bengel, namely, to call attention (as a "dial") to points in the text. The *Notes* are primarily a series of *observations,* not platitudinous comment. Bengel's choice of the term "Gnomon" as the title of his work signifies that he regarded his work as fulfilling the role of "index, or pointer of the sundial."[26] This was the ideal which Wesley set for himself. The Preface to his New Testament *Notes* states that his purpose was brevity, "that the comment may not obscure or swallow up the text." Ten years later, the Preface to the Old Testament *Notes* shows even more clearly the influence of Bengel:

> Every thinking man will easily discern my design in the following sheets. It is not to write sermons, essays or set discourses upon any part of Scripture. It is not to draw inferences from the text, or to shew what doctrines may be proved thereby. It is this: To give the direct, literal meaning of every verse, of every sentence, and, as far as I am able, of every word in the oracles of God. I design only, like the hand of a dial, to point every man to this: not to take up his mind with something else, how excellent soever; but to keep his eye fixt upon the naked Bible, that

---

26 C. F. Fritsch, "Bengel, The Student of Scripture," *Interpretation,* April, 1951, p. 208.

he may read and hear it with understanding. I say again (and desire it may be well observed, that none may expect what they will not find), It is not my design to write a book which a man may read separate from the Bible: but barely to assist those who fear God, in hearing and reading the Bible itself, by shewing the natural sense of every part, in as few and plain words as I can.[27]

Here, as always, Wesley is primarily the evangelist. Everything is subordinate to the dominating purpose of making the Word of God available to the common people. He is not enticed by temptation to display his erudition, nor his rhetorical skill. Brevity was characteristic, almost a passion with him. He remarks that while Matthew Henry's purpose was to say as much as possible, he was determined to say as little as possible. One gets the impression that Wesley's studied simplicity and clarity was not the result of rationalizing his lack of time or of command over the tools of research, but was determined by his purpose of serving the many in the most helpful manner possible. He was not interested in rearing a monument of scholarship for himself which many might admire but few read. At the same time Wesley refrained from "talking down" to his less learned readers. Said he:

It is not part of my design, to save either learned or unlearned men from the trouble of thinking. If so, I might perhaps write Folios too, which usually overlay, rather than help the thought. On the contrary, my intention is, to make them think, and assist them in thinking.[28]

While Wesley was interested in sound doctrine he refrained from "wresting the Scriptures" to bolster his theology. Instead, his exegesis determined his theology rather than *vice versa*. In his *Notes*, therefore, his own doctrinal positions become subordinate to the task of letting the text speak for itself. In 1754 he avowed, "My own conscience acquits me of having designedly misrepresented any single passage of Scripture. . . ."[29] Examination of controversial passages supports Wesley's claim that he did not seek to exploit the situation to buttress Methodist doc-

27 J. Wesley, "Preface," *Explanatory Notes upon the Old Testament* (1765), I, viii.
28 *Ibid.*, p. lx.
29 J. Wesley, *Notes upon the New Testament*, (New York: Land and Tippett, 1847), p. 5.

trinal emphases. He was always ready to distinguish between
sound doctrine and opinions, and to allow much latitude in the
latter. Wesley was far from uncritical in his use of sources. In no
point was he stronger than in his independence of judgment.
He did eliminate from his Old Testament commentary the
passages in which Matthew Henry had expressed his view of
limited atonement or "particular redemption." This he justified
on the grounds that he was clearing the work of a theological
bias without substituting one of his own. In short, Wesley
cannot be justly charged with bending his exegesis to serve a
sectarian purpose.

IV. GUIDING PRINCIPLES OF INTERPRETATION

In summarizing a study of Wesley's use of the Bible it may
be well to summarize, under a series of captions, the basic
principles which characterize his role as interpreter of the Word.

A. A quality which characterizes all of Wesley's Bible exposition is the dominance of the *practical* over the theoretical. Repeatedly he affirmed that he was not concerned with opinions
as such, either his own or others. His sermons and commentaries
do not dwell upon problems of interpretation which belong to
the realm of speculative theology. His independence of thought
is well illustrated in his comment on a passage from the admired
Bengel. To an inquirer he wrote:

> What I said was that Bengelius had given it as *his*
> opinion, not that the world would then end, but that the
> Millennial reign of Christ would *begin* in the year 1836.
> I have no opinion at all upon that head. I can determine
> nothing about it. These calculations are far above, out of
> my sight. I have only one thing to do, to save my own
> soul and those who hear me.[30]

Throughout his own ministry he followed his mother's advice
rather than his father's example in preferring practical divinity
to the "critical learning."[31] Few will deny that he chose wisely;
his *Notes* are far more widely read than his father's commentary
on Job. As true pietists the early Methodists concerned themselves with devotional and moral values. Wesley had little time
for contemplation; his devotional efforts expressed themselves

30 J. Wesley, *Letters*, VIII, 63.
31 Susannah Wesley, "Letter," cited by L. Tyerman, *op. cit.*, I, 32.

in three ways, none of which were in the mood of contemplation — the sacramental, the practical, and the evangelistic. This was not because he was wanting in intellectual curiosity. But the urgency and discipline under which he pressed on his way gave him little leisure, which is the condition of contemplation. The result was that the probings of an alert and curious mental attitude were confined to an occasional entry in his journal, entries which afford fleeting glimpses into his inner soul.

B. With Wesley *obedience* was the condition of spiritual knowledge. The condition for spiritual insight was more moral than intellectual. The Spirit-inspired writer and the Spirit-guided student met in the pages of the Book. In this the early Methodists acted upon John 7:17 — "If any man will do his will, he shall know of the doctrine. . . ." He was one with Bengel and the Pietists in stressing the importance of the spiritual approach to the Scriptures. The student, renewed by the Spirit of God, was regarded as being in rapport with the Author of the Bible and hence able to understand its message better. This emphasis is in line with the apostle Paul's insistence that the avenue to the things of God is the illumination of the Spirit (1 Cor. 2:10-16). It was thus characteristic of the early Methodists to proceed on the conviction that obedience to the will of God must precede and accompany mastery of the Bible — in line with the thought of the couplet:

Light obeyed increaseth light;
Light rejected bringeth night.

C. Wesley believed that the path to spiritual truth was three-fold — Scripture, reason and experience. Sometimes he varied the trilogy to "Scripture, Reason, and Christian Antiquity."[32] Always the Bible was first but he recognized that reason was needed in its interpretation, and also that one's individual interpretation needed to be checked with that of other earnest Christians. In this there was less emphasis on individual interpretation than with the Reformers. There is a kinship between "experience" and "Christian Antiquity" in Wesley's thought. By "experience" he meant primarily the operation of God with the soul, both individual and corporately. By "Christian Antiquity" he meant the same Christian consciousness as expressed by earlier genera-

32 J. Wesley, *Works* (1771 ed.), par. 4.

tions of Christians — the difference was temporal. While there is kinship there is also a distinction. "Antiquity" indicated tradition and reflects Wesley's conservative temperament; "experience" represents Wesley's more venturesome modification of tradition. The latter came to be recognized as Wesley's most distinctive contribution to theology — the "theology of experience."

Wesley, as a Lincoln College Fellow, was a tutor in logic. His father once remarked that John had to have a reason for everything he did. He was an admirer of John Locke and gives evidence of being greatly influenced by his writings. These facts afford substance to Wesley's claim that he used reason to interpret the Bible. It was by the criterion of reason that he opposed the Calvinistic emphasis on particular redemption. Calvin had a legal training and it is interesting to observe that, granting his basic premise of the sovereignty of God, he was led to affirm limited atonement, predestination and final perseverance as the logical consequences, while Wesley, on logical grounds, rejected them all. Wesley assumed that, since God is rational, interpretation of Scripture, if true, should be reasonable; it must cohere with other phases of revelation.[33]

D. Wesley has been widely acclaimed as the theologian of Christian experience, as one who anticipated the modern trend in this respect.[34] Certain it is that the factor of experience was never more influential in Christian theology than now. Wesley cannot be regarded as the pioneer in stressing experience, as Cell regards him, for Paul appealed to experience in addressing the Galatians; but no one more painstakingly or more daringly brought to bear upon his interpretation of Scripture the criterion of the Spirit's work in men's "hearts." Wesley questioned at length, for example, some five hundred witnesses as to their experience of a "second work of grace," in 1761.[35] The factor of experience played an important part in establishing the Biblical basis for one of Methodism's most controversial doctrines, that of Christian perfection.[36] To the Reformer's emphasis upon the

33 See John Wesley, "Free Grace," *Sermons*, I, 488.
34 G. C. Cell, *The Re-Discovery of John Wesley*, p. 72.
35 L. Tyerman, *op. cit.*, II, 417.
36 "Q. But what does it signify, whether any have attained it or no, seeing so many scriptures witness for it?
"A. If I were convinced that none in England had attained what has been so clearly and strongly preached, by such a number of

subjective validation of Scripture Wesley added the interpretation of Scripture gained by the reports of witnesses to the
Spirit's operation within. Underlying all was the conviction that
the direct work of the Spirit and the written testimony of the
Spirit are in agreement.[37]

Experience played a decisive role in the apostles' interpretation of the Old Testament (Acts 15). The report of the Spirit's
work among Gentiles, given by Paul, plus a similar report by
Peter, enabled James to interpret familiar passages in a new
light. Experience was implicit also in Pastor John Robinson's
parting benediction to the Pilgrims — "God shall yet cause new
light to shine forth out of his word." To Wesley experience
provided another criterion that served to assure him whether or
not a given interpretation was in accord with the Spirit of truth.

E. His procedure as an interpreter of the Word is instructive.
Some ten steps are discernible in his approach to the Scriptures.

1. He always approached the Bible with *prayer*. In his Preface
to the *Notes on the Old Testament* he advised prayer before
reading the Bible, and at the close. He also urges interspersing
a period of study with periods of prayer. The principle involved
is that "Scripture can only be understood through the same
Spirit whereby it was given."

2. *Self-examination* is the second step in Bible study. "It might
also be of use, if while we read, we were frequently to pause,
and examine ourselves by what we read, both with regard to our
hearts, and lives."[38]

3. Fundamental in Wesley's exegetical approach was *observation*. Like Bengel the purpose of his exegetical notes on the
New Testament was to point out things of importance in the
text. His purpose was not that of explaining everything in the
verse but only of illuminating it with terse and lucid comment.
His main concern was not to inform the learned but to give
guidance to the unlearned.

---

preachers, in so many places, and for so lang a time, I should be
clearly convinced that we all had mistaken the meaning of those
scriptures: and therefore, for the time to come, I too must teach
that 'sin will remain till death.' " *Plain Account*, p. 88.

37 "Whereas it is objected that experience is not sufficient to prove
a doctrine unsupported by Scripture: We answer, experience is sufficient to confirm a doctrine which is grounded on Scripture." J.
Wesley, Sermon: "The Witness of the Spirit," *Works*, V, 132.

38 J. Wesley, *Notes on O. T.*, p. lx.

4. *Correlation* was another step which Wesley advised. He constantly interpreted a debated passage in the light of the general tenor of Scriptures. Relevant texts were searched out for their possible bearing upon the one in question.

5. The historical *background* of a passage was important to Wesley in explaining many Biblical passages. This point did not weigh as heavily with him, however, as it well might have. He did, on occasion, elucidate the text by placing it in its setting or citing historical parallels.

6. *Literature,* especially the classics and poetry, was quoted rather copiously in Wesley's sermons. They were such as were designed to clarify and make more impressive the truth he was seeking to get across. In his exegetical work he had recourse to the commentaries of other authors. In this he contented himself in familiarizing himself with a few of the best authorities on the subject. His research was by no means exhaustive. An acquaintance with all the literature or all the learned opinions on a particular passage never diverted Wesley's attention from the text itself. The fathers of the first two centuries were usually consulted with more deference than were his contemporaries.

7. *Experience* played an important and distinctive part in interpretation. As his Bible work was always related to experiential piety, and since his conception of religion was subjective — "the life of God in the soul of man" — the states of the soul were regarded as an important commentary on the written Word. In modern parlance, the "ingrafted word" and the "written word" operated under the guidance of the Holy Spirit in harmony, the one clarifying the other.

8. *Conference* was an important and rather characteristic feature of early Methodist Bible study. Much like the early Christians in Acts 15, the preachers who were associated with the Wesleys gathered periodically to seek in group discussion a solution to problems which in isolation seemed difficult. Their doctrine of the Spirit in the individual and in the group made them eager to confer and discuss before they decided what constituted the truth.

9. *Commitment* to the Scriptures was regarded as the condition of illumination. Wesley and his followers believed that they could understand the deep things of God only to the extent that they were willing to "walk in the light." His final advice to the reader of his *Notes* on the Old Testament emphasizes this point.

Whatever light you then receive, should be used to the uttermost, and that immediately. Let there be no delay. Whatever you resolve, begin to execute the first moment you can. So shall you find this word to be indeed the power of God unto present and eternal salvation.[39]

10. *Presentation* was the final step. Self-expression or witnessing was the immediate consequence of a Biblical discovery with this evangelist. To quote his sequence of study again:

Is there any doubt concerning the meaning of what I read? . . . I light up my heart to the Father of lights. . . . Thou hast said, "If any be willing to do Thy will, he shall know." I am willing to do, let me know Thy will. I then search after and consider parallel passages of Scripture, "comparing spiritual things with spiritual." I meditate thereon with all the attention and earnestness of which my mind is capable. If any doubt still remains, I consult those who are experienced in the things of God; and then the writings whereby, being dead, they yet speak. And what I thus learn, that I teach."[40]

There was a masculine objectivity about Wesley. What he understood he lost no time in proclaiming.

Interest in John Wesley as an interpreter of Scripture does not arise so much from any novel methods of interpretation which Wesley originated. It arises rather from the historical importance of Wesley himself. If Wesley was justified in making the claim that he based his teachings entirely upon one book, as he probably was justified, the factor of his daily study of the Bible must not be minimized. It was by no accident that its language became second nature to him. It was rather the consequence of absorbing the Scriptures in Hebrew, Greek, Latin and English, from childhood through a life-time of disciplined study. Most will admit that he received from this source not only a literary style but also a viewpoint remarkably like that of the primitive Christians. He would have regarded that as a compliment.

39 J. Wesley, *Explanatory Notes on the Old Testament*, I, lx.
40 J. Wesley, "Preface to the Sermons," *Standard Sermons*, I, 31-32.

CHAPTER VI

SANDAY AND THE SCRIPTURES

By R. Laird Harris

If we should characterize William Sanday as one of the leading mediating theologians of England in the late nineteenth century, probably no one would be as pleased as Sanday himself. It was his earnest desire to effect a rapprochement between opposing views in all the fields he touched. In this desire he doubtless typified many in the Church of England who desired to hold in the Church's fellowship the best of the traditional orthodoxy and the most necessary (as they thought) of the higher critical scholarship. Especially in the basic subjects of inspiration and Christology Dr. Sanday's mediating views are apparent. It would therefore not be surprising if his exegetical judgments should reflect mediating principles.

Sanday's desire to mediate is interestingly expressed in *Christologies Ancient and Modern* where, after describing orthodox doctrine (which he calls "full Christianity") and modern theology (which he calls "reduced Christianity") he says, "I have no doubt which of the two I lean toward myself; but I can feel at the same time the attraction of the other. Indeed I am perhaps conscious of a certain call to offer to mediate between them — at least so far as to help to bring about a mutual understanding."[1] He remarks that one of his critics "seemed not a little puzzled to understand how I could accept so much as I did of modern criticism and yet work round so nearly to the position implied in the ancient creeds."[2]

He goes so far in his mediation as to feel that the Ritschlian slogan of "God in Christ," though not a sufficient Christology, is at least a step toward a common meeting ground, for the orthodox also believe that God was in Christ. He pleaded that English scholars should approach the then current German

1 William Sanday, *Christologies Ancient and Modern*, p. 97 (hereafter referred to as *Christologies*).
2 *Ibid.*, p. vi.

literature of Harnack and others "not as competing with or directed aggressively against our own beliefs, but rather as cooperating with us in the presentment of the most verifiable portions of those beliefs."[3]

Again Sanday reveals his character of peacemaker in his Bampton Lectures on *Inspiration* when in discussing conflicting claims on the date of Proverbs he says, "I am myself disposed to strike a balance between the conflicting views of critics."[4] The sentence is revealing. Whatever the subject discussed, Sanday sees good on both sides. For this irenic temperament we should feel grateful on many occasions; we do well to seek peace and pursue it. But there come times when with Paul we should draw sharply the alternatives of the true gospel and another gospel — when mediation becomes compromise. And unfortunately Sanday seems quite willing to adopt his mediating positions on the basic questions of Biblical infallibility and the person of Christ.

Sanday stood at the threshold of a new era. The higher criticism was new and becoming popular in England. Germany had largely succumbed to it. America's scholars were not seriously considered, and here criticism had hardly secured more than a foothold. Sanday earnestly felt that the old and the new could be combined. He would find the golden mean.

He drank deeper at the fountain of German theology than many others in England. Referring to the works of Wernle, Bousset, Julicher, von Soden, Johannes Weiss, and Harnack, he wrote, "There is a body of literature in Germany that cannot be easily matched in this country."[5] He quotes with high commendation from the English philosopher, T. H. Green, describing him as a good Hegelian, and declares that the ideas expressed are "not only good Hegelian theology, but also good Biblical theology as well."[6] The quotation from Green, which is very poor theology, begins with the statement, "A death unto life, a life out of death, must, then, be in some way the essence of the divine nature."[7]

Schleiermacher, whom most scholars today would acknowledge as the father of Modernism, is accepted by Sanday as "having

3 *Ibid.*, p. 118.
4 Sanday, *Inspiration*, p. 248.
5 *Christologies*, p. 117.
6 *Ibid.*, p. 88.
7 *Ibid.*

gathered up in his own person a large part of the best culture of his time," but Sanday proceeds to admit that "he rejects the (ordinary) idea of miracle," and adds that he holds that Christ's appearance on earth is not a miracle in the ordinary sense, but "better regarded as the meeting point of God's creative act and the evolution of Man." Sanday regards Schleiermacher's work highly, but not perfect — "rather an effort towards the expression of a truth than the successful expression of it. I cannot see in Schleiermacher's view more than a stage on the road."[8] Subsequent history has made many Christians wonder what is the end of this road!

Sanday's next stage for study is the Christology of Albrecht Ritschl. He admits that Ritschl's view of Christ "differs from the traditional. At the same time Ritschl is thoroughly in earnest in the stress which he lays on Christ as revealing the Father." Sanday seems unconcerned that the Father whom Ritschl speaks of is not the Father of the Christian Trinity, but a Unitarian deity. Sanday admits that the Ritschlians only regard the Trinity as a doctrine of "relative and historical justification," but believes that he could come to terms with them and that "Ideal truth would probably include us all."[9] This is a large admission. He seems quite ready to welcome pure Unitarians into the household of faith.

No whit more serious, but perhaps more striking is his encomium of Rome. After objecting to Hermann's polemics against Roman Catholicism he says, "The book was written many years ago [1886] when the position was different from what it is now [1910]. The 'Kulturkampf' was still fresh in men's minds, and the awakening that has since come over the Church of Rome, and especially over Roman Catholic Scholarship, was still in the future. The more generous spirits in Germany look upon their old antagonists with different eyes. . . . With us, half — or perhaps a third — of the thinking classes in the nation have been converted, but a good deal of the old fanaticism still survives. . . . The time is, I hope, not far distant when Roman and Anglican and Free Churchman and Lutheran will only emulate each other in good works and in the search for deeper truth side by side."[10]

8 *Ibid.*, p. 80f.
9 *Ibid.*, p. 83.
10 *Ibid.*, p. 109.

This ideal of Sanday we are seeing realized today for good or ill in the modern ecumenical movement of which Sanday was one of the early and eminent prophets. It will therefore be of special interest to observe his principles of mediation and to see how his view of Scripture is affected by such principles. We may remark, however, that the history of the past forty years has vindicated Sanday's prophecies better than it has supported his principles. Higher criticism has triumphed in most circles and ecumenicity is triumphing before our eyes. Modernism, however, has not proved to be a welcome ally, but a camel which when given entrance, soon possesses the tent. As to the inherent virtue of the new thought, not a few have had their faith in its power shaken by the cataclysms of our century and the outbursts of brutality which German higher learning or American pacifism were powerless to prevent. Many therefore have recently turned away from Modernism and accepted the Neo-orthodoxy of Barth and Brunner. We may be pardoned if we feel that this panacea also will not work. We may well feel constrained to go back to the Bible itself, see if the plain exegesis of the Scripture is not best and hold to the traditional theology to meet the exigencies of the twentieth century.

Sanday's views as we would analyze them revolve around his conclusions as to higher criticism, verbal inspiration, the doctrines of Christology and the Trinity, and the result of these conclusions upon his exegesis of particular passages.

Although he himself did not specialize in the Old Testament, he is seen to embrace the principles of higher criticism. He faces the question: "It is necessary for the inquirer to take up a definite attitude towards the criticism of the Old Testament. What is that attitude to be?"[11] Contrasting the writings of Driver, Kuenen, and Wellhausen with those of the traditional school he concludes, "It is impossible to resist the impression that the critical argument is in the stronger hands. . . . The cause of criticism if we take the word in a wide sense and do not identify it too closely with any particular theory, is, it is difficult to doubt, the winning cause. Indeed criticism is only the process by which theological knowledge is brought into line with other knowledge; and as such it is inevitable."[12]

11 *Inspiration*, p. 115f.
12 *Ibid.*

Sanday of course will not go the whole way in approval of the German criticism. He recognizes that Kuenen and Wellhausen "wrote in the interest of almost avowed Naturalism";[13] yet he feels that they mapped out the main stages rightly. In particular, he accepts the critical positions of the untrustworthy character of the traditions of the authorship of the Old Testament books and the composite character of many of the books, especially the documents called J, E, D, and P in the Pentateuch which are dated long after Moses. He holds, as critics commonly do, that the Old Testament Canon slowly grew through the centuries as ancient writings became more sacrosanct. He adopts the usual critical dates of 444 B.C. for the Law, third century B.C. for the Prophets, and about 100 B.C. for the canonization of the other writings. These are the essentials of higher criticism, and he accepts the postulate quite freely. His claim is that the higher criticism can be assimilated into orthodox Christianity. Our question is whether the resulting compound is orthodox and the assimilation justifiable.

It goes without saying that Sanday does not believe in a verbally inspired text. He admits that this view was held among the early Fathers: "Testimonies to the general doctrine of inspiration may be multiplied to almost any extent; but there are some which go further and point to an inspiration which might be described as 'verbal.' Nor does this idea come in tentatively and by degrees, but almost from the very first."[14] He quotes Philo, the learned Jew of the first century A.D., to the same effect.[15] But Sanday must differ with the ancient view of inspiration. Because the historians who wrote the Pentateuch were of the much later J, E, D, P schools, he concludes that "it is difficult to claim for the Biblical historians inspiration in the sense of praeternatural exemption from error."[16]

Inspiration is to Sanday a thing of greater or lesser degree. It does not mean exemption from error, but a measure of divine infusion. There may therefore be degrees of it: "There are no doubt well-marked grades of inspiration in the Canon; and there are some books which have their place quite upon the

13 *Ibid.*, p. 120f.
14 *Ibid.*, p. 34. B. B. Warfield comments on this quotation: "He might have spared the adverb 'almost.' The earliest writers know no other doctrine." *Revelation and Inspiration*, p. 54.
15 *Ibid.*, p. 85.
16 *Ibid.*, p. 161.

outskirts of it, and one or two in which inspiration is hardly perceptible at all."[17] Of the Song of Songs he says that it "contributes nothing to the sum of revelation. Its place in our Bibles is due to a method of interpretation which is now very generally abandoned. . . . There can be no question of inspiration . . ." in so questionable a case.[18] Esther, he believes, is in an even worse situation. Of the events at Sinai he says, "The narrative . . . cannot be guaranteed to represent them with literal accuracy."[19]

Instances could be multiplied, but enough have been cited to show that Sanday did not believe that the Pentateuchal narratives were written by Moses or that they are good history, that the miracles of Sinai or the predictions of the prophets were literally true, or even that certain entire books belong in the Canon at all. His mediation has gone to rather an extreme — on the critical side.

It may be added that the conclusions of Biblical scholars have undergone considerable change. Some of the assured results of higher criticism which Sanday was so anxious to assimilate are now discarded. Shortly before the time of Sanday, F. C. Baur had declared that the fourth Gospel could not have been written before 170 A. D. Ritschl had already argued against this, but in 1917 the Rylands papyrus came to light giving us a shred of the actual Gospel of John written at approximately 130 A.D. In the same way, archeological and linguistic studies, especially since the first World War, have been instructive. They have proved the basic historicity of the patriarchal narratives in Genesis — an embarrassment, it would seem, to those who claim that they were not written until the eighth century and not compounded until the fifth. The studies have proved that Aramaisms occurring in literature such as the Psalms are not a mark of lateness after all. Rather, the Biblical poetry shows remarkable parallels in style to the Canaanite literature of Ugarit from 1400 B.C. And more recent studies such as those of Albright and others on the Balaam oracles[20] and on the Song of Miriam in Exod. 15 (material given in class lectures) argue that such poems are quite early — perhaps thirteenth century —

17 *Ibid.*, p. 208.
18 *Ibid.*, p. 211.
19 *Ibid.*, p. 234.
20 *Journal of Biblical Literature.* Vol. LXIII (1944), pp. 207-34.

and that Moses himself was a monotheist.[21] All this leaves less room for the evolution of Israel's religion and means that the traditional views apparently do not conflict with the facts of ancient culture and history as archeology reveals them except perhaps in minor and debatable points. This is not to say that all archeologists are becoming traditional-minded, but it does mean that more and more they are giving up earlier extremes and that the traditional views of authorship and dating are relieved from much of the pressure that Sanday naturally felt when the era of criticism was full-blown.

When Sanday capitulated under the attacks of higher criticism he found himself in an unstable position. The source book of Christian doctrine was gone. It was a question whether the doctrines could still be defended. His answers can be illustrated from his treatment of the doctrines of Christ and the Trinity.

Unfortunately for Sanday's doctrine of inspiration, it not only contradicts the view of the early Church and the apostles and the Jewish scholars such as Philo and Josephus but also the teaching of our Lord. Sanday cautiously observes that Jesus' views come down through the medium of persons who shared the current opinions on inspiration and that therefore the passages might not reflect Jesus' views accurately; but he admits that it is probable that the sayings of Jesus given in the Gospels do represent His teachings on this point. It is too clear that Jesus did share the views of His contemporaries. "The acceptance of the traditional estimate" on Jesus' part, says Sanday, "appears to be the most complete in the region of criticism. It is not possible to point to any anticipation of modern theories in this respect. Moses is repeatedly spoken of as the author of the Pentateuch. A Psalm is quoted as David's which, whatever its true date, it seems difficult to believe really came from him. The Book of Daniel is assumed to be really the work of the prophet of that name. . . . The stories of Noah and of Jonah are both referred to as literal history . . . and to crown all we have in the Sermon on the Mount that strong assertion 'Till heaven and earth pass away one jot or one tittle shall in no wise pass away from the Law till all be fulfilled' " (Matt. 5:17-18) .[22]

21 See Frank M. Cross and Noel Freedman, "The Song of Miriam," *Journal of Near Eastern Studies*, Vol. XIV (1955), pp. 237-50; also W. F. Albright, *From the Stone Age to Christianity* (1940), p. 207.
22 *Inspiration*, p. 409.

This belief of Christ in what Sanday cannot accept, he solves by two methods. First, he adopts the modern kenotic theory (Christ in His self-emptying made mistakes). He speaks diffidently, wishing that a systematic theologian would make the decision, but assures us that "many of the most reverent and most careful of our theologians, men of the most scrupulous and tender loyalty to the historical decisions of the Undivided Church and of our own have pronounced that there is no inconsistency; that limitations of knowledge might be and were assumed along with other limitations."[23] He cites in evidence Gore, Plummer, Swayne, and others. We may question his method of proving his orthodoxy by reference to contemporary opinion. More often orthodoxy has had to stand against the tenor of the day. It is still just possible that the Christian should hold that Christ and the apostles were right and that Sanday and his authorities labored under a misconception.

But even Sanday hesitates to hold that what Christ explicitly affirmed was wrong. He holds only that where Christ was in error it was in matters of no consequence — as if revelation and inspiration were minor matters.

Secondly, Sanday attempts to set Christ against Himself, holding that the verses in the later portion of Matt. 5, which declare the authority of Christ against "what hath been said by them of old time," give a truer insight into Christ's view of the Old Testament and imply that the Old Testament was less inspired than the new revelation.[24]

This is a serious charge, that Christ both affirmed every jot and tittle of the Old Testament and yet proceeded at once to contradict it. Here is perhaps a place where Sanday's opinions clearly influenced his exegesis, to the detriment of succeeding students of the Sermon on the Mount.

There is a better exegesis of the supposed contradiction. Sanday should have noted that Christ contradicted ancient oral tradition ("it hath been said") not a written Scripture (regularly quoted by "that which was written by the prophets" or some such formula). Moreover, in a good example of his usage (Matt. 5:43), it is the portion of the oral tradition not found in Scripture which is denied ("hate thine enemy"). In the famous

23 *Ibid.*, p. 415.
24 *Ibid.*, p. 410f.

lex talionis (Matt. 5:38), the traditional interpretation of the Rabbis had taken a good rule of justice found three times in the Old Testament as a guide for the courts of Israel and had made it into an excuse for personal vengeance. This practice is forbidden also by Paul (Rom. 12:19-21), and Paul cites the Old Testament as proof! The other such verses in Matt. 5, though not so obvious, yield readily to similar treatment. The Pharisees used the regulations on oaths as an excuse for all kinds of chicanery made possible by legalistic codes they had developed on binding and nonbinding oaths (cf. Matt. 23:16f). They had taken Deut. 24:1 as an allowance for divorce — often allowing it on slight grounds. A more natural translation of the Hebrew (followed by the Septuagint) makes it a recognition of the fact of divorce (Moses suffered it) and prohibition of its grosser evil, wife trading. In Matt. 5:28 Christ does not contradict or add greatly to the Seventh Commandment. The Tenth Commandment says as much as Christ does. He was actually rescuing the commandment from the externalizing exegesis of the Pharisees. Likewise in Matt. 5:21 Christ gave no doctrine novel to the Scripture which says "thou shalt not hate thy brother in thine heart" (Lev. 19:17). Sanday very regrettably is *looking* for a variant strand in Christ's teaching rather than bending his theology to the exegesis of the text.[25]

Again, in dealing with John 10:35, Sanday conveniently concludes that the argument is strictly hypothetical and *ad hominem* and need not, he thinks, express Jesus' real view. A different view is given in Meyer's Commentary — one based more carefully on the Greek text. Meyer points out that the truth of Scripture is a basic part of Christ's argument. But Sanday has a second alternative, if his first suggestion fails: "The memory of this had lain for some 60 years in the mind of one who was himself a thorough Jew, and we cannot be equally certain that it came out precisely as it went in."[26] Painstaking exegesis is not cultivated by distracting from the certainty of the text at hand.

Another example of exegesis which is possibly tendential, at least derogating from a high Christology, is Sanday's treatment of the title "Son of Man." He says, "There are places in the

25 These passages are treated at greater length in the writer's *Inspiration and Canonicity of the Bible*, pp. 48-56.

26 *Inspiration*, p. 433.

Gospels where we could almost substitute Humanity for Son of Man."[27] He cites Dan. 7:13 as the most important source of the title but says Jesus read into it another thing than the eschatological figure. Thus to dismiss cavalierly an important title which Jesus used many times of Himself as an eschatological figure is not to deal with the realities of the text. A belief in only the general helpfulness of a text does not normally engender close study as to its meaning.

We offer but one further example. Sanday must share with Headlam, the co-author, responsibility for the treatment of Rom. 5:12-19 in the *International Critical Commentary*. But whichever was responsible, the exegesis opposes the federal headship of Adam over the race, apparently because this would be a distasteful doctrine.

The mediating school of English theology, of which Sanday was an exponent, did not continue to mediate. The camel soon occupied the tent. If inspiration in the high sense of inerrancy is given up, the doctrines of Christ, of God, and of man suffer and become the subject of human opinion rather than divine revelation. May we not feel that the rather unsatisfactory state of exegetical study today both in the Old Testament and New Testament fields is a direct result of opinions such as those of Sanday in which the Old Testament was disbelieved and the witness of Christ to the Scriptures was minimized? Hebrew is a hard language. Why study to read the Old Testament in Hebrew if what you learn to read is quite untrustworthy? We have seen in the last generation numerous theological seminaries of critical persuasion remove Hebrew from their required curricula. Greek has also suffered. Naturally, theology has also suffered. If the Bible is not verbally inspired and true, why labor so hard at its study? Happily there are some signs of a reversal of this course.

Those who do not believe the Bible usually do not even try seriously to exegete it (Barth's exegeses are purely theological, using the Biblical texts as pretexts for statements of his own views), but those who still tremble at God's Word seem again to be awakening to their duty of expounding afresh and ever more faithfully the written Word, which had such authentication of the Living Word Himself.

27 *Christologies,* p. 124f.

Chapter VII

H. H. ROWLEY AND THE NEW TREND
IN BIBLICAL STUDIES

By Merrill F. Unger

H. H. Rowley, Professor of Semitic Languages and Literature in the Victoria University of Manchester, England, and Secretary of the Society of Old Testament Study in England, Scotland and Wales, is recognized both in America and abroad as one of the leading Old Testament scholars and critics of the present day. His importance is accentuated because, perhaps more than any other writer, he has given the fuller expression and interpretation to the change which has come over Biblical studies in recent years.

In open reaction against a mere intellectual and scientific approach, practically divorced from a spiritual understanding of content, which to a large degree has characterized the modern critical study of the Scriptures and stigmatized it with spiritual barrenness, the new movement is an attempt to synthesize the various elements which from the critical standpoint enter into a complete comprehension of these ancient Oracles — the divine as well as the human, the spiritual as well as the scientific, the practical as well as the theoretical, and the religiously relevant as well as the technical.

The task to which the new criticism thus sets itself involves the problem of integrating the alleged findings of modern critical scholarship into a reverent, believing approach to the Bible that will not eventuate, as has heretofore largely been the case, in virtual abandonment of the Sacred Scriptures as the authoritative basis of religious faith, with resultant spiritual bankruptcy. To this end, as Otto Baab has pointed out, "biblical scholars are beginning to evaluate their work, not simply on the basis of the advancement of technical knowledge, but likewise in the light of the religious consequences."[1]

1 *The Theology of the Old Testament* (New York, 1949), p. 15.

In 1944 appeared R. B. Y. Scott's *The Relevance of the Prophets,* Norman H. Snaith's *The Distinctive Ideas of the Old Testament,* G. E. Wright's *The Challenge of Israel's Faith,* W. C. Bower's *The Living Bible* (revised edition) and H. H. Rowley's *The Relevance of the Bible.* In 1946 Rowley published *The Rediscovery of the Old Testament* and H. Wheeler Robinson, editor of *Record and Revelation,* issued *Inspiration and Revelation in the Old Testament.* In 1947 *Revelation and Response in the Old Testament* by Cuthbert A. Simpson came from the press.

The appearance of the word "revelation," moreover, as G. Ch. Aalders notes, "is a remarkable phenomenon of our days: Old Testament study is clearly inclined to reckon with the element of revelation."[2] In dealing with this subject, however, Wheeler Robinson and Simpson are not exceptions. Other authors have written on the problem of revelation in the Old Testament, such as Willy Staerk, Harris Birkeland and Walter Eichrodt.

Aalders correctly traces the emphasis on revelation to two causes: the anti-Judaism of the Nazis and the theology of Karl Barth. Nazism in libelling the Old Testament as a "book of the Jews" led indirectly to a new approach to it and a renewed appreciation of it. Barthianism by its peculiar construction "made it easy for many Old Testament students who cannot abandon literary and even historical criticism of the Divine Book to acknowledge nevertheless its revelatory character."[3]

Another indication of the constructive trend in Old Testament studies stressing the relevance of the Bible for modern life and the value of its distinctive ideas and religious teachings[4] is the revival of interest in Old Testament theology with pertinent discussion of the validity and authority of such theology.[5] A quarter of a century ago "there was scant interest"

---

2 "Old Testament Study Today," in *The Evangelical Quarterly* (Jan., 1952), p. 12.
3 Aalders, *op. cit.,* pp. 12, 13.
4 Cf. G. E. Wright, whose avowed purpose in his monograph (*The Old Testament Against Its Environment,* Chicago, 1950) is to show "that the faith of Israel even in its earliest and basic forms is so utterly different from that of the contemporary polytheisms that one simply cannot explain it fully by evolutionary or environmental categories." (p. 7).
5 W. A. Smart, "The Death and Birth of Old Testament Theology," *Journal of Religion,* Vol. 23 (1943), Nos. 1 and 2. Wm. A. Irwin, "The Reviving Theology of the Old Testament," *Journal of Religion,* Vol. 25 (1945), No. 4.

in this subject "because the very term implied a unity that was felt to be wholly lacking" in the Old Testament.[6] Noteworthy is the appearance of Otto Baab's *The Theology of the Old Testament* (New York, 1949), and Paul Heinisch' *Theologie des Alten Testamentes* (1940), appearing in a revised English edition by William Heidt (Collegeville, Minnesota, 1950).

The task to which the new criticism represented by Professor Rowley has set itself of attempting to harmonize the alleged discoveries of modern critical scholarship with the new constructive approach to the Bible as a spiritual Book demanding a "spiritual" as well as an "intellectual understanding" to its full comprehension[7] is extremely difficult. It may well be that in accepting "substantially the work of Biblical criticism"[8] any imagined harmonization effected between the Bible as a trustworthy guide to faith and practice and the alleged findings of modern criticism will have to be made almost totally at the expense of accepting the Bible as reliable. However, the shifting history of many of the higher critical views, such as the various documentary theories of the Pentateuch, together with the high degree of subjectivity which characterizes them and the questionable assumptions which underlie many of them, well warrant firm skepticism on the part of the conservative scholar toward many of the alleged "findings" of modern Biblical criticism, no matter how widely they are embraced or how loudly they are hailed as "assured results," especially when they compel him to lower his attitude toward the inspiration and trustworthiness of the Bible. So it is that G. Ch. Aalders says, ". . . we feel the more obliged to put forth all our efforts in a real scholarly research of the Old Testament which does not in the least detract from its divine authority."[9]

The basically important critical view of Professor Rowley which has enabled him to integrate modern critical views in what he calls "a spiritual understanding of the spiritual treasures" of the Bible[10] is that which concerns inspiration. He does not hesitate to reject completely the older orthodox position, well defined by B. B. Warfield as "a supernatural influence

6 H. H. Rowley, *The Old Testament and Modern Study* (Oxford, 1951), p. xvi.

7 *The Relevance of the Bible* (New York, 1944), p. 19.

8 *Ibid.,* p. 15.

9 *Ibid.,* p. 13.

10 *The Relevance of the Bible,* p. 19.

exerted on the sacred writers by the Spirit of God, by virtue of which their writings are given Divine trustworthiness."[11] Protagonists of the new, more conservative and constructive Biblical criticism do not conceal their impatience with this "once reputable doctrine of verbal inspiration of Scripture."[12] "Such a view," according to Professor Rowley, "was never free from difficulties, but modern scholarship has made it quite untenable. . . ."[13] He proceeds to lament the fact that "there are not a few who fear that its abandonment means the abandonment of any real belief in the inspiration of the Bible," declaring, on the other hand, "that while modern scholarship has made impossible the old view of inspiration, it does not threaten a truer view of inspiration. . . ."[14]

Since all evangelical Christian doctrines are developed from the Bible and rest upon it for authority, and *the correct Biblical teaching* of inspiration is, as L. Boettner so aptly says, "the mother and guardian of all the others,"[15] and since a faulty view of the inspiration of Scripture is bound to produce unsound views and to permit mere interpretations of men to parade as established facts and genuine discoveries, it is of the utmost importance to examine carefully Professor Rowley's "truer view of inspiration" to see in what sense, if any, it measures up to its claims, or whether it is in reality a mere concession to unsound critical positions rather than a necessary accommodation to the alleged errancy of Scripture.

Fortunately, Professor Rowley is quite explicit in what he means by the term "a truer view of inspiration." He leaves no doubt concerning his contention that "for the New Testament no more than the Old . . . can inspiration be supposed to yield verbal infallibility."[16] Because inspiration is a divine-human process, he concludes that it must therefore be subject to limitation and error from the human side. Regarding "those through whom the revelation of the Old Testament was given," he says: "Not only did their failings mar the word which God spake

---

11 B. B. Warfield, "Inspiration," *International Standard Bible Encyclopedia,* p. 1473.
12 W. F. Albright, *The Archeology of Palestine* (Pelican Books, 1949), p. 255.
13 *The Relevance of the Bible,* p. 21.
14 *Ibid.*
15 *Studies in Theology* (Grand Rapids, 1947), p. 48.
16 *The Relevance of the Bible,* p. 48.

through them, and prevent the perfect revelation reaching men by their means, but those same failings marred their own vision of Him. They had false ideas of God and cherished false hopes, and these false hopes dimmed their eyes. They could neither receive nor communicate the perfect Word of God."[17]

Professor Rowley imagines, moreover, that only through Christ and His perfect human personality could God's perfect Word be given, and that "all that we learn of God in the Old Testament that is in harmony with the revelation given in Christ is truly of God. . . . And all that we learn of God in the Old Testament that is not in harmony with the revelation given in Christ is not of God. It represents the misunderstanding of God by sincere men, whose view was distorted by the eyes through which they looked upon Him."[18]

But Professor Rowley's position becomes inconsistent when he faces the fact that we are also dependent upon inspired men for our knowledge of God's perfect revelation in Christ, since our Lord wrote nothing Himself. If inspired Old Testament writers transmitted their human failings and errors to their writings, did not the Synoptists and the apostle John do the same in writing about our Lord? Is not the "perfect revelation" itself imperfect? How can we be sure the portrait of Christ in the New Testament is not one-sided?

How then can Professor Rowley resort to "the revelation given in Christ" as a standard for evaluating what is "of God" or "not of God" in the Old Testament? An even more serious question is how he can sustain consistently his denial that his position does not "substitute a purely subjective standard for the objective character of revelation," especially when he contends that his view "substitutes as the standard the revelation given in Christ."[19] At most, within the framework of his theory, his standard is defective, and if granted, it can only be less subjective than the one he rejects.

It is no doubt inconsequential to Professor Rowley that his view is utterly at variance with the Bible's own testimony concerning its inspiration. "All Scripture is given by inspiration of God, and is profitable for reproof, for doctrine, for correction, for instruction in righteousness: that the man of God may be per-

17 *Ibid.*, p. 28.
18 *Ibid.*, p. 33; cf. especially p. 47.
19 *Ibid.*, p. 33.

fect, thoroughly furnished unto all good works" (2 Tim. 3:16, 17). This passage not only enunciates the fact of the inspiration of the Old Testament, but stresses its high moral and spiritual value, parts of which Professor Rowley intimates are "spiritually unsatisfying" and involve "dishonoring God."[20]

The important passage in Peter's Second Epistle, which outlines the nature of the inspiration of the Old Testament, clashes even more violently with Professor Rowley's views. "Knowing this first, that no prophecy of scripture is of private interpretation. For no prophecy ever came by the will of man: but men spake from God, being moved by the Holy Spirit" (2 Pet. 1:20-21). First, these verses declare *how* the Old Testament did *not* originate. It is not of "private interpretation," that is, it is neither the result of human research, nor the product of the writer's own thought, containing his errors and miscalculations. It, moreover, did not "come into being by the will of man." Man did not purpose to write it, determine its subject matter, plan its arrangement, or mar the particular revelation God purposed at the time.

Secondly, these verses outline *how* the ancient Scriptures *did* originate. "Men," that is, certain chosen men, "spake from God," the Source — spake as the voice of God. These men spoke because they were being borne or carried along by the Holy Spirit, as a ship is propelled forward by the wind. A strong, definite operation of the Holy Spirit upon the human agent is indicated, making the message *His, not theirs.*

How diametrically opposed to the claims of the Scriptures is Professor Rowley's description of the inspiration of the Old Testament: "They who would understand the Old Testament must read it for what it is, and not for what it is not, must read its stories, not as exact records of history, inerrant in every detail or as authoritative revelations of the future, or as even wholly trustworthy revelations of God, but rather as the experiences and thoughts of men who reached out after God, and responded to God's reaching out after them. . . ."[21]

Professor Rowley would doubtless justify his sharp disagreement with Scriptural testimony by alleging that these ideas of inspiration were the result of the misunderstandings of the

20 *Ibid.*, p. 32.
21 *Ibid.*, p. 43.

apostles Paul and Peter which marred the word which God spake through them and prevented the perfect revelation reaching men by their means. But what will he do with our Lord's witness concerning the inviolability of the Old Testament Scriptures, who said, "And the Scriptures cannot be broken" (John 10:35), and by whom Professor Rowley asserts "the truth of the Old Testament is tested," and who, he declares, "gives the measure of its inspiration"?[22]

In pointing out what we believe to be fatal weaknesses in Professor Rowley's view of Biblical inspiration, we maintain that the difficult question still remains. Is it nevertheless a necessary accommodation to the alleged errancy of canonical Scripture? Are there actually literary and historical inaccuracies[23] and theological imperfections,[24] particularly in the Old Testament, as Professor Rowley would have us believe, that render "the older view of inspiration" now "quite untenable," owing to the discoveries of modern scholarship?[25]

It would be foolish to deny that there are literary problems, seeming historical discrepancies, and other types of difficulties in the Old Testament. The historical-archeological questions alone are sufficient to challenge constructive scholarship for many years to come. But we refuse to believe that the varied problems are of such a nature that, correctly interpreted in the light of the *bona fide* findings of modern Biblical science, they necessitate scrapping the older and higher view of inspiration, which the cumulative testimony of Scripture claims for itself.

While it is not our purpose to cast aspersion upon modern scholarship, but rather to praise its every discovery and to welcome warmly and without bias its every valid conclusion based on objective facts, we cannot but believe that the preponderant mass of the alleged evidence it adduces to show the untenability of the older view of Biblical inspiration is based, not upon the objective findings of modern Biblical science, but upon the erroneous, often highly plausible interpretations of evidence furnished by such findings, and more widely, upon false, highly artificial theories of literary composition, which have been

22 *Ibid.*, p. 50.
23 Cf. *The Growth of the Old Testament* (London, 1950), pp. 114, 154f, 156-58.
24 Cf. *The Rediscovery of the Old Testament* (Philadelphia, 1946), pp. 187-90.
25 *The Relevance of the Bible*, p. 21.

foisted upon the Old Testament, especially the Pentateuch, and which have thrown constructive study completely out of focus. Not until Old Testament scholarship, for example, sees the unsoundness of the presuppositions upon which the documentary theory of the Pentateuch is erected[26] and the vast amount of injury it has inflicted upon Old Testament study, will there be a genuine and far-reaching constructive trend in Biblical studies.

Fortunately, there are definite indications of a decided change in Old Testament literary criticism, especially in Pentateuchal criticism. "Thirty years ago it looked as if the problem of the Pentateuch was reaching a definitive solution. . . . The Graf-Wellhausen theory had triumphed and it seemed that little or nothing remained to be done."[27] But since then attack has been growing, through such names as Erdmans, Redpath, Wiener, Dahse, Löhr, Möller, Cassuto, Dornseiff, Vaccari, etc.,[28] until Ivan Engnell of Uppsala in *Gamla Testamentet* (1945) says, what ought to have been said long since, that the Wellhausian fabric of learning "represents a modern, anachronistic *book-view (boksyn)*, and is therefore an interpretation in modern categories, an *interpretatio europeica moderna*. For a right judgment of the problem a 'modified' or 'moderate' view of literary-critical type is, therefore, not enough; what is demanded is a radical break with this whole method. There never were any parallel continuous documents in the Mosaic books of the kind that are assumed. That large parts of the material in the Mosaic books were from the beginning or at a very early stage fixed in writing is quite another matter."[29]

There is other seeming evidence from the Old Testament besides erroneous interpretation of objective scientific discoveries and false theories saddled upon it by modern scholarship that seems to militate against the older view of Biblical inspiration. There are, as Professor Rowley points out, "difficulties quite apart from any that modern scholarship has created or re-

26 For a discussion of this subject see the present writer's *Introductory Guide to the Old Testament* (Grand Rapids, 1951), pp. 247-75.
27 C. R. North, "Pentateuchal Criticism," in *The Old Testament and Modern Study* (Oxford, 1951) p. 48.
28 For a survey see G. Ch. Aalders, *op. cit.,* pp. 7f.
29 *Gamla Testamentet. En traditionshistorisk inledning* (Stockholm, 1945), I, 189f.
30 *Ibid.,* p. 22; cf. pp. 22-24.

vealed. . . ."[30] These problems, such as the differences between parallel passages in the books of Kings and Chronicles, may be attributable to a variety of causes, such as textual corruption, especially in transmitted numbers, differences in the compiler's or redactor's viewpoint, copyists' errors, and the like, and constitute the legitimate domain of scholarly criticism. Other problems exist simply because of the modern reader's or scholar's ignorance of all the facts that lie behind the seeming difficulty or discrepancy.

Copied and recopied endlessly by hand, some parts for almost three millennia before the discovery of the printing press in the middle of the fifteenth century A.D., the transmitted writings inevitably were subject to the errors of copyists despite extreme precautions taken to avoid them. And yet, although freedom from error is to be attributed only to the original copies of the inspired writings, actually divine providence has faithfully preserved the Sacred Scriptures with regard to their substance. Indeed it may be said that the fact that the Old Testament Scriptures have come down to us in the high state of preservation in which they exist in the Massoretic Text is almost as great a miracle as the inspiration which produced the original inerrant autographs.

This fact ought to inspire greater confidence on the part of scholars, and Professor Rowley in the light of it is unreasonable in concluding that because the present Hebrew text of the Old Testament is in places corrupt, "clearly, therefore, if there once existed an inerrant text as the direct handiwork of God, its Divine Author did not think it of importance to preserve it; and once it is admitted that the Bible now in our hands cannot be relied on to give the authentic word of God, the whole basis of the older appeal to it has gone."[31]

But has the "whole basis of the older appeal" gone simply because inerrancy of inspiration does not assure inerrancy of transmission? Rather, it has served a good purpose in evoking scholarly researches, prodigious and devout, and given impetus to studies in linguistic and archeological science and progress in textual criticism in the last century and a half to give to the present generation a faithful representation of the original text of Scripture. May not the challenge and the blessing of this

31 *Ibid.*, p. 24.

consecrated task have been one reason in the Divine Mind for not causing the Sacred Text to be transmitted inerrantly?

Is Professor Rowley's contention "that the Bible now in our hands cannot be relied on to give the authentic word of God" really true? It was certainly *thought* to be true a generation ago, as Professor Rowley himself points out: "Towards the text of the Old Testament, as represented by the Massoretic Hebrew, there was a rooted suspicion, and commentators vied with one another in the ingenuity with which it was emended. Where any version could be invoked in favor of a change its support was welcomed, but where no version could be laid under contribution it mattered little. Any guess was preferred to a text that was assumed to be untrustworthy."[32]

Professor Rowley confesses that this is an "overstatement; yet there was," he adds, "a very substantial justification for it, and the innumerable emendations that filled every commentary may be appealed to in evidence."[33] But "today," by which he means 1951, he says, "the whole scene is changed, and the student of the Old Testament is living in a very different climate."[34]

Doubtless the climate must have changed considerably also since 1944 when Professor Rowley himself contended "that the Bible now in our hands cannot be relied on to give the authentic word of God."[35] What effected the change? Archeology once again came to the aid of sober scholarship to act as a purge on radical criticism — this time in which is unquestionably "the most important discovery ever made in Old Testament manuscripts"[36] — the recovery of the Isaiah Scroll in 1947, dating from the second century B.C.

Concerning the value of this phenomenal manuscript find, W. F. Albright says significantly: "It cannot be insisted too strongly that the Isaiah Scroll proves the great antiquity of the text of the Massoretic Book, warning us against the light-hearted emendation in which we used to indulge."[37] In his essay, "The Old Testament and the Archaeology of Palestine," in

---

32 *The Old Testament and Modern Study,* p. xv.
33 *Ibid.,* p. xv.
34 *Ibid.,* p. xvi.
35 *The Relevance of the Bible,* p. 24.
36 G. E. Wright, *The Biblical Archeologist* (May, 1948), p. 21.
37 *Bulletin of the American Schools of Oriental Research,* 118 (April, 1950), p. 6.

Professor Rowley's *The Old Testament and Modern Study,* Albright comments even more pointedly on the value of the new Biblical texts: "One thing is certain: the days when Duhm and his imitators could recklessly emend the Hebrew text of the poetic books of the Bible are gone forever; so also when Wutz felt free to reinterpret the original Hebrew *Vorlage* of the LXX to suit himself. We may rest assured that the consonantal text of the Hebrew Bible, though not infallible, has been preserved with an accuracy perhaps unparalleled in any other Near-Eastern literature."[38]

Despite Professor Rowley's skepticism as to the reliability of the Massoretic Text manifest in his statement in 1944 that "the Bible now in our hands cannot be relied on to give us the authentic word of God," the changing attitude toward the consonantal text of the Hebrew Bible was discernible almost two decades before the discovery of the Dead Sea Scrolls in 1947 and was fully justified by this epochal find. As Aalders points out,[39] it was clearly perceptible in the Eighteenth International Congress of Orientalists at Leiden in 1931, where M. S. Daiches of London led a strong opposition against the current craze for emendation of the Hebrew text. The Swedish scholar, H. S. Nyberg, took a similar position in an article, "Das textkritische Problem des Alten Testaments am Hoseabuche demonstriert"[40] and in his book *Studien zum Hoseabuche* (1935).

The changed attitude also made possible the new Dutch translation of the Old Testament from the Massoretic Text begun in 1933 and completed in 1951 under the auspices of the Netherlands Bible Society. When the International Conference of Bible Translators met at Woudschoten in the Netherlands in 1947, those present recommended that the Massoretic Text be followed. It is, moreover, quite understandable why in 1950 J. Philip Hyatt in a review of Elmer A. Leslie's *The Psalms Translated and Interpreted in the Light of Hebrew Life and Worship* should write thus: "Also they [the author's new translations] too often rest upon emendation of the Hebrew text [following Gunkel, Ehrlich, and others]. The first duty of the modern translator should be to give a faithful rendering of MT, whenever that can be made to yield good sense; if not, he may

---

38 *Ibid.,* p. 25.
39 *Op. cit.,* p. 4.
40 *Zeitschrift für die alttestamentliche Wissenschaft* (1934).

then resort to emendation on the basis of the ancient versions. Conjectural emendation should be a last resort, and is seldom necessary."[41] This evidence scarcely supports Professor Rowley's contention that the text of the Bible today is unreliable in giving us the Word of God.

In addition to literary, historical-archaeological and textual difficulties which Professor Rowley claims render the older view of Biblical inspiration untenable he insists on another line of evidence — the theological. The Old Testament, he contends, "says much about the character of God which is abidingly true. At the same time it says much that we can no longer accept as true. For many outgrown beliefs about God were entertained by Old Testament writers and characters, and we must dintinguish between the continuing thread and the passing elements."[42]

There is a differentiation, of course, to be made between truth actually conveyed by inspired Old Testament writers and thoughts entertained by Old Testament characters. Whereas the former may be germinal and undeveloped, we firmly believe it can never contain what is false. The latter, however, may be distorted and erroneous. That which is untrue, especially with respect to that which concerns God, is utterly incompatible with divine inspiration as it is defined in Scripture, and can only be posited of a theory, which, like Professor Rowley's, has no Scriptural support.

As an example of what the Old Testament says about the character of God "that we can no longer accept as true," Professor Rowley cites the unprovoked attack of the Israelites on the land of Canaan, and in particular such an episode as the slaughter of the entire population of Jericho "as an act of religion, because they thought it was well-pleasing to Yahweh."[43] This stricture is of the utmost gravity. In its final analysis it stigmatizes the sacred penmen with duplicity when they represented unequivocally as the actual command and covenant of Yahweh (Josh. 6:17, 18; 7:11) that which was not only His command and covenant, but that which constituted an outrageous calumny upon His character. How can such a view of inspired Old Testament writers be reconciled with the exalted New Testament description of them as "holy men" who "spake

41 *Journal of Biblical Literature* (June, 1950), p. 186.
42 *The Rediscovery of the Old Testament*, p. 187.
43 *Ibid.*, p. 187.

from God as they were moved by the Holy Spirit" (2 Pet. 1:21)?

But what shall be said of the alleged untruth concerning the character of God implied in this and similar Old Testament episodes which are so offensive to modern critics? If Yahweh actually commanded Joshua and Israel to put Jericho under the ban and to exterminate the Canaanites, as inspired Old Testament writers allege, is this contrary to the character of God revealed in Christ? We believe it is not.

There is no doubt that our Lord perfectly revealed the infinite divine love, which is God's essential nature (1 John 3:16; 4:8). His redemptive work made possible the full manifestation of that love because the divine holiness was satisfied in the death of the Son. God can now be just (righteous) and at the same time "the justifier of him that believeth in Jesus" (Rom. 3:26). The Father's love can now be graciously showered upon those who accept the Son's redemptive work. But apart from faith in the Son, God's love is of necessity rendered inoperative toward unbelievers. Because of the demands of His infinite holiness, they are under wrath and judgment because under sin, and they must accept the remedy God's love has provided in dealing with that sin if they are to escape its dire consequences.

God chose His ancient people Israel and manifested His love toward them by virtue of His redemptive purpose for them in Abraham, Isaac, Jacob, and the Promised Seed. He redeemed them out of Egypt as a type of all redemption and established them a priestly nation at Sinai (Exod. 19:5-6). His love toward them was possible by virtue of the fact that they were under His gracious covenant relationships and bound to the types and ceremonies of the Levitical law, which in a most detailed and meaningful fashion pointed to Christ. The Amorites, the Canaanites and other surrounding peoples not under God's electing grace and His covenant mercy, were subject to wrath and judgment as unbelievers in Christ are now under condemnation. This was in a special sense true, as the iniquity of the Amorite (cf. Gen. 15:16) and the Canaanite was now full.

The complete destruction of Jericho and its inhabitants or the extermination of the Canaanites in general is no more a contradiction of God's character than the terrifying divine visitation upon Jerusalem in 70 A.D. or the wholesale slaughter of the godless masses of Christ-rejectors at Christ's second advent (Rev. 19:11-16). Unbelievers and apostates enjoy temporary immunity, but when their iniquity is full, God's wrath, which is the inevitable result of His outraged holiness, is poured out without measure (Rev. 11:18), whether in Old or in New Testament times.

In his discussion of sin in the thought of the Bible, Professor Rowley recognizes clearly the wrath of God as an aspect of sin, and writes: "The sentimental spirit of our age often chooses to ignore this aspect of sin, and to eliminate the wrath of God from its thought of Him. In so doing it dispenses with a real element in the Biblical revelation of God."[44] It therefore seems pointless to claim that such incidents as the divine command to destroy the Canaanites or Jericho and its inhabitants or the Amalekites (1 Sam. 15), all of whom aroused the wrath of God, contain that which is "spiritually unsatisfying" and involve "dishonoring God," who is changeless in His character or that contradicts Him who "is perfectly revealed in Christ."[45]

It must be remembered that it was the same Christ of love who said to those who were called to believe: "Come unto me, all ye that labour and are heavy laden, and I will give you rest. Take my yoke upon you, and learn of me; for I am meek and lowly in heart: and ye shall find rest unto your souls" (Matt. 11:28-29), who also said to those who rejected the grace of God and came under His wrath: "Ye serpents, ye offspring of vipers, how shall ye escape the judgment of hell?" (Matt. 23:33).

At His second advent the same gentle, loving Christ who in His first advent said: "For the Son of man is come to seek and to save that which was lost" (Luke 19:10), will say to those who have rejected salvation: "I have trodden the winepress alone; and of the peoples there was no man with me: yea, I trod them in mine anger, and trampled them in my wrath; and their life-blood is sprinkled upon my garments, and I have stained all my raiment" (Isa. 63:3). And it was the humble Christ of God's love who most clearly warned against the fearfulness of eternal hell, "where their worm dieth not and the fire is not quenched" (Mark 9:42-50).

Taking into account the full Scriptural revelation of sin in the light of the divine holiness and the universal guilt and condemnation of men outside Christ, together with the con-

44 *The Relevance of the Bible,* p. 161.
45 *Ibid.,* pp. 43f.

comitant truth that God bears with sinners until their iniquity is ripe, there is as little warrant for modern critics to reject much that is revealed about God in the Old Testament as the preconceptions of men as there was for the heretic Marcion in the second century to maintain that the God of the Old Testament is not the God of the New Testament. In both Testaments God is "a consuming fire" (Heb. 12:29) against sin and sinners not under the blood of Christ, either typically and anticipatively under the Old Covenant, or anti-typically and actually under the New Covenant. Foregleams of His infinite love in the Old Testament were made possible only because of promise, covenant, ceremony and symbol which pointed forward to Him who was to come. After He who was to come actually came, the same fire of God's holy wrath burned against sin and sinners outside the sphere of faith in Christ. He who in infinite love and pity proclaimed "the year of Jehovah's favor" at His coming in shame and rejection, will proclaim "the day of vengeance of our God" (Isa. 61:2) at His advent in power and glory, when He gives "Babylon the great . . . the cup of the wine of the fierceness of his wrath" (Rev. 16:19).

One more example upon which Professor Rowley lays much stress and which he develops in detail[46] will be considered. It is cited by him to show that inspired Old Testament writers "had false ideas of God and cherished false hopes" so that "they could neither receive nor communicate the perfect Word of God."[47] The incident is that of the death of Uzzah in connection with David's abortive attempt to bring the Ark of God up to Jerusalem (2 Sam. 6:1-15). According to 1 Chron. 15:13, the death of Uzzah is specifically attributed to the fact, whether he was a Levite or not, that the Ark of God was being transported and handled contrary to divine direction. It was not first covered by the priests and then borne by the Levites by means of its staves (Num. 4:5,15,19).

It is quite obvious from 1 Chron. that David failed to acquaint himself with the divine stipulations for removing the Ark. Employing a new cart was simply a Philistine expedient (1 Sam. 6:7,8). When Uzzah put forth his hand to steady the Ark "the anger of the Lord" was kindled against him, "and God smote

46 *Ibid.*, pp. 28-31.
47 *Ibid.*, p. 28.

him there for his error; and there he died by the ark of God"
(2 Sam. 6:7).

The question is whether Uzzah was actually guilty of death or
whether the sacred penmen merely considered him guilty because they shared the popular but perverted notions concerning
God's character. Despite Professor Rowley's insistence on the
latter view, we believe Uzzah was unquestionably guilty. Though
a Levite, he was forbidden under any circumstances to touch
the Ark, "lest he die" (Num. 4:15). His ignorance could not be
pleaded, for he had been so long in the house with the Ark that
he was duty bound to make himself familiar with the law regarding it. Nor can it be urged, as Professor Rowley contends,
that "if the character of God is unchanging, then it can never
have been true that He blazed forth in anger against a man for
the wholly praiseworthy act of trying to prevent the Ark which
had been entrusted to him from falling."[48]

How can it have been a "wholly praiseworthy act" when it
was in direct disobedience to God's law? As F. Gardiner aptly
says: "What may seem, at first thought, an exceeding severe
penalty for a well-meaning, though unlawful act, is seen on
reflection to have been a very necessary manifestation of the
Divine displeasure; for this act involved not only a violation of
the letter of the law (of which David was also guilty), but a
want of reverence for the majesty of God as symbolized by the
ark, and showed a disposition to familiarity with sacred
things."[49]

Uzzah stands as a type of all who, albeit with good intentions
humanly speaking, adopt Philistine ways of doing God's service
in disobedience to His Word. Judgments of this type, like the
sin of Dathan and Abiram at the institution of the priesthood
(Lev. 10), the crime of Achan at the entrance to Canaan
(Josh. 7), and the duplicity of Ananias and Sapphira at the
commencement of the Church's corporate life (Acts 5), involving physical death and not eternal destiny, were dealt with
severely because, standing on the threshold of some new beginning, they serve as a stern warning to later offenders. In this
instance, a new and important period was opening in the conduct of Israel's public worship and David and the people,

---

48 *Ibid.,* p. 30.
49 *A Bible Commentary for English Readers,* C. J. Ellicott, ed. (New
York, n. d.), II, 459.

obviously careless in these matters, needed to be reminded that Philistine ways and disregard of God's Word in holy things demand His judgment.

For tenuous reasons, Professor Rowley rejects Uzzah's culpability. "In the first place," he argues, "the Ark had been kept in the house of Uzzah's father for many years, without calling down divine wrath. In the second place, since by even the chronicler's admission no Levites were employed on this occasion, the Ark must have been placed on the cart by non-Levites."[50]

While it is true the Ark had been kept in the house of Uzzah's father for a very extended period without any manifestation of divine wrath, there is no evidence that anything was done there in violation of the divine regulation under those unusual circumstances, which in any event, certainly constituted a divine accommodation. With regard to transferring the Ark to the cart, the chronicler does not intimate that no Levites were employed in this activity, that is, that Uzzah and his brother Ahio were not Levites, but that Levites were not employed *in the prescribed way* of carrying the Ark on their shoulders with staves, rather than transporting it on a cart. It seems extremely improbable that the Ark should have remained for so long untended by Levites. There is every reason not only to suppose that Uzzah and Ahio were Levites, but that they transferred the Ark to the cart in the prescribed Levitical way.

Professor Rowley, however, offers a further objection to the view that Uzzah was guilty, namely, that "when David decided to desist from the attempt to take the Ark into Jerusalem, he placed it in the house of Obed-Edom, the Gittite, but so far from divine anger being shown for this breach of the Law, marked blessing came to Obed-Edom."[51] But in what way was the Law breached when the Ark was allowed to rest in the house of Obed-Edom, who was a Levite and therefore authorized to take care of it (1 Chron. 26:1-5)? Had it not rested similarly in the house of Abinadab? The judgment of Uzzah and the blessing of Obed-Edom were both to warn David that a holy task must be done in God's way, and then when he had been duly impressed with that lesson, to give him a substantial token of encouragement so that he might actually perform the task.

50 *The Relevance of the Bible*, p. 29.
51 *Ibid.*

It is quite evident that when David finally removed the Ark to Jerusalem it was properly carried by "the children of the Levites" who "bare the ark of God upon their shoulders with the staves thereon, as Moses commanded according to the word of the Lord" (1 Chron. 15:15), despite the weak argument of Professor Rowley that the account in 2 Sam. 6 "says nothing whatever of the Levites."[52] Their presence is clearly implied, in that David was careful to avoid a cart this time, and to conform strictly to the Levitical law.

Professor Rowley also insists that David and not Uzzah would really be guilty as the whole proceeding was in flagrant violation of the law. He asserts: "It would be quite alien to the character of God to blaze forth against Uzzah, because, having been wrongly put by the king in charge of the Ark, he endeavored to discharge his duty."[53] But this objection overlooks the important fact that Uzzah was guilty of death, not because of anything he was required to do by David, but solely because, in touching the Ark, he flagrantly violated the law of God (Num. 4:15), which expressly forbade him so to do, on pain of death.

Professor Rowley attempts to prove the innocence of both David and Uzzah not only on the basis of his unsound view of inspiration, which allows him (almost capriciously it seems at times) to set aside the Sacred Record, but also on the equally shaky basis of modern Pentateuchal literary criticism. According to him: "David was conscious of no wrong in entrusting Uzzah with the task, and Uzzah of none in undertaking it," inasmuch as they knew nothing of the regulations concerning the Ark since the document containing the priestly directions is said by modern Pentateuchal criticism to belong to "the latest strand of the Pentateuch dating from a time long subsequent to the age of David."[54]

But are we to set aside the clear implication of the sacred account in 2 Sam. 6:13 ("they that bare the Ark. . . .") and the definite declaration in 1 Chron. 15:15 that "the children of the Levites bare the ark of God upon their shoulders with the staves thereon, as Moses commanded according to the word of the Lord," in favor of a highly artificial theory of literary criticism that leaves us with no valid reason for a severe divine

52 *Ibid.*
53 *Ibid.*, pp. 29f.
54 *Ibid.*, p. 30.

judgment and in the interests of common morality forces us to reject the account not only as distorted and God-dishonoring, but pointless?

The whole fabric of modern Pentateuchal criticism so easily leads to confusion and uncertainty. Professor Rowley's conclusion is typical: "It is not, indeed, clear exactly what happened, or how Uzzah was killed. . . ."[55] One might observe by way of reply, "Of course not! If the clear-cut God-honoring explanation of the inspired text is set aside by men's theories, how can there be anything but a lack of clarity?"

Professor Rowley's serious misinterpretation of this entire incident furnishes a representative illustration of the fact that subscribing to an unsound theory of Biblical inspiration and permitting oneself to embrace the highly plausible but erroneous theories of modern criticism are bound to lead to faulty interpretations of Scripture. What is even more basically serious is that such an approach, in unavoidably undermining respect for the text of the Bible, must inevitably produce a diminution of interest in the mastery of the Scriptures in the original languages as the ground for careful exegesis. Little wonder theological institutions which pursue the higher critical emphasis show a tendency to gear their curricula to a study *about* the Bible rather than a study of the message and meaning of *the Bible itself,* and at the same time to decrease requirements in Biblical exegesis in the original languages. It is also quite patent why higher critical study has so commonly eventuated in religious irrelevance and spiritual barrenness. These widespread evils in scholarly circles will not be corrected until the Word of God is given its proper place of respect by the scholar as it is by the saint and mystic.

Were the scholarly world to give the Word of God its proper place, intellectual freedom would not have to give way to the fetters of religious bias, and progress in truly scientific research would not necessarily be hampered, as is so often charged. At the same time, Old Testament scholarship would be kept from the radical theorizings which have attended it in bygone years. One could then see the general course ahead that would lead to a safe harbor of constructive achievement and not to the reefs and shoals of destructive hypotheses, which, calling forth a vast

55 *Ibid.*

amount of time and energy in their defense, have to be abandoned later with irreparable loss to sound progress in the study of the Old Testament.

We have surveyed Professor Rowley's view of inspiration at some length and to some degree have illustrated its outworking in actual exegesis of Scriptural passages. What then? Does what he calls a "truer view of inspiration" measure up to its claim, or is it in reality a mere concession to unsound critical positions rather than a necessary accommodation to the alleged errancy of Scripture?

The only conclusion to which we can come is that his position is a concession to his desire to integrate unsound modern critical theories into a constructive and spiritual approach to the Bible rather than a view necessitated by the proved errancy of canonical Scripture.

In reaching this conclusion, however, we would at the same time be most careful to emphasize the brilliant service Professor Rowley is performing in many ways in Old Testament research. Although his views do not coincide with those of conservative scholars, they tend to reinforce the stand of conservatives against the extreme radicalism that has plagued modern Biblical criticism. Such studies of his as "Recent Discovery and the Patriarchal Age,"[56] "The Meaning of Sacrifice in the Old Testament"[57] and "Moses and the Decalogue"[58] are constructive and highly stimulating.

In his article "The Prophet Jeremiah and the Book of Deuteronomy," he fits firmly into the critical groove, favoring the view that Josiah's law book was Deuteronomy and that Jeremiah was influenced by it to some extent,[59] thus subscribing to that date which he acknowledges is "the very sheet anchor of the whole critical position."[60] The same may be said of his volume on introduction, entitled *The Growth of the Old Testament* (1950). His treatment of the relevance of Apocalyptic literature, especially in his strong contention for the historical

56 *Bulletin of the John Rylands Library,* Manchester (Sept., 1949), pp. 44-79.
57 *Ibid.,* (Sept., 1950), pp. 74-110.
58 *Ibid.,* (Sept., 1951), pp. 81-118.
59 *Studies in Old Testament Prophecy,* H. H. Rowley, ed. (New York), pp. 157-74.
60 *Darius the Mede and the Four World Empires in the Book of Daniel* (Cardiff, Wales, 1935), p. 1.

errancy of the book of Daniel,[61] is highly unsatisfying to the student of Biblical prophecy, and would eliminate the possibility of realizing in any adequate sense Jesus' promise that the Holy Spirit, whom He would send, would show us "things to come" (John 16:13).[62]

For our part, in the light of the fact that positions that were once regarded as established have been challenged again and again and "the once 'assured results of criticism' can scarcely be accepted without examination today," as Professor Rowley himself admits,[63] we are persuaded that Old Testament criticism at the present time is in desperate need of a thorough housecleaning, or to use the metaphor that Professor Johann de Groot employed on the occasion of his inauguration in the chair of Old Testament in the University of Utrecht in 1936: "The vessel of literary criticism will have to be docked for entire reconstruction before it will be able again to render reliable auxiliary service; the repair, I fear, will last very long."[64]

Professor Rowley and those following the more constructive trend at the present day, in stressing the necessity of integrating Old Testament critical study with the spiritual relevance of the Bible to our age, are, by the extreme difficulty of their task (impossible we believe within the fabric of present-day critical views), calling attention to the thorough housecleaning and the reconstruction (to use both metaphors) that are needed. As yet the trend is not going far enough, nor entirely in the right direction. With Professor G. Ch. Aalders we repeat: "Therefore, however grateful we may feel in considering the recent tendency towards more conservative views, which makes itself manifest in Old Testament study today, it cannot satisfy us, and we feel the more obliged to put forth all our efforts in a real scholarly research of the Old Testament which does not in the least detract from its divine authority."[65] This is the challenge of the hour to conservative scholarship.

61 *Ibid.*, pp. 178-82.
62 *The Relevance of Apocalyptic* (London, 1944), p. 8.
63 *Darius the Mede and the Four World Empires in the Book of Daniel*, p. 1.
64 Cf. *The Evangelical Quarterly* (Jan., 1952), p. 7.
65 *Op. cit.*, p. 13.

Chapter VIII

EMIL BRUNNER'S DOCTRINE OF SCRIPTURE

By Paul King Jewett

PART I. EXPOSITION

Ever since the days of the Reformation, the Bible has been in the center of the theological picture, at least so far as the Protestant Church is concerned. The reason for this is that the Reformers made the Bible and not the Church the source of religious authority, and there is no more basic question in matters religious than the question of authority. The theological renewal which attaches to the names of Barth and Brunner is no exception in this regard. It purports to be a return to the Bible as the source and norm of religious truth, and though it has been nicknamed the Theology of Crisis, of Paradox, of Dialectic, sometimes even of Pessimism, the designation which undoubtedly best conforms to the intention of these theologians themselves, is that of Kattenbusch, *i.e.*, the Theology of the Word.[1]

The tremendous influence of the new theology is undoubtedly due in large measure to the fact that it has given many a renewed confidence in the authority of the Scripture, without involving them in what they would consider the scientific obscurantism of a wooden orthodoxy.

This juxtaposition of Scriptural authority and critical science brings into sharp focus the problem *par excellence* of the new theology. How is it possible to transcend the orthodox-liberal antithesis? What is the synthesis which will spare the twentieth-century Christian from the impossible choice between theopneusty and the quicksand? Must the preacher choose between an infallible book and a religious relativism in which the law slips from his hands as he approaches the people?

---

1 Kattenbusch, *Die evangelische Theologie seit Schleiermacher* (1926), p. 125.

None of the crisis theologians has addressed himself to this crucial problem with more care, scope, precision and clarity than Emil Brunner. Let us consider, therefore, what he has to say about the Bible.

I. The Bible and Criticism

It is an open secret that in matters of Biblical criticism Brunner aligns himself with a rather liberal school of thought.[2] His works, especially the more critical ones intended for scholarly consumption, are besprinkled with comments reflecting his freedom over the tradition in such matters. That the creation and fall narrative, in fact the pre-Abrahamic history in general, is a late priestly production;[3] that when all is said and done the Wellhausian order of prophets, then law, has remained victorious;[4] that the latter half of Isaiah is post-exilic;[5] that the Lucan account of a census and the Matthean story of the Magi are legendary;[6] that the resurrection narratives are conflicting;[7] that John is not a historical source;[8] and that the pastorals are late;[9] all this is for Brunner the common property of educated minds just as much as Copernican astronomy and Newtonian physics.[10] The Bible "is full of errors, contradictions, erroneous opinions concerning all kinds of human, natural, historical

---

2 In the lectures which he delivered in this country on the new theology, back in 1929, Brunner classified himself as "rather radical." (*The Theology of Crisis* [New York, 1921], p. 41). He is considerably more conservative now, in the sense that he accepts fewer critical hypotheses.

3 *Dogmatik*, II (Zürich, 1950), 235.

4 *Offenbarung und Vernunft* (Zürich, 1941), p. 283, note 29.

5 "Der Erfüller," *Zwischen den Zeiten*, 8:4 (1930), p. 275.

6 *Dogmatik*, II, 281.

7 Cf. *Der Mittler* (Tübingen, 1927), p. 525, where he says that anyone who talks about a harmonious representation of the resurrection developments in the New Testament is either "ignorant" *(unwissend)* or "unscrupulous" *(gewissenlos)*. Brunner himself seems to favor the Galilean hypothesis. *(Ibid.,* p. 524).

8 *The Theology of Crisis*, p. 41.

9 *Offenbarung und Vernunft*, pp. 8f.

10 In his earlier publications he did have some good things to say about Fundamentalism. The movement numbers too many scholarly and devout men to be considered as simply a manifestation of the *via inertiae*. Though it is a petrification of Christianity, it is not, as is modernism, its dissolution. *(The Theology of Crisis,* pp. 8-14). This was before he tangled with the conservative students at Princeton during his guest lectureship.

situations. It contains many contradictions in the report about Jesus' life, it is overgrown with legendary material even in the New Testament."[11]

At no point does Brunner do less credit to his erudite name than in his polemic against the doctrine of verbal inspiration, much of which is but glorified innuendo.[12] Its meaning, in his thinking, is exhaustively expressed with such formulas as mechanical dictation, inspired vowel points and Holy Ghost Greek. The whole idea goes back to a late Jewish innovation whereby the Word of God was equated with the words of Scripture.[13] On such a basis one believes the Bible before he reads it.[14] He likewise believes everything in the Bible because it is in the Bible. It is an "all-or-nothing-faith."[15] Belief in Scripture thereby becomes not an article of faith, but its principle, the axiomatic presupposition of all the articles of faith, as we find in Johann Gerhard (*Loci theologici*, I, 9.).[16] In fact, it becomes not only

---

11 *Religionsphilosophie* (München, 1927), pp. 77-78.
12 The attack frequently spills over into a general indictment of Protestant Orthodoxy. Orthodoxy lacks ethical power *(Der Mittler*, p. 540) and missionary zeal *(Wahrheit als Begegnung*, p. 28). It has a Byzantian Christ (because it takes John as history) *(Der Mittler*, p. 165). It does not foster fellowship among believers (a hard judgment for one who belongs to the *Landeskirche* of German Switzerland) *(Offenbarung und Vernunft*, p. 143). It is little better than liberalism ("Die Andere Aufgabe, etc.," p. 271) or relativism *(Religionsphiloso-phie*, p. 96). In short, it is "one of the most frightful things recorded in the annals of intellectual history." The catechism teacher took the place of God *(Die Mystik und das Wort*, p. 100). While it is no doubt true that Brunner's perspective is that of one who has experienced the inertia of the state-church system, a factor which might conceivably ameliorate the bitterness of his polemic, yet significantly he rarely suggests that this aspect of the life of the post-Reformation Church on the Continent is culpable. The all but universal procedure is to trace the curse of Orthodoxy back to one fountain head, a belief in the verbal inspiration of the Scripture, an analysis that takes no account of the fact that the Pietist-Wesleyan reaction to the deadness of the contemporary religious establishments, a reaction which certainly possessed as much dynamic as Kierkegaardian existentialism, derived its vitality from a verbally inspired Bible. Cf. *Ante*, p. 96, note 2.
13 *Offenbarung und Vernunft*, p. 117. Brunner at this point appeals to Schürer, *Geschichte des jüd. Volkes*, II, 365.
14 *Ibid.*, p. 164.
15 *Ibid.*, p. 164.
16 *Dogmatik*, II, 401.

the principle of faith, but of all knowledge — "The Bible along in all questions."[17]

When faced with the problem posed by critical science, orthodoxy at first cut the Gordian knot by declaring a given text (Luther or Jerome) the final norm, and then when textual criticism had become established, posited a hypothetical primal text, a Bible-X, of which very little was known, since it was considerably removed from all available manuscripts, except that it was the infallible word of God. "This solution, in the long run, was untenable. It ekes out a miserable existence still in certain fundamentalistic circles."[18] Recourse to such slovenly apologetic in the interest of Biblical authority justly exposed theology to the contempt of science. We owe a debt of gratitude to Biblical criticism for having made such a *sacrificium intellectus* impossible. "Orthodoxy," says Brunner, "has become impossible for anyone who knows anything of science. This I would call fortunate."[19]

All this does not mean that Brunner is totally indifferent to the results of Biblical criticism. Here and there in his writings he engages in discussions of particular problems as they fall within the orbit of his universe of discourse. But for the most part they have an academic tone. The one problem posed by criticism, for which Brunner is vitally concerned to work out a solution, is that of the apparent difference between the Jesus of the synoptics and the Jesus of Paul and John.[20] In Jesus, eternity became time, God became man, as the apostles taught, or else Christianity is a fiction. Any major discrepancy, therefore, be-

17 Cf. "Falscher und wahrer Biblizismus," *Kirchenblatt*, 100:134-40 (1944), where Brunner observes that the most Biblicistic-minded find it necessary to use Euclid, not the Bible to teach their children geometry and no one goes to the Bible to learn atomic weights, star distances, and the nature of cell development.

18 *Offenbarung und Vernunft*, p. 271.

19 *The Word and the World* (New York, 1931), p. 38. Brunner in one place compares the service of criticism against the ossified orthodoxy of the letter, to that of the French Revolution against a corrupt patriarchal system (*Zur Sozialethik*, p. 327). About the only good thing which he ever had to say for the doctrine of verbal inspiration was that it is better than nothing. Better to hold to it than to lose "the Christian church's principle of Scripture." (*Der Mittler*, p. 292).

20 "There exists between both [the Synoptics and John], likewise also between the doctrine of Jesus and the apostles, a major, thoroughgoing difference. That is, I think, the most important result of the whole of Biblical criticism." (*Offenbarung und Vernunft*, pp. 285-86).

tween the Jesus of history and the Jesus which the early Church preached, constitutes in the very nature of the situation a major challenge to Christian faith. Broadly speaking, Brunner's solution is that it was the task of Jesus to *be* the Christ, while it was left to the apostles to *preach* Him. Thus, he feels, we can adequately account for the difference between the way in which Jesus Himself speaks and the way in which the disciples speak about Him. Brunner is not concerned in the main, however, with the solution of critical questions *in concreto*. He will never write a book on the theme, "Archeology proves the Bible." His interest lies rather in another direction. Granted that one can no longer talk of the Bible as an infallible norm of faith and practice, what place does it have, or at least, should it have, in our present-day thought about God and his self-disclosure to man?

II. THE LOCALE OF SCRIPTURE IN THE DIMENSION OF THE IMPERSONAL

It is impossible to understand Brunner's view of the place and function of the Bible in our religious thought apart from his view of history and faith.

As for history, Brunner concedes that the time-space *continuum* is one of flux. "History is the dimension of the relative."[21] Revelation, therefore, in the Christian sense of the word, can never be identified with the historical as such. Christianity stands or falls with its claim to a *transcendental* revelation, a revelation whose *termini a quo* and *ad quem* can never be reduced to or made a part of the world process as such. Such a revelation we have in Jesus Christ. As a bolt out of the blue, as a perpendicular from above, bifurcating the horizontal plane of human history, God broke into time in the person of Christ. In Him the Divine became human; the Eternal, temporal; the Absolute, finite. Hence Brunner can say, "Jesus Christ Himself is the revelation, not a doctrine about Jesus Christ."[22]

But this revelation is complete only in the response of faith on the part of the individual as he is confronted by God in Christ. The revelation which *happened* in the Jesus event, *happens* in the crisis of faith.

21 *Die Mystik und das Wort* (Tübingen, 1924), p. 269.
22 *Dogmatik*, I, 63.

The revelation in Christ is not complete with the life, death and resurrection of Jesus; it attains its goal only in that is becomes really evident, viz., in that a man *recognizes* Jesus as the Christ. Revelation is not an objective entity in itself, but a transitive event: God reveals Himself to someone. This revelational act of God is a double condescension to man: a historically objective one, in the incarnation of the Son, and an inwardly subjective one, in the testimony of the Son through the Spirit in the heart of man. . . .[23]

When the individual, confronted by God in Christ, responds with the affirmation of faith, he is thinking, as Kierkegaard would say, existentially. Existential thinking is the opposite of abstract, theoretical thinking. Abstract thought, whether it be that of the metaphysician seeking to reduce reality to his system, or of the scientist probing the secrets of nature, ever moves in the cool atmosphere of objectivity. I observe objects, I contemplate ideas, but I *meet* God and in that encounter I must *decide,* I must say *yes* or *no* and that decision involves more than my theories; it involves *me* in my concrete existence. It makes the difference between heaven and hell to *me.* Because revelation is consummated in this encounter between two persons, God and man, Brunner calls it "personal correspondence," the "fundamental category of all Biblical thought."[24]

His celebrated Uppsala lectures, in which he first began to develop this approach in a systematic way, appeared significantly, in the German, with the title, "Truth as Encounter,"[25] and in these studies he draws a sharp distinction between what he calls thou-truth *(Du-Wahrheit)* and it-truth *(Es-Wahrheit).* It-truth is truth in the ordinary sense of the word, truth that moves within the framework of the subject-object antithesis, as Brunner styles it, *i.e.,* the knowing subject and the object known (it) , define the scope of the knowledge situation. Thou-truth, on the other hand, is a relationship between two subjects, the divine "Thou" and the human "I" in face-to-face encounter.[26]

23 *Dogmatik,* I, 33-34.
24 "Schicksal und Freiheit," p. 534.
25 *Wahrheit als Begegnung* (Berlin, 1938), translated as *The Divine Human Encounter.*
26 "The Biblical concept of truth is truth-as-encounter." *(Wahrheit als Begegnung,* Vorwort.). *"The Biblical understanding of truth cannot be grasped through the subject-object antithesis, but rather is thereby falsified." (Ibid.,* p. 14).

It is impossible, within the limits of our assigned task, to trace the implications of this bifurcation of truth for Brunner's approach to the religious problem as a whole. Suffice to say that the Bible, though it be in close proximity to the personal dimension of revelation, is, nonetheless, on the impersonal side of the great divide. The Bible is truth expressed in an objective, impersonal form. It is truth about *God,* but it is truth *about* God, not God Himself as He confronts me in Christ. We must ever remember, Brunner says, that there is an "abyss" between human words and God's Word.[27] The Bible is a human word about the Divine Word, and for that very reason it participates in the inadequacy and fallibility of all that is human.

The question, then, is this, How does one get from the Word which is Christ, to words about Him, *i.e.,* the Bible, and how are these words related to the Word? The rise of "it-truth" from "thou-truth," or to cast the proposition theologically, the rise of doctrine (the Bible is primal doctrine) from revelation occurs in a quarter turn *(Viertelsdrehung)* on the part of the apostles, a turn from the God who addresses them, to the men whom they address.[28] Faith is, as we have observed, an integral part of the revelational event. It is on the personal side of the dimensional divide. It moves in the sphere of encounter, of confession. "Verily thou art the Christ, the Son of the living God!"[29] Every genuine testimony *about* Christ must be grounded in and stem from such personal encounter *of* Him. The primal form of all witness to Christ is faith "in the form of the thou-answer to the addressing thou-word of God."[30]

> The first prerequisite, therefore, for the rise of the witness of doctrine, is the stepping out of the thou-relationship to God, a turning of the face, as it were, away from God and toward the world. In doctrine man speaks no more in the *thou*-form *to* God, as in the original confession of faith — but he speaks now in the *it*-form *about* God. Doctrine is no more the spontaneous personal answer of prayer to God's word, but even in its simplest form al-

27 *Offenbarung und Vernunft,* p. 415.
28 This distinction was first clearly drawn in *Offenbarung und Vernunft (Zürich,* 1941), p. 146.
29 *Dogmatik,* I, 44.
30 *Ibid.,* p. 44.

ready, reflective speech about God. Stepping out of the dimension of personal meeting into the impersonal realm of reflection, is the presupposition of all doctrine. God is now no more the one who speaks, but the one who is spoken about; no more is God the one who is addressed, but a man or a plurality of men.[31]

Strictly speaking, then, the inmost ring about the personal center of revelation is the apostolic witness *(Zeugnis)*. Such witness is not revelation in the absolute sense of the word, and yet it is a complement of that "mute" act-revelation in Jesus Christ, the latter being, in and of itself, insufficient. God's act-word *(Tatwort)* in Christ, must be interpreted to us in the witness of the believing apostles.[32] Upon occasion Brunner observes that this testimony has a double character. It is not only "teaching about Jesus," but also "report concerning Jesus."[33] We must have report because of the historical character of Christian revelation. Revelation in the Christian sense of the word is event, *Faktum*, "the life, suffering, death and resurrection of Jesus Christ the Son of God."[34] But *mere* history is never capable of awaking faith. We must always have, as observed, an interpretation of the event.[35]

The Bible is the fixation of this faith-confessing, faith-creating, interpretative testimony of the apostles. This *viva vox* of the apostles stands in much closer relationship to the Word of God than the Bible, but the Scriptural fixation of this living testimony, which was necessary to preserve it from being completely altered and thereby lost in the moving stream of historical tradition, participates in the authority of that revelation. It is, so to speak, the rim, the border of that unique *revelational event*

---

31 *Ibid.,* p. 45.

32 *Offenbarung und Vernunft*, p. 159. It is because of the interpretative character of this apostolic witness, that it is to be classified as doctrine. It is teaching about Christ, it is reflection in its simplest form concerning the meaning of the revelation in Christ. Therefore it is not revelation.

33 *Dogmatik*, I, 40-41.

34 *Offenbarung und Vernunft*, p. 22.

35 *Ibid.,* p. 159.

of which it bears record.[36] It is this participation in the once-for-all character of revelation as an historical event that gives the written documents superiority over the subsequent oral tradition and grounds the idea of a canon. "We have the word of revelation as something unique and finished, therefore, as canon."[37] The once-for-all spoken word of revelation meets us as a *Perfectum praeteritum* in the Scripture, which is therefore the norm of revealed truth. Brunner affirms his stand with those who make the Holy Scriptures the sole norm of their faith according to the fundamental principle of the Reformation. "The source and norm of all Christian theology is the Holy Scripture."[38]

III. The Nature and Limits of Biblical Authority

Having fixed the locale of Scripture in the dimension of the impersonal, we are now in a position to address ourselves to the important question of how Brunner conceives the nature and limits of Biblical authority. We have in our outline already made the important discovery that for him the Bible is not the Word of God in the unqualified sense of orthodoxy. It is, strictly speaking, a record of the apostolic witness to the Word, which participates in the authority of that witness. Or we could say, it is a word about the Word.[39] It is this side the dimensional divide, so that when all is said and done, howsoever it may differ from other human formulations of revealed truth, the distinction cannot be an absolute one, but only a relative one. Remembering also his desire to escape not only rational autonomy, but also authoritarian heteronomy in religious questions, we are in a fair way to anticipate the basic contour of Brunner's approach to the question of Biblical authority.

Jesus Christ is Himself the Word of God. The Bible, therefore, is not the ground of Christian faith, but its means. I do not believe that Jesus is the Christ because I believe the Bible. The order is exactly the reverse to Brunner's way of thinking. "Be-

---

36 ". . . the Biblical account itself belongs to the history in which God realizes His relationship to man, viz., His Kingdom." *(Wahrheit als Begegnung,* p. 38.). Cf. also, *Offenbarung und Vernunft,* p. 22, 121-25; also *Dogmatik,* I, 94).

37 *Christlicher Glaube nach reformierte Lehre* (Stuttgart, 1926), p. 254.

38 *Wahrheit als Begegnung,* p. 32. *Vom Werk des Heiligen Geistes,* p. 7.

39 "God's Word is never exhaustively contained in words." *(Offenbarung und Vernunft,* p. 93).

cause I believe in Christ, I believe in the Scripture."[40] Nor does
it help any to say that I believe Jesus is the Christ because an
apostle says so. It is all the same.[41] Are not apostles men? Could
they not err? Indeed they could and they did. Their testimony,
as we have it preserved in Scripture, is, to be sure, "inspired by
the Spirit of God, but it is at the same time a human word, and
therefore laden with the frailty and incompleteness of all that is
human."[42] Hence, to seek the ground of faith in the inscripturated witness of the apostles, is to subject faith to the uncertain
results of historical criticism, which is the surest way to religious
skepticism. The only alternative to skepticism is to close one's
mind to the difficulties. This way of authority is, no doubt, the
easiest road. But the trouble is that anyone can believe anything
if he wants to take another's word for it. It was the genius of
Luther, having broken the shackles of Romish heteronomy, not
to become enslaved to a paper pope.[43] We should not conclude
with the Enlightenment, however, that the solution to the
problem of religious authority is no authority at all. If there is
anything worse than heteronomy, it is the autonomy of the
natural man who will not be told anything. Brunner seeks to
get above this disjunction by viewing the Scripture as the
indispensable *means* of faith.

> We do not believe that Jesus is the Christ *because* the
> apostles say so. However, *without* their witness we could
> not know it ourselves. The picture that the apostles give
> us of Jesus and their witness that He is the Christ, are
> *the means* through which we know Him and God in Him.[44]

40 *Ibid.*, p. 166. It was, according to Brunner, Martin Kahler who first
   stated clearly the all-important reversal of the tradition, in his declaration, " 'We do not believe in Christ because of the Bible, but in
   the Bible because of Christ.' *(Der Sog. hist. Jesus. S. 75, 1. Auf).*"
   (Ibid., p. 166, ft. 8).

41 "I do not believe in Jesus Christ because an apostle says to me, he
   is the Son of God, so that I believe in Jesus Christ because I believe
   first of all in the apostle." *(Ibid.,* p. 165).

42 *Dogmatik,* I, 40.

43 "It constitutes one of the most magnificent proofs of the truly spiritual freedom of Luther, that he did not allow himself to be misled
   into championing a literalistic concept of Scripture, though this
   would have been most natural in view of the struggle in which he
   was involved." *(Ibid.,* I, 115).

44 *Dogmatik,* II, 307.

Ergo the authority of Scripture is an instrumental authority. The Bible is authoritative "insofar as therein is brought to me, that, before which I must in truth bow, that is, that which itself awakens in me the certainty of truth."[45] The Bible, in other words, becomes the Word of God to me in the moment of revelation when I become contemporaneous with Christ. The ground of my faith in Christ, therefore, is not the Scripture, but Christ Himself, addressing me through His Spirit in the Scripture. ". . . I know at one and the same time that Christ is truly the One whom the apostle testifies him to be and that the apostle is a faithful witness. In one and the same act of revelation there is created in me faith in the Christ and faith in the Scripture which testifies to Him."[46] The relativism attaching to the merely historical (that is, the inscripturated apostolic testimony) which makes impossible final recourse to the Scripture as such, is overcome in the act of faith, whereby the historical becomes "other than the historical . . . an organ of the revelation of the eternal God."[47]

But, it may be replied, the Scriptures speak of many things. Is all which the Scriptures teach equally capable of bearing the truth of revelation to me? Brunner's reply to this inquiry is not difficult to anticipate at this stage of our investigation. Jesus is Himself the Word of God. Hence the Scriptures become a means of revelation insofar as they testify to Christ.[48] Brunner's motto here is Luther's *Christus rex et dominus scripturae*.[49] The Bible bears witness to Jesus Christ. It *points* to *Him*.

The formula which Brunner uses to describe the relation of the words of Scripture to the personal Word is the same, therefore, as that which he employs with respect to doctrine in general, that is, "pointer," *(Hinweis)*, for the Scripture is, as we

---

45 *Dogmatik,* I, 115.
46 *Offenbarung und Vernunft,* p. 166.
47 *Dogmatik,* II, 307.
48 ". . . we believe in the Scripture, because and insofar as it teaches Christ. The authority of Scripture is not a formal, but a material one: Christ, the revelation." *(Dogmatik,* I, 115).
49 Cf. *Dogmatik,* I, 53. Also *Offenbarung and Vernunft,* pp. 166, 272. Also Luther's reference to the Scriptures as "the crib in which Christ lies." *(Ibid.,* p. 166, 172; *Wahrheit als Begegnung,* p. 131; *Dogmatik,* 1-40). Again from Luther, "that which fosters Christ, is apostolic." *(Ibid.,* 55).

have seen, primal doctrine. No word of man is itself adequate to the revelation of the mystery of God's person in Christ.[50] The personal relationship which I sustain to God in revelation is no "it-belief," but a "trusting Him."[51] Hence the pointing to that which is beyond it, is of the essence of the teaching of Scripture. Brunner in one place defines *Zeugnis* as that which "points to something behind and above it."[52] He compares doctrine to a pointing finger which guides one's seeing,[53] and to a telescope which focuses the eye of the mind upon Christ.[54]

This testimony of the Scriptures to Christ is the key to Brunner's solution to the problem of the unity of revelation. There are times when he speaks of the differences in various authors of Scripture as simply differences of perspective. Who can deny that the apostles at the first only gradually apprehended the significance of that which happened in Christ?[55] As time elapsed the Church naturally came into a fuller appreciation of the implications of its message. But the notion of different perspectives, which are mutually complimentary, is by no means sufficient, according to Brunner, to cope with the situation. Not only the differences between the Old and New Testaments, but also the differences within them, the differences between priestly and prophetic religion on the one hand, between the synoptic and the Johannine tradition, Pauline and Petrine theology on the other, involve logical contradictions. The Epistle of James contributes that "which effects not only a complement, but also a corrective of Paul."[56] This state of affairs proved, of course, for orthodoxy, an impossible one, because orthodoxy equated the Word of God with a system of

---

50 *Dogmatik*, I, 19.
51 *Ibid.*, I, 30.
52 *Der Mittler*, p. 542.
53 *Dogmatik*, I, 63.
54 "Doctrine is only a pointer, even when it is a clear telling pointer. Therefore faith does not cleave to it, but glides along it, as a bullet in a gun barrel, toward the mark. Doctrine is the telescope through which we should see Jesus Himself. Hence it is never the object of faith, but faith's expression, faith's confession." *(Offenbarung und Vernunft*, p. 153).
55 Cf. *Die Absolutheit Jesu* (Berlin, 1926), pp. 12f., and especially *Dogmatik*, II, 295, where he argues that were the difference [*Andersheit)* in the apostolic witness a matter of contradiction (*Gegensatzlichkeit)*, the disciples would have been the first to perceive it.
56 *Offenbarung und Vernunft*, p. 286.

doctrine. The only escape in such a position was to ignore the difficulties or coerce the Scripture with allegorical exegesis. But with the onward progress of Biblical criticism this has become impossible for any informed student of Scripture.[57]

But a truly Biblical faith is not shaken by the difference between old-Israelitic and post-exilic religion. Faith, as we have repeatedly observed, does not have as its object a logical system of truth. The unity of the Bible, therefore, is not one which exists for science.[58] The *analogia fidei* is something which can be grasped only with the eye of faith.

> What, according to faith, belongs together in revelation, can be recognized only through faith, just as the coherence of rational truth itself rests on the evidence of this coherence and hence can be recognized only in the carrying of thought through to its completion.[59]

Faith recognizes that the divine revelation was broken in the human medium, even in the primal witness of Scripture and hence reaches beyond the contradictory perspectives of Scripture to that One to whom they all point, Jesus Christ. The unity of Scripture is "wholly and solely in Him, the one to whom testimony is borne, not, however, in the teaching of those who bear the testimony."[60] Precisely the most antithetical elements, according to Brunner, belong together because the truth as it is in Christ is thereby made known, that truth which lies behind and beyond all doctrine.[61]

> Just as a sentence has many words, but one meaning, so the revelation of God in the Scripture, in the Old and New Testament, in the law and the Gospel, has one meaning: Jesus Christ . . . stammeringly or clearly all the books of the Bible spell this one name, they instruct us, on the one hand, prospectively, on the other, retrospectively, of this meaningful fact of the incarnation. . . .[62]

Brunner readily concedes, as the above quotation indicates, that not all the Scripture equally bears the Word of God. Some

57 Cf. *Wahrheit als Begegnung*, p. 131.
58 *Religionsphilosophie*, p. 80.
59 *Ibid.*, p. 55.
60 *Dogmatik*, I, 54.
61 *Offenbarung und Vernunft*, p. 287.
62 *Religionsphilosophie*, p. 76.

parts of Scripture "stammer" in spelling the name of Jesus.
That is to say, not only is the authority of Scripture the authority of means, but it is not all equally binding even in this
instrumental capacity. "Not all that is Biblical, not even all that
is in the New Testament, is in like manner and to the same
degree a bearer of God's Word."[63] Paul, for example, frequently
distinguished between what he ordained as an apostle and what,
as a word of the Lord, was binding upon the conscience.[64] All
must concede that there are certain pronouncements of Paul's
that are not to be understood from his faith in Christ, but from
particular patriarchal views which prevailed in ancient times.[65]
There is nothing in Holy Writ which does not stand in some
relation or other to the "matter" of Scripture, which is the
revelation of God's name in Christ, but there are certain kernel
utterances in the New Testament, which sustain maximal
contiguity to the Word itself.[66] It would be absurd, says Brunner,
to assert that the greeting list in Rom. 16 is the word of God in
the same sense as, for example, Rom. 3:21-31. The Bible is not
an even plane, but as it were, a funnel, in which all is oriented
around one point. The nearer anything is to that point, the
nearer it is to that which is of fundamental concern. Brunner
sees a maximum of contiguousness in the Johannine formula,
"The Word became flesh and we beheld his glory. . . ."[67]

63 *Offenbarung und Vernunft,* p. 128.
64 *Das Gebot und die Ordnungen,* p. 531.
65 *Ibid.,* p. 364. Brunner is reflecting upon Paul's ideas respecting the
   relation of the sexes.
66 *Wahrheit als Begegnung,* p. 88.
67 *Wahrheit als Begegnung,* p. 86. Since the Bible is simply primal
   doctrine, Brunner introduces the same principle in evaluating doctrine in general. All doctrine is but a paradox which points beyond
   itself and yet there is a distinction between the degree of directness
   with which various doctrines function as pointers. There is, in other
   words, pure and impure doctrine. "It [pure doctrine] is a matter
   of proximity to the immediate address of God in Jesus Christ
   Himself. The more clearly and univocally the doctrine points to
   that one center, the more the 'something' said compels the thought
   to look away from the 'something' which is said, to 'Him Himself,'
   that is, the more witness about Him, makes the address of God
   itself audible, so much the more immediately is the something, the
   doctrine, bound up with that with which the Holy Scripture is
   concerned." *(Ibid.,* p. 86).

PART II. CRITIQUE

I. BIBLICAL INSPIRATION

Introduction. When all the utterances of Brunner concerning verbal inspiration are amassed, there is a striking dialectic (to borrow a leaf from Brunner's book) which runs through the corpus. Brunner is, in a way, attracted by what he repudiates. While God's Word is more than a word, yet he is anxious that revelation should not evaporate into mysticism. He calls the human word the "locale of revelation,"[68] because there is a basic likeness between the two. "The likeness between the human and the divine word grounds the presupposition that the former can bear a testimony to the latter."[69] After all, music is not a medium of revelation. Nor can we paint what God has to say to us. In this regard the human word is not a means among others, since human speech alone is able clearly to point to the will of God.[70] While, therefore, it is fortunate that one can no longer believe in verbal inspiration,[71] yet we read that it is better that "one hold fast to it, than on account of its incorrect form, cast off its precious content, which is the Christian church's principle of Scripture."[72]

In his earlier writings Brunner simply identified the position of the Reformers with his own, in contrast to the orthodox tradition. By the time his *Offenbarung und Vernunft* appeared in 1941, he was obviously losing his grip on them a bit. He distinguishes between the first and second generation. Luther and Zwingli were not devoted to the doctrine of verbal inspiration as were Melanchthon, Calvin and Bullinger.[73] Finally, in the first volume of his *Dogmatics,* he concedes that even with Luther one finds, along with Luther's revolutionary new concept of Biblical authority, the traditional view of verbal

68 *Der Mittler,* p. 545, note 1.
69 *Dogmatik,* I, 184.
70 *Das Gebot und die Ordnungen* (Tübingen, 1932), p. 489.
71 *The Word and the World,* p. 38.
72 *Der Mittler,* p. 292.
73 *Offenbarung und Vernunft,* p. 126, note 1. Here he observes that Calvin especially loved to speak of the *oracula Dei.*

inspiration.[74] In fact, verbal inspiration is the "classic" doctrine.[75] It is almost as old as the Church itself. So strongly did the early saints feel the revelational power of the words of the apostles that they designated their words simply the Word of God, which is true, if one means thereby "a definitive form of revelation. . . ."[76]

Brunner cannot convince himself, however, that the early saints were always careful to make such nice distinctions. He sees even in the Pastorals, especially 2 Tim. 3:16, the beginning of the false identification of the Word and doctrine.[77] Yet this fateful error is "most comprehensible."[78] By the time he wrote his *Dogmatics*, Brunner was ready to allow verbal inspiration more than the niche on the periphery of the canon to which it was entitled by virtue of its appearance in the Pastorals. Verbal inspiration is the mode of revelation found in the Old Testament. In the prophets God really speaks in human language. "Hence the word of God is there in the form of revealed human words, not behind them . . ., but in direct identity, in a complete correspondence of man's word and God's word."[79] This

74 (Zürich, 1946), p. 117. As noted above, Brunner sees this revolutionary insight of Luther succinctly summed up in the words, *Christus rex et dominus scripturae*. Not everyone is convinced, however, that he should be allowed even this precarious claim to the reformer. Cf. Armin Moellering, "Brunner and Luther on Scriptural Authority," *Concordia Theological Monthly*, 21:801-18 (1950).

75 *Offenbarung und Vernunft*, p. 126.

76 *Dogmatik*, I, 21-22.

77 *Offenbarung und Vernunft*, p. 9, note 13.

78 *Das Gebot und die Ordnungen*, p. 530. It should be, since Brunner himself does not always maintain the proper distinctions. Cf., for example, his sermon "Der allmächtige Vater," where he refers without qualification to Isa. 45:6,7 with the formula, "in this word of God as found in the book of Isaiah. . . ." *(Ich Glaube an den lebendigen Gott* [Zürich, 1945] 20).

79 *Dogmatik*, I, 26. The movement in Brunner's thought is patent when the above statement is compared with his mode of expression in a popular presentation appearing seven years prior. Speaking of the writers of Scripture, he said, "God threw his fiery word into men's hearts, and they sought publicly, for the benefit of others, to pronounce in their own speech, what God secretly whispered in their ear. They sought in human speech to spell God's word after Him. One succeeded more, another less." *(Eiserne Ration* [Zürich, 1939], p. 22). Even as late as *Offenbarung und Vernunft* (1941), he insisted that in the time of the apostles as well as among the Old Testament prophets, revelation was understood not as a book or document, but as a history of salvation, the event of the divine self-disclosure of God. "Revelation is no book or doctrine, but revelation is God Himself in his historical self-testimony. Revelation is an event, the living history of God with humanity." *(Ibid.,* 8).

really brings not only the camel's nose, but also his head into the tent, inasmuch as it would be exceedingly difficult to establish any significant difference between the view of revelation found in the Old Testament and that of the writers of the New Testament, for all of whom the Old Testament was normative. It is not surprising, then, that Brunner, having conceded verbal inspiration in the Old Testament, also admits that Paul and the other apostles accepted the doctrine. He can only insist, calling attention to 1 Cor. 9:9, that the force of the doctrine was curbed by a very free and at times arbitrary use of the allegorical method of exegesis.[80]

The net result of this review is to leave Brunner standing pretty much alone. His affinity with the tradition has become increasingly tenuous, so much so that he cannot make a *bona fide* appeal either to the Reformers or the apostles for a view of Biblical authority which avoids on the one hand the traditional doctrine of verbal inspiration, without, on the other hand, reducing the Bible, as is the case in religious liberalism, to the level of any other inspirational book. It would, then, be a truly Herculean achievement were Brunner to succeed in framing a new synthesis, by carrying through an alleged insight of the top-flight Reformers, a task which they themselves, on his own confession, were unable to achieve.

The Inspiration of the Spirit. Our review of Brunner's attempt to reconstruct the doctrine of Scriptural authority so as to maintain that authority against modern scientific criticism without the theory of verbal inspiration, need not be repeated *in extensio* at this juncture. The crucial point is Brunner's two-dimensional concept of truth ("thou-truth" and "it-truth"), more particularly the passage from the former to the latter. Revelation moves in the dimension of the personal. It is divine-human encounter. The Bible, on the other hand, is "it-truth," the inscripturated form of the apostolic testimony *about* the Word of God who is Jesus Christ. The transition, as we have seen, from the personal to the impersonal, is accomplished by a quarter turn *(Viertelsdrehung)* on the part of the apostles to whom God revealed Himself in Christ. All witness *to* Christ must stem from a personal encounter *of* Him. And yet the witness is not itself revelation, because it involves a stepping

80 *Dogmatik*, I, 113.

out of the dimension of the personal, a turning one's face, as it were, from God to the world. In the statement, "He is the Christ," we have doctrine in its simplest form, reflection *about* revelation. God is no more the One who *speaks* but the One who is spoken *about*.

It is a trifle difficult, however, to see why such stupendous significance should be attached to the difference between the proposition, "*Thou* art the Christ" (faith) and the proposition, "*He* is the Christ" (witness). Brunner makes much of the fact that the one involves direct personal encounter with God in Christ, while the other is testimony to one's fellows and is therefore truth *about* something. But not even Brunner can deny that both the confession of faith, "Thou art the Christ," and the testimony to that faith, "We have found Him who is called the Christ," are propositions cast in the form of human words and subject to the laws of coherent speech. It would seem then that whatever dimensional divide there may be, would be not between faith and theology, but between the personal Word and the word of faith as it becomes a spoken word. This observation is not intended to solve any problems, but rather to bring one into clearer focus, for it draws attention to the fact that the real difficulty with a two-dimensional concept of truth such as the one with which Brunner operates, is not a passage from the personal pronoun in the second person to that of the third person. The fact that a man, in turning from God to his neighbor, says no more, "Thou art," but, "He is," is relatively inconsequential. The problem, on Brunner's structure, is how to get from the personal Word which is Jesus, to the spoken word of confession. Brunner in one place reflects on this question. He asks, "Is there a point of identity between the Christ-revelation and the spoken word, between the person-revelation and the word-in-human-speech?" His reply is that there is such a point of identity, namely, "the testimony of the Holy Spirit."[81] The *prius* of all genuine, valid testimony about Jesus is the divine witness given to Him "in" the human spirit. The answer to the question, Whence the apostolic witness which we have in Scripture? is, "The Spirit of God testified in *them* [the apostles] Jesus as the Christ."[82] This is what happened, perhaps for the

81 *Dogmatik,* I, 33.
82 *Ibid.,* p. 33.

first time, in Caesarea Philippi. Hence Jesus' word, "Flesh and blood hath not revealed it unto thee, but my Father which is in heaven."[83] This also, affirms Brunner, is what Paul referred to when he spoke of God's having revealed His Son in him.[84] The condescension of God in revelation consists not only in His taking on a human form *(Menschengestalt)*, but also in His speaking in human words *(Menschensprache)*, in the testimony of the Spirit to the Son.[85]

> The revelation of God in Jesus Christ, becomes to him [namely, the human witness] the genuine, real *word* of God, the literal *Deus dicit*, in which the figurative[86] *Deus dixit* of a historical revelation becomes discernible, for the first time, in this word of the Holy Spirit.[87]

Are we then to infer that the confession is inspired? Most assuredly, Brunner would reply. Inerrantly inspired? If Brunner answers this latter question in the affirmative, the principle of verbal inspiration has been reinstated. Not, to be sure, in the extensive sense that all which stands in the Bible is without error, but in the intensive sense that at least one proposition in Scripture, *i.e.,* Peter's confession at Caesarea Philippi, is. But if God can infallibly inspire a man to say, "Thou art the Christ," there is no reason why He could not inspire him to say, "He is the Christ." The Holy Ghost is certainly able to decline the personal pronoun. The foundation of Brunner's polemic against theopneusty would then deteriorate into a merely quantitative issue.[88] Awareness of this situation is no doubt what forces Brunner into a kind of double talk. He proceeds to make a distinction between the witness of the Spirit and the echo of that

83 Matt. 16:17.
84 Gal. 1:16.
85 *Dogmatik*, I, 33. ". . . God humbles Himself in that He Himself speaks in human language, in the witness of His Spirit, who testifies to the Son."
86 By the adjective *figurative* Brunner alludes to the fact that to call Jesus *Himself* the Word, is a figure, an unreal expression. *(Ibid.,* I, p. 32).
87 *Ibid.,* p. 35.
88 At this juncture, Brunner makes the (dialectical) point that inspiration does not involve the union of the divine Spirit with the human. Such an observation would seem to be irrelevant, since the question is not a metaphysical, but an epistemological one, namely, inspiration does not involve a oneness of the divine and human spirits, but a oneness of meaning in God's mind and man's mind.

witness in man's heart. There *may* be identity between the echo and the divine original, but the possibility remains that that identity will fail to materialize.

> The identification can take place but man does not control this possibility. The witness of the Spirit can, therefore, be correctly apprehended by the human spirit so that the "echo" corresponds to the word whose echo it is: there is the possibility, however, that that identity will *not* take place; it is possible for the human spirit more or less to miss the testimony of the divine Spirit. An unambiguous criterion for the one or the other is not to be found. The apostolic witness to Christ has, indeed, its divine ground in inspiration, but it nowhere raises the claim, *eo ipso,* because it is apostolic witness . . . therefore to be inspired.[89]

This statement is bristling with difficulty. In our present discussion the primary question is, When and if the identification between the Spirit's witness and the human echo takes place (and without such identification revelation is impossible) wherein would that differ from the doctrine of verbal inspiration which Brunner has made the butt of his ridicule? Is the testimony of the Spirit the Word of God? It most certainly is, according to Brunner. But it is also a human word. It is, Brunner has assured us, the point of identity between Christ-revelation and the spoken word. Now if this spoken word of the Spirit is correctly apprehended by the human spirit, if identification takes place, it would take a double dialectic to avoid the conclusion that in that instance there was an identification of God's word and man's word, which is verbal inspiration. The dimensional divide is broken down. It-truth has become thou-truth.[90]

Inspiration and Incarnation. Passage from the dimension of the personal to the impersonal, from revelation to words about revelation, is not the only aspect of Brunner's thinking that makes it difficult for him to maintain his repudiation of ortho-

---

89 *Dogmatik,* I, 36. The allusion to the fact that the apostolic witness does not claim to be inspired *because* it is apostolic, is begging the question. Whatever the ground of the claim, the claim itself is clearly expressed by Paul in 1 Thess. 2:13.

90 Witness the complaint of Nels Ferré that Brunner is on the verge of becoming a non-literalist Fundamentalist. "Present Trends in Protestant Thought," *Religion in Life,* 17:343 (1947-48).

doxy. The problem again emerges in connection with his doctrine of the person of Christ. Let us see how this is so.

At the basis of Brunner's rejection of verbal inspiration is the insistence that the Bible, though indeed a vehicle of the divine Word, though inspired by the Spirit of God, is a human book and as such laden with the imperfections and defects which necessarily attach to all that is human.[91] The Scripture is not just the Word of God, but rather man's word about God's Word, and we must ever keep in mind that while it is divine to forgive, it is human to err. God's Word of revelation is broken in the element of the world. Unfortunately the dogmatizing Church has never taken seriously Paul's famous dictum, "We know in part." This means, according to Brunner, that even what we know by revelation is absolute truth only insofar as it is God's Word; formulated by us as our knowledge, it at once becomes part of the whole weakness and imperfection of our human condition.[92]

> Naturally the Scripture is an historical document, written by men and, to that extent, also participating in the frailty of all that is human, in the relativity of all that is historical. Men must first have forgotten what to come in the flesh, to become historical, meant, to be able to set up a doctrine of an infallible Bible book.[93]

What Brunner nowhere makes clear is why this dualism, which renders impossible an infallible written revelation, is no barrier to an infallible personal revelation in Christ. The greatest religious genius, insists Brunner, must be reconciled to God, but Jesus needs no reconciliation to God. He rather reconciles us to God. The most pious man needs forgiveness, but in Jesus we have One who can forgive sins because He had no sins to be forgiven. Now if God can reveal Himself in a man who never sinned, and yet is truly human, why could He not reveal Himself in an infallible book which would yet be truly human? Brunner is untrue to his own canon, "The church must formulate its

91 *Dogmatik*, I, 40.
92 *Christianity and Civilization*, I, 41.
93 "Christlicher Glaube nach reformierter Lehre," *Der Protestantismus der Gegenwart* (Stuttgart, 1926), 254.

doctrine of Scripture after the analogy of the incarnation of Christ."[94]

Jesus' View of Inspiration. Closely related to this subject is the question of Jesus' view of Biblical inspiration. History has shown how difficult it is to hold to a Jesus who is morally and religiously impeccable, while at the same time admitting his fallibility in other areas of human knowledge.[95] But this is the tightrope that Brunner assays to walk. He definitely rejects the statement of Barth in the third edition of his commentary on Romans, "as an earthly appearance Jesus is a sinner."[96] While it is true that Jesus' sinlessness is veiled by His human incognito, it is nonetheless emphatically asserted by Brunner as a proposition of faith. Faith cannot be grounded in the sinlessness of Christ, but His sinlessness can be asserted on the basis of faith.[97] It would certainly seem, however, that even faith could not sustain the scientific infallibility of Jesus. Brunner never reflects directly on this problem, save in a passing allusion to Jesus' mistaken views respecting the calendar date of His return, but it is the clear inference from his own view of science and Scripture. Jesus obviously took the primal history of the Old Testament at its face value, as His references to Noah, Lot's

---

94 *Offenbarung und Vernunft*, p. 272. Volken, reflecting on Brunner's refusal to recognize an external ground of absolute divine authority, well observes, "The chief reason consists ultimately in Brunner's presupposition that the Divine cannot really unite itself with the human. That, however, is an unfounded dogma, against which the facts cited above speak. How can he honestly hold this, when he affirms the much closer, in fact, essential unity of God and man in the person of Christ?" (*Der Glaube bei Emil Brunner*, 218).

95 Evidence of the difficulty which Brunner has in maintaining the religious infallibility of Jesus is reflected in his sermon on the parable of a sower (Mark 4:1-2). He refers to Jesus' statement about those who are without being taught in a parable, so that they might *not* see and be converted (vv. 11-12), as "riddle-like, terrible words." ("Die vierfache Ackerboden," *Saat und Frucht*, p. 8). Calvin's idea, however, that God wills that men harden their hearts rather than be converted, which is just another way of saying what Jesus has said, "is an insane and blasphemous exegesis. . . ." (*Ibid.*, 12). It is apparently a matter of who says a thing.

96 *Der Römerbrief* (3d ed.), 5. This rejection took place in a personal interview with the writer.

97 *Der Mittler*, pp. 199-200. Here Brunner argues that though Christ assumed a human nature He did not become a human person. Ergo, He is not a sinner. (*Ibid.*, 283ff).

wife, and the like, show, and was therefore involved in the error which Brunner ascribes to the "alphabet" of revelation.[98]

More than the "alphabet" of revelation would seem to be involved, however, when we come to such a vital religious issue as the nature of divine revelation. It would certainly be more than anomalous, if Jesus Christ, who is God's revelation *in persona,* should Himself have faulty views on this subject. And yet, if we are to follow Brunner in his analysis of the revelation problem, it is impossible to come to any other conclusion. He has branded that view of revelation which identifies the Word of God with the words of Scripture as "the error having the most serious consequences of any development in Christianity. . . ."[99] He has categorically asserted that "recourse to a pronouncement of Scripture as the final court of appeal is impossible."[100] The reason for this is obvious. Such a final appeal to Scripture would be possible only on the traditional view of verbal inspiration. And yet this is precisely what Jesus does. His appeals to Scripture are always final. So far is the Scripture from being laden with the imperfection which Brunner ascribes to all that is human, that for Jesus it is the one thing which cannot be broken.[101] Brunner complains of those "Christians of the letter, who suppose, when they simply hold, in a slavish way, to the Bible book, that then they are disciples indeed, while actually in so doing they have nothing at all of the spirit of the Master about them. . . ."[102] When discussing the reasons for his rejection of the virgin birth, he observes that such arguments would formerly have been cut short by the phrase, "it is written," a procedure which rests on the doctrine of verbal inspiration, and is therefore no longer possible.[103] Yet this is

---

98 When we say that Jesus took the primal history of the Old Testament at its face value, we do not intend to commit Him to some particular interpretation of the details. We mean simply that Jesus understood these events as time/space history, not as primal history. Brunner would have to concede that by accepting the historic form in which the revelation in Genesis is mediated, Jesus was *eo ipso* involved in scientific error.

99 *Offenbarung und Vernunft,* p. 8.

100 *Dogmatik,* 1, 58.

101 John 10:35.

102 "Vom klugen Haushalter," *Saat und Frucht* (Zürich, 1946), p. 115.

103 *Der Mittler,* p. 288.

precisely the formula used by Jesus against the devil.[104] Brunner in one place refers to the place where Jesus "expresses Himself definitively on the subject of marriage. . . ."[105] When we turn to this definitive utterance of our Lord we find a most interesting situation. Certain Pharisees have come to Jesus with the question of divorce, and He replies, "Have ye not read, that he which made them at the beginning made them male and female, and said, For this cause shall a man leave father and mother and shall cleave to his wife: and they twain shall be one flesh?" The point to be noticed in this "definitive" utterance is the way in which Jesus appeals to Scripture. "Have ye not read, that he which made them . . . said, For this cause," etc. The reference is to Gen. 2:24. But the Genesis narrative does not purport to give us a direct word of Jehovah, nor is there any place in the Old Testament where this saying is ascribed directly to God. What Jesus is doing is quoting a word of Scripture and declaring, God said that. The only hypothesis which will do justice to such a situation is that Jesus regarded the Scripture itself as the Word of God.[106] And this occurrence is not isolated. Everywhere Jesus appeals to Scripture, to each part of Scripture and to each element of Scripture as to an unimpeachable authority.[107] It may be that such considerations have figured in Brunner's recent concession that in the prophets there is identity between the divine and human word. In any case, so long as Brunner maintains a sinless Jesus whose teaching has "partici-

---

104 Matt. 4:4, 7, 10; Luke 4:4, 8. Curiously enough in a sermon (*Gott und das Brot* [Bern, 1930], p. 10), Brunner appeals with approbation to the example of Jesus who answered the devil with "it is written." Further evidence of the zigzag of Brunner's thought is the way in which he himself appeals to Scripture when it is convenient. Jer. 3:30 and Ezek. 18:5-9, we are told, make it clear that no one shall be declared guilty for what he has not done. (*Der Mensch im Widerspruch*, p. 121). We cannot solve the marriage crisis "with the biblicistic proof text method" (*Das Gebot und die Ordnungen*, p. 620, note 4), and yet marital asceticism is ruled out because it contradicts 1 Cor. 7:5 (*Ibid.*, 354).

105 *Das Gebot und die Ordnungen*, p. 329. The passage is Matt. 19:3-9. Cf. also Luke 16:18.

106 Interestingly Paul (1 Cor. 6:16) quotes the same passage as a divine word: "For, The twain, saith he, shall become one flesh." Cf. B. B. Warfield, "The Biblical Idea of Inspiration," *Revelation and Inspiration* (New York, 1927), pp. 86-89.

107 Witness, for example, His inference of the resurrection from the statement of Scripture, "I am the God of Abraham," etc. (Matt. 22:32).

pated in the absolute authority of the Son of God,"[108] the pendulum of his thought will periodically gravitate to the orthodox side of the theological arena.

II. Biblical Authority

Let us conclude our critique of Brunner's view of Scripture by analyzing those elements in his thinking which tend to the left of theological center. We shall attempt to show that Brunner halts his break with the tradition short of a complete abandonment of the authority of the Bible, only by an act of will.

In a popular presentation Brunner may make an unqualified appeal to the normative authority of Scripture. The Bible is the measure by which we judge all claimants to revelation.[109] The difficulty is that this standard by which we are to determine what is and what is not God's Word, the Bible, is not absolute; in fact, it is not even itself the Word of God, according to Brunner. In the last analysis, there is no objective criterion of the divine Word. While the theology stemming from the Reformation was right in elevating the authority of the Bible above that of the Church, yet it erred in making the Bible the final norm of religious truth, from which there was no appeal. By thus identifying God's word and the Bible's word, it returned in principle to the error of Catholicism.[110] To avoid this heteronomous faith, Brunner, as we have seen, insists upon the mediacy of Biblical authority. The Bible is not the Word, as orthodoxy teaches with its doctrine of verbal inspiration, but rather a *means* thereto. Even in his most recent statement, Brunner maintains this distinction. "The Scripture is not the authority on the basis of which one believes in Christ, but it is the instrument of God, by means of which he shows and gives us Christ."[111] While we are unconditionally bound to the apostolic

---

108 *Offenbarung und Vernunft,* p. 120.
109 "But not everything that pretends to be the Word of the Holy Spirit is what it claims to be. We need a measure to know what is of the Spirit of God and what is not. This measure is the Bible, the document, the original Word of the Holy Spirit, the normal meter upon which all that claims to be God's Word must be gauged. Whatever fails to agree with it, cannot be God's Word." *(Our Faith,* 86). Cf. also *Wahrheit als Begegnung,* p. 32, "The Holy Scripture is the source and norm of all Christian theology."
110 *Dogmatik,* I, 63.
111 *Dogmatik,* II, 402.

witness as a *means* of revelation, we are only in a relative sense
bound to the *authority* of that witness as it becomes the vehicle
of God's Word to us.[112] There can be no last recourse to a
passage of Scripture because human fallibility attaches to the
Scripture itself. It is interesting to observe this principle in
operation, in the case of the resurrection of Christ. Does Brunner believe in the resurrection? Of course. Why? Because the
Bible says so and because he is convinced of the veracity of the
Biblical witnesses? Should he concede this, then the Bible would
become willy-nilly the ground of faith. But what else can he
say? He argues, unconvincingly, as follows:

> The report of the apostles concerning their meeting
> with the resurrected One is not the ground, but an element
> in the witness of that revelation which is the ground of
> our faith in Christ and therefore of our faith in His
> resurrection.[113]

In other words, I do not believe in the resurrection because the
apostles report that they met the risen Lord, but I believe in it
because of the revelational witness of which that report is an
element. A couple of pages later he observes that it is possible
to say that we would believe on the resurrected Lord, even if
there were no reports of the resurrection, only we must ever
remember that we have the apostolic testimony only because
the apostles met the resurrected Lord and without that
testimony we ourselves could not believe.[114]

A further difficulty with the idea that the Bible is a means of
revelation is that it reduces the authority of the Bible over the
voice of the preaching Church to a matter of chronological
priority and dignity. Though the Bible has the temporal priority
of *"primal*-witness," in principle it is on the same plane with
the "witness of the church."[115] Brunner admits that mere *historical* priority is not the equivalent of normativeness. The

---

112 "While we, however, are bound in an absolute sense to the medium,
to the *means* of revelation, which is the witness of the apostles, we
are only in a relative sense bound to the *authority* of this witness."
(Die christliche Lehre von Gott, p. 55). Brunner in one place makes
the Scripture an objective means of revelation to the unbeliever. (Cf.
Offenbarung und Vernunft, p. 69.) Just how something can be a
means of revelation, to those who do not accept it, is a paradox.
113 *Dogmatik,* II, 439.
114 *Ibid.,* p. 441.
115 *Offenbarung und Vernunft,* p. 143.

element of "essential priority" must be maintained, but even this does not rise in the last analysis beyond the category of special dignity, which, he concedes, cannot be precisely defined.[116]

At no point does Brunner's adeptness at illustration, the mark of a truly great teacher, evidence itself more felicitously than at this juncture, when he speaks of the function of the Bible in mediating to us the Word of God, in the figure of a phonograph record. Because of the attractiveness of this thought and the importance of its implications for Brunner's doctrine of Scriptural authority, we repeat it here *in toto.*

> On every street one sees advertisements of the phonograph company, "His Master's Voice," which means in German, "Seines Meisters Stimme." This is the way the phonograph company takes of saying, buy a disc and you will hear the master Caruso's voice. Is that true? Certainly! Really his voice? Yes, indeed. And yet, — ah yes, the phonograph persists in making its own sounds. It is not the voice of the master, but the scratching of hard rubber. But do not find fault with the hard rubber (disc) ! Only by means of the hard rubber phonograph disc can you hear "the master's voice." And lo, so it is with the Bible. It enables you to perceive the real voice of the master, really his voice, his words that he wishes to say. But there are extraneous sounds along with it, even for this reason, that God speaks his word through man's mouth. Paul, Peter, Isaiah and Moses are men. But through them God speaks His word. And as man, God came into the world, really He, but really as man. Therefore everything (in their writings) is His voice to be sure, but with all the disturbances which belong to the human as such.[117]

It is unfair to press an illustration as though it were the thing itself. But there is one matter which obviously is not covered by this illustration, but needs to be, and that is this: If no one had ever heard Caruso in person, how would we

---

116 "This priority, however, is not to be absolutely and sharply defined." *(Dogmatik,* I, 53-4). Thus the Bible slips into the category of Euclid's geometry. We must learn geometry from Euclid only in the sense that his work has the superiority of chronological priority. Brunner's attempt to make the Bible participate in the absoluteness of the once-for-all revelational event cannot be carried through.

117 *Unser Glaube,* p. 15.

know that this reproduction of his voice was really a reproduction of *his* voice? Record collectors tell us interesting stories of disputes as to who is actually singing on certain old cylinders. Sometimes it is impossible to settle the argument by comparing the record in dispute with other records. The only way to resolve the difficulty is to call in some older person, preferably one who made recordings of artists for Edison or Victor, but in any case someone who has heard the living voices of the singers, over whose recordings the debate reigns. But, Brunner would say, that is just it. The inspired apostles did hear the voice of God and have given us an account of what they heard in the Bible. But did they really hear the very voice of God as it really is, or was their hearing also broken and defective because human? If Brunner replies that their hearing was not blurred by the element of the world, wherein then would his position differ from verbal inspiration? Hence, Brunner must answer that the hearing of the apostles, since they were human, is also, like all that is human, an imperfect and faulty hearing, but then the analogy breaks down.[118] The Bible is not a record of His voice, but only the record of a record, so to speak. No one has ever heard the voice of God apart from the record. But then how do we know that the record of God's voice is really a record of *His* voice?

It is but a step further in the same direction to say that God may reveal Himself apart from and outside of the Bible. Though *we* may be bound to a given means, God is sovereign. Why should He be bound to means? Since the Bible is not itself God's Word, but only a means of revelation, who is to say that God could not speak through other means, other books? With great hesitancy and obvious reluctance Brunner admits the possibility.

> However, what then is the situation with regard to those other books, which also claim to be the word of God? I answer two things. Firstly, are you a Mohammedan, a Hindu? Then those books do not concern you. Secondly, if you still want to know how it stands with those other books, I can say only one thing to you; it is another voice

---

118 "The breaking of divine revelation in the human medium of the knowledge and witness of faith, is already present in the primal witness. . . ." (*Dogmatik*, I, 54).

which speaks in them from the voice which is to be heard in our Bible. It is not the same God, not the good Shepherd that comes to His sheep. It is a strange voice. It may be that it is, somehow or other, also God's voice, but then one that is scarcely recognizable, like a very bad photograph, that is "he" indeed, and yet no, "it is not he."[119]

Here the doctrine of Biblical authority is dwarfed to the vanishing point; here the pendulum of Brunner's thought moves to the opposite extreme of theological possibility from that noted above. And thus the question of Biblical authority is still oriented in the orthodox-liberal either-or in which he found it. His attempted synthesis must therefore be pronounced a failure.[120]

119 *Unser Glaube*, p. 15. This statement is in direct contradiction to his assertion of the exclusiveness of Scripture made some eight years before. *(Der Mittler*, p. 147).
120 Having come to the end of the way, it is difficult to see how Brunner's attempt to save the normative character of Scripture, while insisting that it is only a means of revelation to which no final appeal can be made, differs materially from the effort of Kant to maintain the principle of responsibility to the transcendental self. If, in the latter instance, as Brunner alleges, the concept of responsibility disintegrates, by the same token, in the former case, the doctrine of authority in religion evaporates.

Chapter IX

REINHOLD NIEBUHR'S VIEW OF SCRIPTURE
By Edward John Carnell

To compose an essay on Reinhold Niebuhr's view of Scripture is far from easy, for the topic (to my knowledge) is nowhere an object of direct attention in the vast and stimulating Niebuhrian literature. The reason for this omission is the "nonexistential" character of the topic. The significance of this will be clarified in due time.

If one were to follow ideal lines in defining Niebuhr's attitude toward Scripture, he first would review the whole of Niebuhr's philosophy of religion. After this, he would find the precise relation between this restricted question and the larger system. Since so ambitious a project would not be practical in this compendious account, however, a substitute plan must be arranged.

In the absence of the larger procedure, the best alternative is to devise a guiding criterion. If such a standard can be found, we will have a norm by which to advance our particular problem.

In the interests of economy, I choose the following as a working criterion: *Religious thinkers will submit to the Bible only as they despair of learning the meaning of life without assistance from God.* Before this criterion can be either accepted or rejected, it must first be understood.

The norm sounds more complicated than it really is. It simply means that since sin is a personal rebellion against God, and since rebellion is an expression of human self-sufficiency, it follows that the natural man will not yield to the revealed Word of God until it interests him; and it will never interest him until he discovers profit in such a submission. Whenever God's voice is of neither interest nor profit, man remains autonomous. Only as one *hungers* for Scripture will he conform to its teachings.

Let us illustrate this point, using humanism, orthodoxy, and Roman Catholicism as examples. Let us indicate in each case whether, and to what extent, there is dependence on the Bible.

Since consistent humanism believes it can solve all its problems by a more critical application of methods devised by man, it owns *no* instance of dependence on special revelation. This is one end of the scale. Orthodoxy lies at the other. Convinced that nothing can be known about the destiny of a rebellious society unless God reveals it, orthodoxy cheerfully yields itself to *every* teaching of Scripture. If humanism has no interest in special revelation, orthodoxy has every interest. Roman Catholicism is a case unto itself. Although it accepts Biblical authority in the abstract, it materially submits only at those places where the interests of the Church are advanced. It is the living Church, not the written Word, which is the supreme court in all decisions.

With these preliminary observations behind us, let us apply our criterion to Niebuhr's system. *To what extent, if any, does Niebuhr cast himself on the authority of Scripture?* If we can find an answer to this question, our assignment will be finished.

I. Niebuhr's Rejection of Immanence

Humanism says that man either does have, or could have, all the clues needed to explain everything worth explaining. The philosophy behind this optimism is called *immanence*. Immanence is the confidence that history contains its own meaning. Man needs only time and patience to acquire all significant truth. The Logos of history dwells within history.

The alternative to immanence is the spiritual admission that we cannot solve the meaning of life until some extra-historical source of knowledge and power is found — which, in our case, is the Bible. Using our illustrations again, we note the following: humanism is built on immanence; orthodoxy rejects it at all points where questions about an offended God's attitude toward man are involved; and Catholicism courts it wherever it buttresses the interests of the Church.

Although it does not follow that the rejection of immanence implies a submission to Scripture, it can be said that only as a man despairs of solving history's problems within history will he long for a Word which proceeds from heaven. This is why it is crucial to discover Niebuhr's stand on the question. If he accepts immanence, we may safely conclude that he rejects any serious dependence on the Bible, and our study is finished; while if he rejects it, we may assume that he at least is open to the possibility of Biblical authority.

Niebuhr emphatically rejects all forms of consistent immanence. "Man in his strength and in his weakness is too ambiguous to understand himself, unless his rational analyses are rooted in a faith that he is comprehended from beyond the ambiguities of his own understanding."[1]

To assist in the explanation of this quotation, let us grasp what Niebuhr means by "freedom." Freedom refers to man's simultaneous potentialities for creativity and destruction. Wherever one enjoys transcendence above nature, he is free. This is why Niebuhr asserts that *a solution to the problems raised by human freedom cannot be found by an extension of human freedom.* Since man is already out of harmony with the law of life, it follows that freedom cannot be its own redeemer. Freedom spreads its evil on every new level of life. Let us delay naming this disease until we have first observed its symptoms.

Classical liberal theology cites science and universal education as proof that man's control over existence is as inevitable as the hardening of the muscles in the arm of the blacksmith. Niebuhr rejects this sanguine optimism because it overlooks the element of corruption in all expressions of freedom.

Science cannot solve our problems for at least two reasons. *First,* it is not equipped to recognize the difference between neutral, empirical data and the prejudiced affections of the scientist. "The usual basis for this hope is the belief that there is no essential difference between the stuff of history and the stuff of nature and therefore no real distinction between the application of the 'scientific method' to nature and to history."[2] But there happens to be a qualitative difference between bunsen burners and the self-love of a technician. *Second,* a failure to perceive this difference encourages the error that mankind's troubles stem from a poor use of science, rather than from the evil which inheres in the will of man. This blindness fosters the very pride and self-sufficiency which cause history's sickness. "The rise of the natural sciences was at first merely a by-product

---

1 *Faith and History* (New York: Scribner, 1949), p. 101.
2 *Ibid.*, p. 82.

of this sense of human self-reliance, for nature was regarded merely as the mirror of the greatness of man. But as science gradually contributed to man's actual mastery of natural forces it gave a new impetus of its own to the idea of human self-sufficiency."[3]

Next comes education. By lying nearer spiritual vitalities, education is more easily confused with values which only faith can safeguard. Whenever education is equated with virtue, man betrays himself into the error of thinking that his life is natively in harmony with the right. But there happens to be a conflict between the mind's perception of truth and the egoistic interests of a very stubborn will. Education may tell us what is true, but it cannot affectionately conform man to the truth. At this point secular science and education join in falsely presupposing that man's life is causally continuous with nature. "The reason mechanistic psychiatry and psycho-analysis run easily into a justification of license is because they labor under the illusion that the higher self (they would scorn that term) is able to put all internal forces in their proper place, if only it knows their previous history and actual direction."[4]

But why are science and education agents of self-interest? Answer: man is a sinner. Sin is man's stubborn refusal to accept the limitations of human nature. "Sin is to be regarded as neither a necessity of man's nature nor yet as a pure caprice of his will. It proceeds rather from a defect of the will, for which reason it is not completely deliberate; but since it is the will in which the defect is found and the will presupposes freedom the defect cannot be attributed to a taint in man's nature."[5] Since man participates in both time and eternity, he is tempted to pretend securities and finalities which are neither secure nor final. "The brutality with which a Pharisee of every age resists those who puncture his pretensions proves the uneasiness of his conscience. The insecurity of sin is always a double insecurity. It must seek to hide not only the original finiteness of perspective and relativity of value which it is the purpose of sin to hide, but also the dishonesty by which it has sought to obscure these. The fury with which oligarchs, dictators, priest-kings, ancient and modern, and ideological pretenders turn upon their critics

---

3 *Human Nature* (New York: Scribner, 1941), p. 66.
4 *Does Civilization Need Religion?* (New York: Macmillan, 1927) p. 21.
5 *Human Nature*, p. 242.

and foes is clearly the fury of an uneasy conscience, though it must not be assumed that such a conscience is always fully conscious of itself."[6]

It now ought to be clear why Niebuhr rejects consistent immanence. To repeat: *a solution to the problems raised by human freedom cannot be found by an extension of human freedom.* "Where there is history at all there is freedom; and where there is freedom there is sin."[7] Every individual and collective pretension to finality illustrates man's contentious refusal to accept limitations that are native to creatureliness.

The desperation of our predicament can only be understood as one recognizes that sin soothes man into believing that evil in history is the fault of others, never his own. Any *personal* repentance before God is either superfluous or dangerous: superfluous because it suggests that man is not sufficient unto himself — while he is; and dangerous because it substitutes reliance on God for human industry. With stentorian boldness Niebuhr speaks against the complacency of modernity. He voices judgment against a decaying bourgeois-liberal culture; he indicts its pretensions and securities on every level of life.

Let us now return to our initial criterion: *Religious thinkers will submit their minds to the Bible only as they despair of learning the meaning of history without assistance from God.* Since Niebuhr rejects consistent immanence, we are safe in concluding that he at least is open to the *possibility* that the answer to life is found in Scripture. Whether this possibility eventuates in personal appropriation must now be investigated.

II. The Twilight Zone of Transition

Although both Barth and Niebuhr share the existential presuppositions of Soren Kierkegaard, Niebuhr refuses to follow the Barthian stress on the complete discontinuity of time and eternity. Man is depraved, but he is not so depraved that he is unaware of his depravity. If sin were to blot out man's memory of original righteousness, man could never be goaded into creativity by a feeling of his own moral shortcomings. Niebuhr, thus, affirms a clear point of contact between God and the secular world.

6 *Ibid.*, p. 256.
7 *Human Destiny* (New York: Scribner, 1943), p. 80.

In developing a philosophy of natural revelation, however, Niebuhr is careful to guard against immanence. A penumbra borders nature and grace. It may be identified with neither immanence nor transcendence. It is not in immanence, for it speaks against human self-sufficiency; and it is not in transcendence, for man is able to discover it apart from special revelation. Natural revelation points toward, but is not part of, special revelation.

The contents of natural revelation cannot be laid on the table for curious eyes to inspect. Before a person can be sensitive to the voice of God in his heart, he must learn to think *existentially;* that is, from within the sensitive center of his own inner responsibilities and conflicts, and not after the manner of objective speculation. An existential perspective is a concerned perspective — a concern for what it means to be a responsible, existing individual: to tremble when friendships and loyalties are betrayed, to fear when duties are neglected, to grieve when ideals are dethroned.

When Niebuhr finished analyzing the sickness of society, he concluded that harmony is destroyed because pride inflates each one to believe himself finally secure over against his neighbor. No other thesis can account for the piety with which men defend their own interests. Whether in driving a car down the street — where one is angry at another for inconsiderateness — or in a collision between national interests that leads to war, the same sinful disease of pride is at work. It soothes man with the comforting assurance that his interests are universally valid — taking care, of course, to conceal the radical disparity between pretense and conduct.

Evil in history can only be eliminated as individuals and nations substitute sympathy for belligerency and intolerance. But such spiritual modesty is not possible until one appreciates the distance which separates his own evil ways from the perfection of the "law of life." This, however, is an existential insight. If one refuses to view the problem from within his own evil life, he will never submit to God's righteousness. He will never perceive how greatly his devotion to duty is corrupted by personal interest and finite perspective. He will never realize that the law of perfection stands in opposition to, rather than in harmony with, the vitalities of his own ego. It is the strategy of pride to urge the ego to believe that a lovely harmony unites its own with universal duty.

Niebuhr is careful to show that the law by which we judge others, and hence the law by which God judges us, is *the law of love*. Tolerance, forgiveness, and pity are the basis of a just society. The law of love is the law of life.

Existential experience testifies that whenever an individual courageously tests his life by the law of love, he is confronted by two important facts. *First,* that the law of love stands in judgment upon the pretensions of the ego. Interests are sinful whenever they are entertained at the expense of the rightful securities of others. *Second,* that judgment comes from the person of God. Conscience is an outlet for eternity's dissatisfaction with the raw elements which nest in the bosom of the heart.

The more existentially one analyzes the elements in this moral confrontation, the more accurate will be his definition of the God who deflates pride. Man is able to know God in three complementary ways. "The first is the sense of reverence for a majesty and of dependence upon an ultimate source of being. The second is the sense of moral obligation laid upon one from beyond oneself and of moral unworthiness before a judge. The third, most problematic of the elements in religious experience, is the longing for forgiveness."[8]

But what is the significance of this discussion? What is the relation between natural revelation and Niebuhr's view of Scripture? Now that our findings have become complex, how shall our original criterion be applied? Two observations must be made.

First, having despaired of discovering the meaning of life apart from a rule of eternity that is discontinuous with tribal particularities, Niebuhr submits to whatever Biblical insights support this need. The Bible authoritatively witnesses to the fact that God stands in judgment over all human pretensions. Jehovah is *never* an extension of personal interests. He is eternally wrathful against all claims to individual or tribal virtue. Human acceptance is by grace, not merit. No man is worthy to look on God. "Israel does not choose God. God chooses Israel; and this choice is regarded as an act of grace for

8 *Human Nature,* p. 131. If the reader has an opportunity to study Niebuhr's own arguments, let him check the entire context here. Niebuhr goes to great length to clinch his point.

which no reason can be given, other than God's own love (Deut. 7:7-8). In Biblical thought, the grace of God completes the structure of meaning, beyond the limits of rational intelligibility in the realm of history, just as divine creation is both the fulfillment and the negation of intelligibility for the whole temporal order."[9] Modernity's disease is a result of its proud insistence that eternity is morally continuous with finite interests, a view which leaves the particularities of culture in perpetual war with each other. Finitude has no norm by which one partiality can be judged superior to another. It has no resources of forgiveness when hostilities end. The Bible is God's Word because it is not an extension of either individual, tribal, or national pride. God simultaneously judges and completes history.

Second, and more important for our study, there is a *dialectical* necessity for Biblical revelation. Here is our predicament: if we *deny* the law of life, we court moral skepticism; but if we *admit* this law, we place both ourselves and society under a condemnation from which there is no earthly deliverance. We cannot keep the law of love; yet we corrupt our own dignity if we cease to try. This is the basis of a dialectical tension.

A "dialectical tension" is formed by contrary relations — as when two individuals take exception to each other's opinions. Their manner of speech is a dialogue; its purpose is to bare a truth that is acceptable to both parties. There are, in Hegelian terms, three parts to the dialectic: the thesis, the antithesis, and the synthesis. Thesis and antithesis are the contrarieties. The synthesis develops as contrarieties elicit latencies from each other. Niebuhr's theology rests on a formal acceptance of the principle that time and eternity are related dialectically, *i.e.,* after the manner of a dialogue: time creates polarity tensions which are resolved only as eternity speaks — a process which is never static and completed, but which is repeated at every moment within the spiritual life of the penitent.

Niebuhr's social theology is premised on the following dialectic. *Thesis:* nothing less than the law of love can define righteousness. *Antithesis:* neither the individual nor the collective mind meets the terms of this righteousness. These are the contrarieties of the dialectical tension. But this is the limit of the human perspective, for only *Christ* can elicit a synthesis.

9 *Faith and History,* pp. 102-3.

Throughout the two volumes of the Gifford Lectures, Niebuhr persuasively argues that only Biblical Christianity correctly comprehends and resolves the dialectic. The sweep of non-Christian, religio-philosophical literature betrays familiar, nondialectical conclusions: either the law of life is misunderstood and some furious, demonic vitality replaces the cohesions of fraternity — as in the Nazi ideology; or the law is understood, but its implications misunderstood —as in all forms of immanence. "The fact that a culture which identifies God with some level of human consciousness, either rational or super-rational, or with some order of nature, invariably falsifies the human situation and fails to appreciate either the total stature of freedom in man or the complexity of the problem of evil in him, is the most telling negative proof for the Biblical faith. Man does not know himself truly except as he knows himself confronted by God. Only in that confrontation does he become aware of his full stature and freedom and of the evil in him. It is for this reason that Biblical faith is of such importance for the proper understanding of man, and why it is necessary to correct the interpretations of human nature which underestimate his stature, depreciate his physical existence and fail to deal realistically with the evil in human nature, in terms of Biblical faith."[10] Only Biblical Christianity is truly dialectical, for it alone announces the law with perfection, while yet judging all pretensions to fulfillment.

This is not to suggest that the Biblical witness is *consistently* dialectical. Like other human writing (so Niebuhr argues) it is corrupted here and there by finite perspective and personal interest. But faith overcomes these inconsistencies and seizes the announcement of heaven that in the epoch of Christ's life and death a dialectical solution to the relation between God's justice and His mercy is defined — a solution which the Old Testament prophets sought but could not find.[11]

III. Dialectic and the Authority of Scripture

Remembering the terms of our criterion *(that religious thinkers will submit to the Bible only as they despair of learning the*

10 *Human Nature,* p. 131.
11 It is impossible to document these propositions within the short compass of this chapter. Those who are interested in pursuing the theological ramifications should read the primary sources.

meaning of history without assistance from God), we are now
ready to sum up the relation between Niebuhr's dialectical
theology and the authority of Scripture. Since he believes that
nondialectical truths can be developed within immanence, Niebuhr interacts with Scripture only at those places where the
Bible is dialectical. In order that we might understand how
this takes place, let us set down a series of steps, using each as a
point of departure for the next; this procedure to continue until
our goal has been reached.

First, Niebuhr breaks from the liberal doctrine that the Bible
was developed within immanence. It is not a record of the
religious experiences of men. "This historical revelation is by no
means simply the history of man's quest for God or the record
of man's increasingly adequate definitions of the person of God,
interpretations to which modern liberal thought has sometimes
reduced Biblical revelation."[12] Scripture *judges* the pretensions
of immanence.

Second, the Bible is an account of the covenantal (dialectical)
relations between God and Israel. It tells of the moral obliga-
tions upon the part of a responsible, responding people and the
twofold, personal Word of God — mercy and grace when men
walk humbly before Him, and judgment when they persist in
sin. The Bible is "the record of those events in history in which
faith discerns the self-disclosure of God."[13] God comes into
history and reveals Himself through Israel.

Third, although the Bible is a record of how God deals with
a covenant people, it is not a system of propositional truth that
can be tested by the law of contradiction in the light of
regenerate experience, as in orthodoxy. Its truth is perceived
existentially-dialectically, not critically-historically. Scripture
illuminates and interprets the confrontation which faith experiences whenever the transcendent self meets God on the edge of
history. "What it discerns are actions of God which clarify the
confrontation of man by God in the realm of the personal and
individual moral life. In personal life the moral experience
consists of the moral obligation as being laid upon man not by
himself, nor yet by his society but by God; as a judgment upon
man for failing in his obligation; and finally as the need for

12 *Ibid.,* p. 136.
13 *Loc. cit.*

reconciliation between man and God because of the estrange-
ment resulting from man's rebellion against the divine will."[14]

Fourth, as an objective book, therefore, the Bible is marred
by the same errors and inconsistencies that corrupt any human
document. Niebuhr accepts destructive higher criticism as a
legitimate tool when examining Scripture. "Yet early Biblical
history has many facets which relate it to lower particularistic
religion. The canon of the faith contains an 'Old Testament' in
which we find the usual 'story' of a particular people, seeking
to comprehend their history in terms of their origin. Their God
is the God of 'Abraham, Isaac and Jacob,' who seems to be, on
some levels of their history, simply their champion against
competitors and foes, both allowing and enjoining them to the
most ruthless actions in order to encompass the defeat of the
foe and to establish their own security."[15] "The Deuteronomic
code was an effort to place legalism in the service of prophetism
and to give to prophetic insights the permanence of legal
codes."[16] "The suffering servant figure is not a Messianic symbol;
or, if so, only in a very secondary sense. Most probably it was
meant to designate the nation rather than any individual. If so,
it represented a profound effort to give the sufferings of Israel a
higher meaning by the suggestion that its mission and triumph
in the world would not be achieved by the usual triumph over
others but by its vicarious suffering for the sins of others."[17]
The truths of the Bible lie behind the time-bound forms in
which they are expressed. They can only be "existentially"
perceived.

Fifth, since transcendence has no more rights over immanence
than immanence has over transcendence, it is illicit for Christians to use the Bible as an authority in fields which are
accessible to the unaided intellect: science, history, philosophy,
and the like. Unless faith succeeds in disengaging the accidental
from the essential and the marginal from the central, it will fall
into a literalism which converts the paradox of Biblical Christianity into complete absurdity. Let us enlarge upon this matter.

Faith must separate nondialectical elements — genealogies,
the dimensions of the temple, and the like — from those that

14 *Ibid.,* pp. 136-37.
15 *Faith and History,* p. 24.
16 *Human Destiny,* p. 39.
17 *Ibid.,* pp. 44-45.

are richly dialectical, though garbed in terms appropriate to immanence (Biblical stories, such as creation and the fall of man). The latter are depth insights. Wherever they may be found, and under whatever conditions they may appear, depth insights are true. Take the fall of man, for example. When tested as history, it turns out to be an artless Hebrew narrative which betrays the prescientific mentality of an early mind; but when tested existentially, it mirrors profound truth. It accurately explains the transcendental experience of a morally sensitive individual. Although one may earnestly *assent* to the law of life, he nevertheless experiences a "fall" whenever he tries to conform his conduct to this perfection. The Biblical account of Adam and Eve is "religiously," though not scientifically or historically, true. It is a "myth" of the Hebrew mind, a trans-cultural truth which is stated in terms drawn from an earlier culture. Faith accepts the story as a "symbol" of its own experience. Sagas and myths represent the transcendental effort of both individuals and groups to "seek a deeper or higher dimension of meaning than the mere record of their continuance in time."[18] The Bible is rich with symbols: Babel, the Ark and the Temple, the Son of Man, the Cross, the Resurrection, the Second Coming, the Antichrist — symbols which lose their value the moment they are taken literally. Niebuhr believes that the literalizing of symbols is the capital error of orthodoxy.

Let us illustrate Niebuhr's philosophy of symbolism by the following rather meaty passage:

> The symbol of the second coming of Christ can neither be taken literally nor dismissed as unimportant. It partici-pates in the general characteristic of the Biblical symbols, which deal with the relation of time and eternity, and seek to point to the ultimate from the standpoint of the condi-tioned. If the symbol is taken literally the dialectical conception of time and eternity is falsified and the ultimate vindication of God over history is reduced to a point in history. The consequence of this falsification is expressed in the hope of a millennial age. In such a millennial age, just as in a utopian one, history is supposedly fulfilled despite the persisting conditions of finiteness. On the other hand if the symbol is dismissed as unimportant, as merely a picturesque or primitive way of apprehending the rela-

18 *Faith and History*, p. 23.

tion of the historical to the eternal, the Biblical dialectic is obscured in another direction. All theologies which do not take these symbols seriously will be discovered upon close analysis not to take history seriously either. They presuppose an eternity which annuls rather than fulfills the historical process.[19]

Sixth, in summary: the Bible is the record of a redemption history *(Heilsgeschichte)* that completes life from a perspective beyond history. Redemptive history mirrors individual history by dialectically balancing the following triad: the eternal justice of God (law) ; the failure of man to abide by law (sin) ; and the grace and mercy of God in Christ (forgiveness). The Biblical testimony about Christ is what a pious soul experiences in Christ. But if we confuse a "witness" to truth with a corpus of infallibly revealed propositions, we convert a profound understanding of Scripture into a distressing literalism.

> The Reformation insistence upon the authority of Scripture, as against the authority of the church, bears within it the perils of a new idolatry. Its Biblicism became, in time, as dangerous to the freedom of the human mind in searching out causes and effects as the old religious authority. But rightly conceived Scriptural authority is meant merely to guard the truth of the gospel in which all truth is fulfilled and all corruptions of truth are negated. This authority is Scriptural in the sense that the Bible contains the history, and the culmination in Christ, of that *Heilsgeschichte* in which the whole human enterprise becomes fully conscious of its limits, of its transgressions of those limits, and of the divine answer to its problems. When the Bible becomes an authoritative compendium of social, economic, political and scientific knowledge it is used as a vehicle of the sinful sanctification of relative standards of knowledge and virtue which happen to be enshrined in a religious canon.[20]

CONCLUSION

Here is the sum of the matter: *Since he is pessimistic about the success of immanence, though not about man's ability to develop a dialectical philosophy, it follows that Niebuhr retains*

19 *Human Destiny,* p. 289.
20 *Ibid.,* p. 152.

a critical autonomy over the system of Scripture. Whether such autonomy is good or bad depends upon how seriously one accepts or rejects the Bible as a system of thought. Orthodoxy is persuaded that one has no final truth about God until he submits to the Bible's self-testimony. Neo-orthodoxy judges the Bible by dialectical insights; orthodoxy judges dialectical insights by the Bible.

Let us remember the *interests* which encourage Niebuhr to reinterpret the Biblical system after the lines of myth and symbol. He does not come to Scripture to learn whether sin is so awful that Christ's atonement propitiates an offended element in the nature of God; not whether the rejection of this blood results in the judicial sentence of the sinner to hell; not whether God has so committed His will to writing that those who love Him prove their affection by a complete and unreserved submission to the whole counsel of Scripture. Rather, he has sought an answer to this one question: "Is it possible to join the existential experiences of man with a hopeful philosophy of both history and society?" Niebuhr feels that apart from Biblical presuppositions, this simply cannot be done. Therefore, he defends the Bible as the Word of God.

CHAPTER X

DIVINE REVELATION AND THE BIBLE

By Carl F. H. Henry

The relationship which prevails between divine revelation and the Hebrew-Christian Scriptures is perhaps the most vigorously debated theological question of our century.

In some circles, confessedly, it is scarcely a live concern. The Communist ideology thrusts the question aside as wholly irrelevant to the cultural crisis.

But the problems which dialectical materialism ignores are likely to be the cardinal ones. The scornful way in which Soviet-sphere thought dismisses supernaturalistic considerations creates a proper suspicion that they are by-passed rather than judiciously measured. Precisely because Communism deals so artificially with the supreme concerns of life, it is an undesirable option for most of the Western world.

Where the reality of the supernatural is dogmatically excluded, the reality of any Word of God is, of course, concealed along with the actuality of God's existence. But the fact of God and of His self-revelation cannot be evaporated simply by naturalistic denials.

Despite its repudiation of Communism as a way of life, the West is plagued nonetheless by the fact that naturalism as an interpretative philosophy of reality is on the ascendancy. The idealistic philosophies are in a state of retreat, if not of actual collapse, and naturalistic schemes are seeking pre-eminence.

In this crisis, the theological viewpoint again has the responsibility and strategic opportunity of addressing the modern mind in behalf of the theistic perspective.

To speak dramatically to the Western world for the standpoint of theism inevitably brings into focus once again the problem of Hebrew-Christian revelation and of the Sacred Scriptures. Wherever God is acknowledged, the question whether He has spoken, and what if anything He has said, belongs in the forefront. For that reason the question of the

Bible and of its relationship to divine revelation continues with uncompromised relevance into the last half of the twentieth century.

The terms "revelation" and "Scripture" assuredly are not synonymous. No era of Christian thought has made the egregious error of equating them absolutely, although modern opponents of historic Christianity frequently gain sympathy for their low views of the Bible by imputing excessive and obviously objectionable claims to the theological tradition. When Christianity speaks of the Word of God, it designates not only the *rhēma theou,* the spoken and written word of God in the grammatical sense, but also the *logos theou,* the personal Word, or the speaking Logos, the agent in creation and the mediator of divine revelation in all its forms and the supreme revelation of God incarnate. Therefore, alongside of special divine revelation in its Scriptural form, Hebrew-Christian theology emphasizes as an indispensable corollary the general divine revelation given in nature, history and conscience. Moreover, the Biblical view traces both the general and special revelations to the Logos, Jesus Christ. As the divine revealing agent in creation and preservation He manifests God in the general revelation of nature, history and conscience. By the Sacred Scriptures, divinely outbreathed through the Holy Spirit to prophets and apostles, He discloses truths about God and His redemptive purpose, inclusive of that salvation history consummated at last by the incarnation and atonement.

Whatever Hebrew-Christian thought affirms about the Scriptures, therefore, it does with the firm consciousness that (1) Jesus Christ is the divine agent in all revelation, (2) revelation is not merely special but also general,[1] and (3) special revelation involves unique historical events of divine deliverance climaxed by the incarnation, atonement, and resurrection of Jesus Christ, the supreme disclosure of God in the flesh. The divine revelation of stupendous redemptive truths, and of the gracious purpose of salvation for sinners, includes the interpretation of these special saving acts, and is, among other things, a mirror of particular revelations vouchsafed by the Spirit of God to chosen prophets and apostles.

---

1 The Bible itself teaches the reality of this general revelation (Ps. 19, Rom. 1:19ff., 2:15ff).

The category of revelation is therefore broader than the category of the spoken and written words of Scripture, since it covers special historic events which the Bible normatively interprets, including the incarnation, and moreover, extends beyond special revelation to include the sphere of general revelation as well. Special revelation is broader than the Bible in an added sense. In view of the era of pre-written disclosure existing from Adam to Moses, and from Christ to the apostolic writings, special revelation may be conceived as non-written as well as inscripturated; Abraham had special revelation, but no Bible, and our Lord's spoken word conveyed special revelation, though not written. Nothing less may be said than that the category of revelation is identical with the whole unveiling of God, whatever forms that disclosure may assume. Revelation cannot, therefore, be equated simply with the Hebrew-Christian Scriptures; the Bible is a special segment within a larger divine activity of revelation.

The important question which remains is whether the Bible may be identified with special revelation, and hence described as the written form of redemptive revelation. Let it be granted that God discloses Himself universally and perpetually in nature and in history and in man in the course of general revelation, and uniquely in miracle-history and incarnation-history. The further question is, Does His special revelation confront us in the form of divinely communicated ideas and words authoritatively recorded by inspired writers? While acknowledging that divine revelation is larger than the Bible, and not exhausted by it, does Christian theology contend that the Bible is identical with divine revelation? Is the Bible the written form of revelation? Is it the only form in which special revelation is available to us today, and one by which the Spirit of God has mediated to us whatever is of permanent importance in God's redemptive disclosure?

The verdict of historic evangelical Christianity is unequivocal in these matters. Augustine, Aquinas, Luther, Calvin, and lesser expositors before and after them, held firmly to the revelatory character of the Word written. The message of the Bible is not the message of men merely; it is the veritable Word of God, since all Scripture is God-breathed. Special revelation is not broader than the Bible in the sense that non-biblical avenues of divine redemptive disclosure are now available to us; the Bible is special revelation in its trustworthy form.

Three succinct affirmations convey the distinctive elements of the evangelical view of the Bible:

(1) The Bible is no mere record of revelation, but is itself revelation. Revelation is inscripturated. Scripture is a mode of divine disclosure, a special written form of revelation. The Bible is an integral part of God's redemptive activity, constituting a unitary and logical whole alongside the general revelation in nature, in history, and in man. Without the Scriptures all knowledge of God is sullied by man's religious experience as sinner. God speaks to us today by the Scriptures; they are the trustworthy and adequate bearer of His revelation. The Scriptures are not higher or lower than other modes of revelation in the sense of being more or less perfect than they for the specific purpose each was ordained to fulfill. They are, however, fuller and more explicit than revelation in its general form. The Bible is indispensable for fallen man, therefore, as is the general revelation, and as is the salvation history which Scripture relates and to which it belongs. It is the final factor in presenting God's redemptive activity as a unified and comprehensive whole, an indispensable mode of revelation through which the redemptive events become coherent. In the sense that Scripture sets before us both God's acts and words, saving events together with their meaning, special revelation becomes equivalent with the Bible. It is therefore misleading to designate the Bible as only a part of special revelation. If anything, the Bible, in exhibiting both the saving acts and their interpretation, is clearer than the acts viewed in isolation. The meaning of the saving events is given trustworthy expression in the inspired Scriptures, and is not merely suspended upon the inferences of experts in historical research. The inscripturation of special revelation is the objective culmination, therefore, of God's redemptive disclosure in special historical events and in propositions communicated to chosen prophets and apostles. This identification of written sentences and propositions with special divine revelation — the recognition, that is, of the Word in the form of words — evangelical Christianity holds to be not merely the historic Christian view, but an indispensable element in a proper Biblical theology.

(2) The formation of a canon of inspired literature fulfills God's original intention in the communication of special revelation. The collection of Biblical books arose not by accidental accretion nor by human impulse but by divine purpose. The Bible is a complete unit because of its divine authorship. Special revelation is inseparable from any and all of the books, Genesis through Revelation. They are its locus, giving to redemptive revelation a tangible, objective, and comprehensive form which confronts regenerate and unregenerate humanity alike. Hence, while the process of revelation is broader than the Bible, the content of special revelation is for us identical with the Biblical message. The canonical books are what the Holy Spirit says to fallen man, insofar as we designate an epistemological or intellectual content of special revelation. By the historico-grammatical exegesis of these writings alone, and in their entirety, the content of special revelation is to be determined.

(3) The Biblical writings differ from other sacred religious literature not in degree merely, but in kind. A special divine activity of inspiration has been operative in their production. No distinction of inspiration exists between parts of the Bible. All are inspired, although not for the same immediate purposes. The Spirit, in His redemptive outgoing to fallen man, has outbreathed the Scriptures by a special relationship to chosen prophets and apostles. Hence these sacred writings are not to be dismissed merely as the highest form of a religious expression everywhere latent in the spiritual history of mankind.

Before the end of the nineteenth century, liberal Protestant theology in Europe, and then in Great Britain and in the United States, revolted against Christian supernaturalism. It vigorously attacked the high view of the Bible, with its emphasis that a divinely intended identity exists between Scripture and special revelation. To speak of "the liberal perspective" is difficult, since liberalism was not always unified in its voice. But the liberal negation of the historic Christian appraisal of the Bible was abundantly clear in its outlines:

(1) The Bible is not in its totality identical with special revelation, but in some of its parts contains divine revelation.[2]

2 This form of expression, namely, that the Bible contains divine revelation, is found among evangelical writers also, and occurs even in the Westminster Catechism, although within a very different

Whatever higher criticism excludes, especially scientific and historical segments of the Bible, and much of the theological and ethical also, cannot be regarded as divine disclosure. The words of the Bible and the Word of God are, therefore, in a substantial measure, separable and even contrary. Much of Biblical teaching must be dissociated from divine revelation; only what has survived higher criticism may be retained, and even that only on a tentative basis. But the moral precepts of the Bible, especially the Commandments and the teaching of Jesus, are to be prized as divine truth. The historical Jesus in selected moods of expression, rather than the Bible in its totality, is the locus of divine revelation. Certain aspects of Jesus' teaching, the Sermon on the Mount especially, and numerous particular sayings of Jesus, but supremely the morality of love, are to be regarded as the Word of God in the Biblical form. In many of its parts, therefore, the Bible is not identical with special revelation, but is a fallible human interpretation of things and events, and even of God and of the moral order.

(2) The canon is an essentially human collection. It is an anthology of the highest ancient religious and moral insights, which are admittedly to be found in the Hebrew-Christian spiritual tradition. The books are a unit not because they have a common divine author, nor a unified system of theology and ethics, but because of their enlarging devotion to ethical monotheism and to the theology of love. The canon does not gain its existence through uniquely inspired writers; moreover, it is theoretically open and revisable.

(3) The Bible is not qualitatively unique literature in comparison with other sacred writings differing in kind from them. Rather, it represents, by its superior insights, a higher degree of general divine revelation than is elsewhere mirrored in religious experience.

---

postulate. The thesis "The Bible contains revelation" does not, for the evangelical school, suggest a distinction between content and essence. For evangelical writers, the thesis has for its background the prior conviction that the whole of Scripture is uniquely inspired, being divinely constituted a trustworthy objective authority, in contrast with the liberal insistence on the fallibility of Scripture. The evangelical does not distinguish parts of the Bible which are trustworthy from parts which supposedly are not, but rather distinguishes modes of divine communication of revealed truth.

As a reaction to this classic liberal view the second quarter of the twentieth century has witnessed the theological initiative and aggression of the theology of crisis, or so-called dialectical theology. It is professedly a "theology of the Word," reasserting the reality of special divine revelation. But it proposes to relate the Bible and divine revelation in a manner which contrasts strikingly with the classic liberal view, and at the same time with historic evangelical theology. The following emphases make this contrast apparent:

(1) The Bible is the indispensable witness to special redemptive revelation. It is the testimony of prophets and apostles who were contemporaneous with the events of salvation history, supremely the event Jesus Christ. Contrary to liberal theology, the Bible is not simply the highest form of general divine revelation, but witnesses to a special divine revelation. Contrary to evangelical theology, the canon of Scripture is based not on the unique inspiration of chosen writers, but is a human collection bearing a unique witness to special or redemptive revelation and distinguished by the chronological priority attaching to the prophetic and apostolic testimony.

(2) No identity exists between the Bible in its written form of words and sentences and special divine revelation. To identify the Scriptures with revelation is, in the framework of this thought, to commit idolatry and is to regard the Bible, assertedly a fallible human product, as a paper Pope. As propositional statement, the Bible is not to be identified with special divine revelation. Neither all Biblical statements and words, nor any of them, are identical with special revelation. The Bible in its entirety is finite and fallible in its moral and theological, as well as in its historical and scientific propostions. Not even the words and teachings of Jesus are to be identified with special divine revelation.[3]

(3) The Bible is to be "correlated" with special revelation. Scripture is the frame within which God addresses man, the atmosphere of witness in which God speaks in the moment of His personal revelatory encounter with us. The Bible may

3 It is the postulate that "special" revelation is "dynamic" (hence non-propostional), which requires the further break with the old liberal view. Liberalism denied that any of Jesus' teaching is special revelation in the sense of miraculous impartation, but it held that some of Jesus' teaching is "special" revelation in the sense of the highest expression of general divine revelation.

"become" revelation in the subjective experience of the soul's personal meeting with God — not revelation in the form of concepts, words and sentences, but revelation in the form of dynamic spiritual response. The Bible has the quality not of "inspiredness," nor of authoritative and inerrant propositions about God and His purposes, but of "inspiringness." It serves in the important role of a catalyst for our immediate experience of God. The Bible holds, in this view, a purely instrumental role. The content of special revelation is to be determined not by exegesis of Scripture, since not the Bible but the Spirit presently encountered is regarded as the locus of revelation. Special revelation is a continuing process, not a completed product identical with the Bible.

From this review of these three contrasting conceptions of the relationship assumed to prevail between the Bible and revelation, it is obvious at once that widely discordant assumptions in the spheres of metaphysics and epistemology underlie these competitive views.

The classic liberal view is not any longer, in the mid-twentieth century, a conspicuous option in influential theological circles. But for earlier generations it held a fascination through two basic concepts: the doctrine of an exaggerated divine immanence, and the philosophy of evolution. Alongside this may be mentioned the anti-metaphysical mood engendered by Kant's theory of knowledge. The combination of radical divine immanence and evolution disallowed the Biblical miraculous. Hence it ruled out a unique canon, and in fact, the unique inspiration of any sacred writings. Its end result was the denial of special revelation and the consequent assimilation of the Bible to the movement of general revelation. What the God of extreme immanence reveals anywhere He necessarily reveals everywhere, even if in lesser degree. Divine uniformitarianism allows no special events, no special revelation, no special writings.

The dialectical theologians are likewise devoted to basic assumptions which control the appraisal of Scripture in relation to divine revelation. While they revolt against the liberal theology of immanence, their controlling tenets are the extreme transcendence of God, and the doctrine that revelation is subjectivity. The reality of God, we are told, eludes conceptual reason; the tension between time and eternity, in view of their radical contrariness, is such that they cannot be rationally synthesized. God is "wholly other," He is hidden to man even in His revelation. The dialectical theology, insisting that the spiritual realm can confront human conception only as a paradox and antinomy, disparages as "rational gymnastics" every venture of dogmatic theological pronouncements. The complete discontinuity of God and man, of the eternal and temporal realms, is affirmed. Alongside this doctrine of exaggerated divine transcendence, which displaces the older liberal formula of exaggerated divine immanence, appears a corresponding doctrine of special divine revelation, namely, that revelation is subjectivity. The synthesis of the eternal and the temporal, a synthesis which is the event of revelation, is conceived as a dynamic divine-human encounter. As an existential moment of subjective faith-response, it involves no conceptual grasp of spiritual realities. In revelation, God assertedly communicates Himself, rather than truths about Himself. Revelation is identified with redemption, as functional or dynamic, but not in the traditional sense with Scripture as the indispensable conveyor of the saving knowledge of God. The revelation-sphere of "I-Thou knowledge," or of divine disclosure patterned by the anti-intellectualism which Schleiermacher inherited from German romanticism, is contrasted with the phenomenal sphere of "I-It knowledge" to which the relevance of coherence as a criterion and of rational consistency as a test is restricted.

Likewise the evangelical forging of the relation which prevails between Scripture and special revelation also is part and parcel of a larger atmosphere of metaphysical and epistemological conviction. The controlling ideas of the evangelical statement of the Bible and revelation are first, the rational Creator-God, second, the *imago Dei* borne by man on the basis of creation and surviving the fall despite its distortion by sin, and third, the conviction that God intends the whole man as an object of His revelation.

Biblical theology assigns to the Logos a status in the very reality of the Godhead. The rationality of the self-revealed God and His intellectual attributes provide evangelical Christianity a framework which makes possible both the conceptual knowledge of God and an inscripturated propositional revelation. As a bearer of the *imago Dei*, man experiences rationally and morally. Experience in this form is an intended consequence of man's distinctive origin, having a specific view to his fellowship with his Maker. Hence all significant human experience is cast in rational and moral form. The fall of man does not vitiate the rationality of knowledge, but rather impairs the human effort to know. Man is subject to error and has a distorted apprehension of truth and goodness. But what man knows, whether in the sphere of general revelation or of special revelation, he knows within the bounds of the laws of consistency and contradiction or he does not have genuine knowledge or meaningful experience. The fact of the *imago Dei* gives to man's cognitive experience its relevance to the sphere of metaphysical knowledge, while the fact that both man and the space-time universe are creations of a rational God gives coherence its relevance as a test for truth in the phenomenal world of things and events. The divine image in man did not, in the fall, suffer to such an extent that man's *ratio* is now unable on the basis of general and special revelation to receive conceptual knowledge of the supernatural spiritual world; rather, divine revelation is addressed to man as a totality, both in its general and special forms, and hence with a view to the rational as well as the volitional and emotive aspects of his existence.

Historic Christian theology has therefore defended the possibility, necessity and actuality of a revelation addressed in conceptual form to man. Special revelation is adjoined to general revelation, and revelational knowledge in all its forms belongs to the genus of knowledge generally. Special revelation is addressed to the whole man, and involves the communication of truths about God and His purposes as a factor in man's redemption; hence redemptive revelation comes by conceptual mediation through chosen prophets and apostles, is communicated in the form of words and propositions, and is inscriptured in canonical books.

The difficulties which arise from the manner in which the Bible and revelation are correlated by the classic liberal, neo-liberal or dialectical, and historic evangelical views are apparent enough.

In the case of liberal Protestantism, in fact, the difficulties proved insurmountable. The loss of a uniquely inspired Bible led, through successive alternatives, to the loss also of the self-revealing God. This in turn led to the contemporary revolt

against classic liberal theology as a significant Christian position. The inner difficulties of the liberal account of the Bible
and revelation were obvious and numerous. But none was more
persistent and perplexing than the problem of authority. How,
in an assertedly fallible religious literature blending divine
and human elements, are revelation and non-revelation to be
objectively discriminated? What criterion shall be found for
distinguishing what is revelation from what is not revelation
in a book which professedly contains both? How is the Bible's
"truth" to be convincingly "sifted" from its "error"? Are we
not reduced to value judgments, to a merely subjective determination of "revelation" by individual interpreters whose
arbitrary preferences legislate what is "the word of God"?
Liberal writers may be quoted at length to exhibit their
indignation over such complaints, coupled often with excori-
ations of the high evangelical view of the Bible, and also with
a flabby and unconvincing reply to the primary theological
questions. One liberal expositor differed from another in the
identification of what parts of the Bible survived the onslaught
of higher criticism and could, for the time being at least, be
confidently received as revelation. Where liberal scholars agreed,
there was no convincing exhibition of an objective basis for
their concurrence. By an act of will the recognized strategists
of the position shifted first from one line of defense to another:
the fallibility of the scientific and historical coupled with the
trustworthiness of the theological and ethical teaching; then
the fallibility of much of the Old Testament ethical and doctrinal teaching as well; then the reliability of the theological
and ethical teaching of Jesus only; then the fallibility also of
some of Jesus' views, for example, the existence of Satan and
demons, and the reality of hell and of eternal punishment.
So the wheel of theological progress turned in liberal circles,
around and around, until one authority could be cited against
another. It became evident at long last that if man himself
is left to delineate the Word of God, then the idea of special
revelation collapses.

The point is not that the surrender of the divine inspiration
of the Bible automatically required the surrender of the fact
of special divine revelation and of the gospel of redemption.
Those who waive Biblical inspiration are not to be comforted with the view that thereby they have dispensed with

the realities of redemption. Treated simply as sober narratives of historical actualities, the Biblical records confront the reader with a unique view of God and human destiny, calling man to the bar of repentance or doom. To discredit this, one must dispense with more than Biblical inspiration. One must make a further negation: not only inspiration, but additional Biblical teaching must be repudiated. True enough, scholars who repudiated the high view of inspiration have almost invariably surrendered much more. They have proceeded, that is, on a bias against miraculous supernaturalism which robs Christianity of much more than the doctrine of inspiration. But theological relativism is not an unavoidable implication of the rejection of an inspired Bible, although liberalism was reduced at last to poverty in the sphere of religious knowledge because of its anti-miraculous bias. Christianity is supported by far more than a Book; the whole tide of nature and history is to be ranged on its side, as best interpreted from the Hebrew-Christian point of view. To repudiate Biblical theism, one must repudiate not only the Bible, but the whole of reality. The gospel of redemption has a broader base than inspiration, and its central issues are creditably affirmed by the Biblical writers, even if their inspiration be ignored. But the denial of the inspiration of the writers, while it does not exclude the gospel, invariably places it in jeopardy. For one thing, an alternative view of Biblical origins is then inevitable, and the interpretation of redemptive history is moved into the dimension of fallibility and error. The authoritative note is gone, and the trustworthiness of the writers is reduced to a matter of personal subjective determination. Such an approach may modify the Biblical message only in details, or it may threaten its intrinsic content. That is why the connection between special revelation and the Bible is strategically important, and why it must be stressed that the Scriptures are no mere appendage to special redemptive history, but an essential and climactic phase of it.

Internal inconsistencies in the liberal view should have given abundant warning of its ultimate untenability. How could a professedly Christian idea of revelation be maintained, when everywhere in the Bible, as the fundamentum of the record, that idea is correlated with the miraculous, which liberalism repudiated? For nothing stands more obviously in the forefront of the Biblical narratives than that their whole concept of revelation turns on the admission or exclusion of the reality of miracle, in view of the claim to particularity and once-for-allness attaching to God's redemptive manifestation. Moreover, in its essential disregard for exegesis of the Bible in the formulation of the strategic content of divine revelation, liberalism set itself in opposition to the Hebrew-Christian movement's historic understanding of itself. And, equally distressing, the liberal view of religious knowledge came to impugn the stature of Jesus. Once the miraculous was set aside in deference to the scientific method, which forged only tentative conclusions, by what consistency could absoluteness be ascribed to Him and His teaching, in part any more than in its entirety? If the crucial and determinative reference-point for historical credibility and actuality was to be found in present experience, in contemporary experimental verification of all claims, then how in any sense could it be contended that revelation had reached a climax in Jesus of Nazareth?

The liberal view of the Bible was in the main a reflex, as we have seen, of an undergirding philosophy of religion, as well as of nature and history, which has now fallen on days of judgment. Hardly a year passes but that the last defenses of this position are weakened by an exodus of former advocates to opposition territory.

It is the dialectical alternative, rather than the evangelical alternative, to which many of these deserters have resorted. The weaknesses which inhere in the correlation of the Bible with revelation in this more recent view must therefore be candidly examined, to determine if a theology which builds upon Schleiermacher's anti-intellectualistic formulation of revelation can supply a stable alternative to the deteriorated liberal defenses. The neo-liberal[4] position, it will be recalled, considers the Bible a fallible human witness to a dynamic contemporary revelation-encounter possible to faith, not an inspired canon

4 No denial is intended of significant differences between the theology of crisis and classic liberalism. The term is used to indicate the writer's judgment that, in the statement of the relation of the Bible to revelation, it is the liberal rather than orthodox view which prevails. On the broader issue, both Van Til in his *The New Modernism* and the Catholic theologian Balthasar, who has followed Barth from the first, share the verdict that the similarities of the dialectical theology to the older liberalism are, in the total approach, more fundamental than the differences. But that question is not here debated.

of authoritative revealed truths unveiling God's special redemptive purposes. If we ask what difficulties obviously
confront this view, these should not be hard to discern.

Despite its profession of a higher role for the Bible than
liberalism allowed, dialectical theology can retain no decisive
significance for Scripture as normative. The Bible is assigned
a mere chronological prophetico-apostolic priority as testimony.
If revelation is not divinely communicated in objective propositional form, then obviously the Biblical writings can no
longer be regarded as authoritative criteria in that sense. What
remains to them is, so we are assured, the mirroring of the
prophetic and apostolic witness to revelation, happily in written
form to guard against an accretion of legendary elements. And
yet on the view of the dialectical theologians themselves these
same records are not merely fallible, and prone to error in
theology and ethics as well as in science and history, but
actually include legend and myth as well. The restoration of
a high reverence for the Bible is, therefore, more a fancy than
an actuality. This is apparent not merely from the circumstance that the Bible is allowed by the neo-liberal view only
a conditional normative role, but from the equally obvious
fact that, taken even as a witness to special revelation, the
testimony of the prophets and apostles is set aside by its
approach. For the repeated witness of the writers is that their
very words are the words of God; that it is permissible to
assert that God has spoken only because He has spoken
these precise words and sentences. What they witness to, indeed,
is not special revelation in the anti-intellectualistic vein of the
post-Schleiermacher mood, but to a special revelation which is
conveyed in the form of concepts, of words and propositions.
One may dismiss the prophetic "thus said the Lord," which
recurs with almost wearying regularity, as a "low order of
revelation," as Brunner curiously puts it, but special divine
revelation and nothing less it is with which the writers identify
their utterances. The notion that the content of special revelation is not to be determined from what God has spoken to
the ancient prophets, or to the apostles in New Testament
times, is not one which the Biblical witness endorses. For the
possession of the Word of God in written form is, according
to the Biblical witness, the glory of the Judeo-Christian community; hence Paul rejoiced that the Hebrews possessed "the

oracles of God." The frequent Biblical interchange of the phrases "it says" and "God says" evidences the confidence that the Word of God was given in objective verbal form; and nowhere in the Bible, it may be pardonable to add, is there the slightest uneasiness on the part of its sensitive and reverent spirit that such a conviction is a form of idolatry — an evidence that the real reasons for hostility to this confidence in verbal revelation proceed from quite alien motivations. The fact that Jesus Christ validated the Hebrew assurance of a canon of uniquely inspired writings, and appealed decisively to "the law and the prophets" as authoritative teaching, stands in supreme contradiction to the neo-liberal restatement of the Biblical witness. The contemporary exclusion of exegesis as determinative of the content of special revelation involves a resort to eisegesis in the construction of the Biblical witness to special revelation, and in fact an outright denial of that witness.

The neo-liberal view of Scripture, as we have already indicated, is an adjunct of broader metaphysical and epistemological tenets. The radical transcendence of God, and revelation as subjectivity, are its controlling biases. Set in this context, the problem of religious knowledge gravitates between three non-Christian options which hover invitingly over the sphere of religious experience.

The first is mysticism. Hebrew-Christian thought had been able to characterize the spiritual world with assurance and definiteness on the basis of revelation. But the anti-metaphysical bias of recent theology, and its consequent repudiation of doctrinal revelation, together with the emphasis on the existential encountering of God, dissolves the supernatural into a formless and nebulous mysticism. The God of Barth and Brunner emerges more in the role of the God of Kant and Kierkegaard than of the God of Abraham, Isaac and Jacob. The point is not that Kant, Kierkegaard and the crisis theologians are mystics; Kant surely was not, Kierkegaard professed to be anti-mystical in at least one of his letters, and the dialectical theologians are avowed enemies of mysticism. But they share the primal atmosphere out of which mysticism rises: the denial that the supernatural world can be grasped by the discursive reason. The self-revealing God of Biblical theology does not exist in this misty zone of rational antinomy, inaccessible to conceptual thought, and incapable of trustworthy characterization by representative ideas. Such are the gods of mysticism, and the Living God of Biblical theology is the antithesis of them.

But the neo-liberal formula involves more serious consequences still. The surrender of conceptual knowledge of the metaphysical world inherits always the task of avoiding agnosticism as its discomforting estate. The spiritual Other with which the non-conceptual aspect of the self contends may, after all, be simply the higher self of moral aspiration, impelling the subject onward to unrealized ethical heights. The encounter with a sphere of which nothing is cognitively knowable only unconvincingly avoids a flirtation with spiritual nothingness.

An even more distressing option haunts the neo-liberal formula. The encounter on which it relies may be equally serviceable for a resurgence of demonism. Of course, if one begins with the optimistic but profoundly anti-biblical assumption of the unreality of the demonic, of Satan and of evil spirits, the possibility of encounter with false gods is automatically ruled out. But a theology which maintains the standpoint either of Moses or of Jesus is entitled to no such premise. And a philosophy of revelation which abandons the relevance of all objective evidences, and which excludes any test for truth, on the ground that special revelation is paradoxical and supraconceptual, cuts itself off in advance from any rational means of discriminating God from Satan, as well as of detecting Satan in the role of an Angel of Light. The competitive deities which contemporary theology professedly encounters should be unnerving enough: Brunner's insistence on a deity confronting all men by general revelation; Barth's insistence on a deity whose revelation is exclusively saving; John Baillie's claim that the deity's revelation is not only saving, but universally so. What, from the standpoint of Biblical theology, could more obviously disqualify a proposed deity as false, than the denial that this deity is universally and perpetually revealed in the creation? Equally false is the assertion that this deity redeems men universally by an immediate self-communication. And yet both notions are vigorously espoused today by advocates of confrontation-theology. The dialectical dismissal of empirical evidences and rational consistency as factors in evaluating valid spiritual experience is a vulnerable point in the neo-liberal philosophy of revelation. The arbitrary confinement of the criteria of coherence and consistency to the realm of phenomenal truth, and their detachment from any relevance to metaphysical realities, involves more than the lamentable loss of any apologetic for the Christian view of God with which theology may venture into the market place of competitive views. This surrender of a rationally consistent theology is, in fact, but one aspect of a larger and even more disastrous capitulation, growing out of the repudiation of conceptual revelation, and involving therefore the abandonment of any claim to revealed doctrines, and along with it discounting the unity of Bible teaching. Such a rejection of revealed doctrinal truths marks a basic and radical departure from the Biblical comprehension of special revelation and its implications.

While the elimination of metaphysical knowledge would be the consistent outcome of the neo-liberal approach, that view has not in fact completely destroyed such knowledge. It constantly borrows, in stating its position, features which are integral elements of the Biblical revelation, but to which it is unentitled on the ground of its own professed existential access. What the neo-liberal view surrenders is any test for truth in the spiritual world. For that reason it unwittingly restores to centrality, because of this deficiency, the question of the ontological status of reason, of the *imago Dei* in man, and of the relationship of special Biblical revelation to human experience in its cognitive aspect. The anti-intellectualistic theories characteristically ignore both the persistent necessity of human nature to relate itself consistently and meaningfully to the whole of experience, and the fact that the demolition of a test for truth in relation to the spiritual world gradually nullifies the force of the latter in man's life and outlook.

If the historic evangelical Christian view of the relation between the Bible and special revelation also involves difficulties, they are nevertheless gratifyingly different from those which plague the classic liberal and neo-liberal perspectives. The evangelical difficulties, happily, do not grow out of the liberal sacrifices of miraculous revelation, nor out of the neo-liberal surrender of the intelligibility of the spiritual world. Problems there will always be in human experience while the shadows of sin remain and the shades of finitude endure. Even special Biblical revelation, on its own witness, is not yet a knowledge "face to face," but rather "in part." Nor are the difficulties of the evangelical view what its theological opponents have frequently made them out to be, for example, that it involves the worship of a "paper Pope," or that it requires faith in a Book at the expense of faith in God, that it involves the divine dictation of the Biblical text and the exclusion of every human element, or that it blindly assumes the present text to be inerrant and assumes the futility of lower criticism as well. The orthodox view doubtless faces problems, but they are not problems such as these, which belong to the order of propaganda rather than of apologetics, and which throw the evangelical position into extreme statement, so that its desirable features may then be incorporated as adjuncts of an objectionable and compromising alternative.

By historic Christianity, special divine revelation is comprehended at once as personal, propositional, historical, once-for-all, and inscripturated. The problems which arise in the modern mind over this representation are: (1) the reconciliation of Biblical with contemporary science and history; (2) the presence of admitted errors in the present text, coupled with the absence of an infallible original; (3) the problem of the canon; and (4) the patent fact of diverse interpretations of the Biblical revelation. In comparison with these problems, others are of a minor nature and fade into the background.

It would, of course, require a specialized volume adequately to state and to reply to each of these matters. The fact is that a competent and extensive literature already exists, having emerged in the course of evangelical Christianity. Though obscured from significance during recent decades because liberal and neo-liberal thought has operated on alien assumptions, much of it is still fully relevant to the theological controversy. All that will be ventured here is a series of comprehensive observations, suggesting the outline of a reply to acknowledged evangelical difficulties.

Before this is attempted, a delineation of the temper of the modern man is in order. Contemporary civilization refuses to bow the knee before divine authority. This revolt against God is more conspicuous because, rather than repudiating all authority, there is a willingness to bow to false and human authorities. This anti-authoritarian mood is as apparent in the theological sphere as elsewhere; indeed, it would perhaps be true to our cultural situation to say that in relation to the spiritual world the revolt againist authority is especially conspicuous.

Yet the sovereignty of God must always be the background from which Christian theology begins. He is Creator and Lord, and His freedom to reveal Himself if and as He will must be maintained. He may write His glory in the stars, and, if He desires, He may inscribe Ten Commandments on stone. If He can create man, the communication to him of ideas and words in man's language is no great burden. If God's Spirit breathed into man the gift of a unique life, qualifying him for an eternal destiny, that same Spirit assuredly can breathe out to sin-ensnared man the redemptive words of God.

Perhaps the hour is propitious in which to seek a rapprochement of Biblical theology and science and history. That the God of creation and the God of redemption are one and the same God both the Old and New Testaments proclaim. When exegesis departs from the text, when science strays from the data of reality, problems arise in each area. In both instances speculative philosophy intrudes, even if it be dignified with the authority of revelation on the one hand or of science on the other. But it must be apparent even to the non-religious spirit that the whole movement of science has been subject to staggering revision and reversal in our century. Many of the bold thrusts against the very possibility of creation and miracle are now more widely acknowledged as expressions of a biased philosophy. Precisely when the Darwinian alternative is toppling, when the loud boasts of convincing paleontological evidence of missing links bridging the kinds of life are quavering, and when the theory of emergent evolution gains popularity as the secular explanation of beginnings, it is regrettable that many theologians today depreciate Genesis as an account of actual empirical origins. While the newer philosophy of science cannot settle decisively the question of Hebrew-Christian miracle, the old anti-miraculous dogmatism is largely a thing of the past. The hesitancies of modern man are once more seen to turn not on a conflict of the Bible with the prevailing world view, but on spiritual indecision. In the sphere of history, the old Wellhausen perspective has long been in retreat; what in 1925 was regarded as the indubitable achievement of criticism, that the prophets preceded the law and sacrificial system, is now repudiated, and the significance

of Jesus Christ is interpreted once more from the standpoint of
the Cross. As a science, archaeology confessedly can never reach
a final verdict, whether in contradiction or support of the
Bible. But its total impression is one of overwhelming confirmation of trustworthiness of the Scriptures. When one sets
the cardinal contentions of the liberal criticism of a half
century ago side by side with the evangelical perspective of
traditional Christianity, it is the former position which has
been deflated, and those who carry on the revolt against historic
Christian theism still must reckon with the latter position as
that to which they formulate their alternative.

The tension between a fallible text and an infallible original
brings simultaneously into view a number of important issues.
The reproach that "nobody has seen the infallible original" is
frequently intended to suggest that the inerrant autographs
are simply evasive devices of evangelical apologetics. To this it
may once be replied that it is equally true that "nobody has
seen fallible originals." This may not quite be a head-on
reply to the taunt, "we have infallible copies, nothing more,"
but it does emphasize that both judgments about the original
writings turn on something more than the available copies.
In the neo-liberal theology, the controlling idea is that the
finite and historical are by definition sinful and relative, a
dogma with abominable implications for the doctrine of the
incarnation as well as for the significance of the Biblical
writings. In evangelical theology, the governing idea is the
special divine self-revelation conveyed by the Bible, including
its statement about the nature of authoritative Scripture and
its original inspiration.

Precisely this insistence on a trustworthy and authoritative
Scripture poses for evangelical Christianity the problem of the
fallible translation. It should be noted that this descriptive
term "fallible translation" is forged from the perspective of
modernity; it suggests, what historic Christianity could not
allow, the essential untrustworthiness of the Bible, or the corruption of the translation. But it is quite impossible to think
in terms of a corrupt text. Find what variations they will in
the presently available copies, the critics must reckon still with
Westcott and Hort's past verdict that a question exists regarding but "a thousandth part of the whole New Testament." The
doubts concern mainly grammatical forms, and in no case is a

major doctrine imperiled. The decisive factor contributory to the emphasis on fallibility was the liberal bias against the supernatural Jesus, which identified the original writings with a non-miraculous tradition, and then labelled all verses supernaturalistic in tendency as later accretions or interpolations. This dogma, although it had the sanction of many distinguished seminaries and theologians, led to the breakdown of liberalism rather than of the New Testament. The present text is essentially continuous with the original. Subsequent progress in textual criticism may confidently be expected to confirm this verdict, and not to dislodge it.

In the matter of authoritative translations, the world of faith has before it the significant attitude of Jesus Christ toward the Old Testament. For responsible Christian belief, the example of Jesus is of decisive import. The Bible of Jesus' day was in use centuries after the completion of the Old Testament canon and, from the circumstance that copyists were perhaps less careful, if not less intelligent[5] than translators, and from the fact that inspiration did not extend beyond the original writers, the texts in everyday use in our Lord's time most probably contained, like our own, variations from the original. The fact that the Old Testament in ordinary use was the Septuagint form removes this from doubt. Yet one does not find in the teaching of Jesus, despite His constant appeal to the law and the prophets, in details as well as in the large, the peculiarly contemporary tension between the original writings and the particular text at hand. Interestingly enough, one can find in the parallel sections of Kings and Chronicles textual difficulties of the same order as those occurring later in synoptic Gospels, and yet they were not made the basis of an argument against the authority and reliability of the Old Testament. The Church's Founder and Lord bequeathed to it, in His manner of appeal to the Old Testament writings as authoritative, a confidence that the authority of the originals resides also in copies and translations and that, while the original writings alone are inspired, the copies may with propriety be regarded as the veritable Word of God. When a translation so obscures the sense of the original, whether through theological bias or

---

5 The Dead Sea scrolls of Isaiah do not confirm the prevalent thesis that the Jewish copyists of the Old Testament were less competent than the translators.

linguistic incompetence, is perhaps a delicate question. But the distrust and depreciation of the sacred writings has no parallel in the example of Jesus, nor of the apostles, nor of the long ages of Christian faith. Until the rise of modern higher criticism, to discredit the Bible was characteristic only of those who spoke from the standpoint of unbelief, and not of those inside the circle of belief, except for Roman Catholic apologetics after the Reformation, which sought to enhance the authority of the Church by stressing the margin of error in the Biblical texts in general use. As over against the probable disparity between the Scriptures in use in Jesus' day and the Old Testament originals, it may be argued with force that the modern science of textual criticism offsets the longer period which intervenes between the composition of the New Testament and our own day, so that if anything, we have a purer text.

This consideration leads on naturally to the discussion of the canon. For Jesus validated not merely the Hebrew confidence in inspired writings, but in a collection of authoritative books, a sacred canon, to be contrasted with all other literature as uniquely inspired. The idea of a canon did not first originate, therefore, with the early Church, but the community of faith had before it the Old Testament in a unitary form, referred to by Jesus as "the law and the prophets," and appealed to as a canon, in judgment even upon the religious tradition which surrounded it. The Old Testament canon lacked its climax; it ended with promise and anticipation, but halted short of fulfillment. Jesus Himself taught His disciples to look for an enlargement of the canon; He would have somewhat to say to His followers even after His death. The apostles impose their letters authoritatively on the churches in His name, as divinely inspired. This is the spirit in which the writings were received from the very beginning. The idea of a gradual recognition of the New Testament writings as divine is not one which the New Testament itself vindicates; disputes appear, such as Paul's controversy with the Judaizers, and even his rebuke of Peter's conduct, but the acceptance of the apostolic writings as authoritative is even made a test of faith. The problem of the canon needs therefore to be recanvassed, not on the liberal assumption that uninspired letters came gradually to be regarded as divine, and that no canon could have arisen until late because of a supposed second-century authorship of numbers of the writings.

The whole approach to the question of the canon has been unfortunately obscured in recent years by the radical liberal bias against miraculous supernaturalism, which required the notions that the theological views of the New Testament reflect a late authorship, and hence a gradual acceptance of the writings.

The so-called "phenomena" of Scripture, that actual textual data with which lower criticism is continually occupied, are usually held today to contradict the high view of the inerrancy of the Bible. The apparent contradictions in the text itself, especially the seemingly irreducible Synoptic variations, are constantly brought to the fore. It is argued on the basis of the characteristics of the writings that the Biblical doctrine of inspiration could not conceivably involve a claim to inerrancy.

The high view of inspiration is easily disqualified in advance, as least likely, because most supernatural, especially in an age which is cautiously retreating from a naturalistic stand. But if Christian faith may find in the divine-human relationship in the incarnation a clue to the character of inspiration, then the divine achievement of an infallible end product in human nature is not excluded as a possibility. An examination of the Biblical texts from which a Scriptural doctrine of inspiration may be derived indicates as their common element the recognition of the divine authorship and quality of Scripture. Nowhere is any hint to be found of the compatibility of inspiration with error, or that some parts of Scripture are to be segregated from others as more, or less, trustworthy.

The Scriptural emphasis falls on the reliability of the end product, of the Word as written, and not on the detailed *modus operandi* of inspiration. The Biblical and pagan delineations of inspiration differ remarkably in this very fact, that the pagan emphasis falls, often in great detail, on a subjective psychological experience characterizing the moment of exaltation, whereas the Biblical emphasis falls on the divine authority of the written Word.

At the same time, there is abundant reason for caution in categorizing the methodology of inspiration. In view of the stylistic differences and personality factors which distinguish the various writings, it would be clearly erroneous to conceive of inspiration in terms of divine dictation. Yet the fact remains

that, in the giving of the Law, written on stone, we are confronted by the recording of revelation by absolute miracle
entirely apart from human means. But this is hardly the
representative divine method of providing a reliable text.
Indeed, a generous variety in method is obvious: from a dependence on other sources, and a certain looseness in quotation
which is not in some instances inconsistent with the purpose
of inspiration, to much more rigid patterns. But the claim
to divine authority and trustworthiness is nonetheless cast
over the whole.

The Biblical approach to the phenomena of Scripture is
one of confidence in the supernatural authority of the writings
suspended upon a rational delineation of the precise manner
in which the divine and human were in each instance related.
If it were necessary to know the divine methodology in detail,
before confidence in the end product becomes possible, then
the mysteries of the virgin birth would stand as a barrier to
faith in the incarnation as well. The emphasis of speculative
philosophy may fall on method, but the Bible centers its
attention on an authoritative content.

Textual problems do exist, and while they raise no doctrinal
issue, they are often made the determinative factor in reaching
a decision for or against Biblical inerrancy. These textual difficulties are characteristically exaggerated by the modern mind.
Our Lord's remark, "Ye do err, not knowing the Scriptures,"
affords a caution against a hasty negative verdict. In the case
of debatable items — questions of history or geography in the
main — the science of archaeology can hardly hope to confirm
every last jot and tittle of ancient books. In such unconfirmed
areas archaeology, as an empirical science, is unable to give a
dogmatically negative judgment. Its conclusions are subject
always to revision, and never final. No absolute verdict of
error can, in fact, be directed against a Biblical passage, simply
on the ground that confirmation is lacking; what is necessary
is proof of the impossibility of such an event under the circumstances indicated. And yet it is remarkable, indeed, what
confirmatory verdicts the past century of archaeological endeavor has given in support of the accuracy of the Bible. The
real struggle appears more and more to be one between the
Bible and non-biblical views of God, nature, history and man.

The approach to the Bible, in whole and in part, is ventured from only one of two standpoints, that of faith or that of suspended judgment. One has either a regard or disregard for its authority. In the one case, its trustworthiness is assumed unless conclusive evidence for the contrary appears; in the other, any and every passage in the Bible is called in question, and its trustworthiness acknowledged only for some other reason than that it belongs to the sacred record. The latter approach begins with apparent errors, and endeavors to arrive at a view of inspiration from this orientation. This is, of course, an almost infinite process, owing to the present limitations of knowledge, and subject to constant retraction; it casts over the whole reservations which attach only to a part; and it quite overlooks the fact that by citing examples of accuracy one could not in actual fact prove the reality of inspiration, but only exclude it by negative examples. And it falls easy prey to the fallacious formula, "One proved error in the present manuscripts, and the case for Biblical authority is shattered," especially since the possibility of such error in the copies is conceded in advance by the evangelical view.

The Biblical view and its alternatives are to be judged as comprehensive wholes, and not primarily by isolated and peripheral skirmishes which need not furnish decisive tests of strength. The Christian view of inspiration is part and parcel of a Christian view of God and the world. The answer to the question, "Where, in a debatable matter, shall the benefit of the doubt go?", will reflect the pattern by which one approaches the problem. Does the benefit fall to the modern view, with its bias toward the fallibility of Scripture? Does it fall rather to the side of Biblical authority and reliability?

The latter mood alone is consistent with competent exegesis of the Bible's claims concerning itself. It is consistent with the claims of the prophets. It is consistent with Jesus' attitude toward the Old Testament. It is consistent with the apostolic view of Scripture. It is consistent with the regard of the historic Christian Church for the Biblical writings. These all commend to our generation the presumption of the trustworthiness of Scripture.

Alongside the justification which this revered precedent gives to the approach of faith rather than to that of incredulity or suspense of judgment, must be ranged the positive contribution of the high view of the Bible, in contrast with alternative views. It has retained the heart of the gospel, which liberalism sacrificed, and without this, Christianity is a hollow shell. And it has perpetuated the living unity of revealed doctrine. Whatever difficulties the high view poses, they are as nothing alongside the frustrating and overwhelming difficulties of its competitors. It does not ask for faith in the absence of all evidence, nor does it plead for anti-intellectualism in theology. Those approaches belong to the non-evangelical and neo-liberal schools. What evangelical Christianity purposes to offer is a faith which fits the requirements both of the empirical scene and of the sphere of rational consistency, while at the same time it exhibits the world's most sacred message.

The biggest obstacle to faith, as the evangelical view measures the modern scene, is the hardness of men's hearts in relation to the Word of God revealed and written. The man in the street, wholly apart from critical negations, does not long read the sacred Book without detecting even today the imprint of that special divine authority with which it confronts him. The Bible is, and doubtless will continue to be, the most controversial book in history. But its potential for debate is two-sided. The controversy raised by what men say about the Bible is a matter of changing fashion. But the controversy engendered by what the Bible has to say about man is agelong, and upon the way each man settles this turns the eternal destiny of the human soul.

INDEX